Off Balance

THE REAL WORLD OF BALLET
OFF BALANCE

BY SUZANNE GORDON

WITH PHOTOGRAPHS BY EARL DOTTER

McGraw-Hill Book Company

New York   St. Louis   San Francisco   Bogotá   Guatemala   Hamburg
Lisbon   Madrid   Mexico   Montreal   Panama   Paris
San Juan   São Paulo   Tokyo   Toronto

Author's Note

This book was researched and written between the winter of 1980 and the summer of 1982. Since that time, many dancers, teachers, and choreographers have left companies and schools. Dancers have retired or divorced or moved on. Alexander Minz and Madame Messerer are no longer with American Ballet Theatre; Alexander Godunov was fired from ABT; and Barna Ostertag is no longer Gelsey Kirkland's agent. Both Benjamin Harkarvy and Barbara Weisberger have left Pennsylvania Ballet, and Robert Weiss no longer dances with New York City Ballet. Robert and Rachel Maiorano were married when I interviewed them; now they are divorced.

I cannot predict how many others will change company, spouse, or even profession. Ballet, like everything else in America, seems to be in constant flux. What has not changed are the basic facts of ballet life.

Reprinted by arrangement with Pantheon Books

First McGraw-Hill Paperback edition, 1984

1 2 3 4 5 6 7 8 9 DOCDOC 8 7 6 5 4

ISBN 0-07-023770-0

Library of Congress Cataloging in Publication Data
Gordon, Suzanne, 1945–
  Off balance.

  1. Ballet. 2. Ballet dancers—Employment. 3. Ballet dancers—United States—Attitudes. 4. Ballet—Vocational guidance. I. Title.
GV1787.G62   1983b   792.8'2   83-24397
ISBN 0-07-023770-0

"FOR MY MOTHER AND THE DANCERS OF THE AMERICAN BALLET THEATRE."

Contents

LIST OF ILLUSTRATIONS

ACKNOWLEDGMENTS

So many people encouraged and supported me in the writing and researching of this book that I can barely begin to thank them all for their help. But they are a part of this book, just as they have become a part of my life.

First, I would like to thank Clifford May, who was editor of *Geo* and who gave me the assignment—and later the encouragement—that led to my writing this book. I would like to thank my agents Georges and Anne Borchardt, who understood that there was far more to ballet than what appeared onstage; and Nan Graham, my editor, who was constantly available to discuss, sympathize, shape, and encourage throughout the entire two-year span.

Then there are the dancers and their advocates. Lenny Liebowitz and Michelle Benash cannot be thanked enough. They were absolutely boundless in their support. I would like as well to thank Kristine Soleri, Joel Timm, and Lisa de Ribere, all of whom helped me understand the realities of the ballet world. I would like to thank Hilda Morales and Frank Smith for their time and energy. The conversations I had with Nancy Bielski, Clare Duncan, and Dick Kutch were of enormous help to me and clarified many issues.

I would like to give special thanks to Gunilla Rumpke, Dan Rudholm, and the Royal Swedish Ballet for the help they have given me, but mostly for what they are doing to help their dancers. Thanks also to Jane Salier at the Royal Swedish Ballet and Carolyn Humpston at London Festival Ballet. Selma Rudnick at Pennsylvania Ballet provided me with invaluable assistance, and Barbara Weisberger was kind enough to share her insights with me.

I also owe an intellectual debt to the work of the great American sociologist Erving Goffman, whose book *Asylums* provided the intellectual framework for the understanding of ballet and the problems it poses. And, of course, I feel deeply grateful for the help and suggestions offered, over the course of these two years, by my friend Isabelle Marcus.

The people above have given me a great deal of help. But two people must be singled out. While I was writing this book, Patsy Vigderman was unstinting in her suggestions. She helped me reformulate ideas, rewrite copy, and reorganize my thoughts. She commiserated and was always willing to put down her other work to make sure I refined my ideas and met deadlines. And finally, my husband, Steve Early, was my greatest support. While I was struggling to figure out whether or not to pursue this project, he was utterly confident of its worth. While I anguished over wording, he came up with the right phrase at the right moment. He edited and commented, held my hand, and kept me going. The book is not dedicated to him, but rather to my mother, who, as I said, brought me to ballet. But it is as much a gift to him as it is to her.

INTRODUCTION

I was raised on ballet. Not to be a dancer but to love the dance. When I was four years old, my mother started filling our Wednesday and Saturday afternoons with ballet. We watched everything at those matinee performances. During intermission, my mother attached a note to her playbill, tipped an usher, and asked her to deliver it to that day's prima ballerina. She politely requested an audience and an autograph for her young daughter, the budding fan. In those days, when ballet fans were rarities, most ballerinas agreed.

So my mother and I would go round to the stage door, and there, backstage, I met Maria Tallchief and Alicia Alonso. When I was only five or six, I met Alicia Markova, a dark-haired woman dressed in a white tulle gown, its heart-shaped bodice hugging her torso. And I will never forget meeting Leslie Caron, who was then dancing with a French company, before she quit ballet to become an actress. When I fell shyly silent, she pulled a rose from an impressive bouquet and gently offered it to me, a memento that I quickly pressed between the covers of a book I lost long ago.

I grew up on ballet. But I never wanted to be a dancer. When I was thirty I saw the Joffrey Ballet perform a Frederick Ashton pas de trois to Erik Satie's *Trois Gymnopédies*. The slow precision, the way the dancers melted into the music, converted me. I resolved to take ballet lessons. If I learned only to move an arm, one hand with fluid grace, that would be enough.

The Yellow Pages gave me the numbers of several schools; and at the first call, I found the wonderfully unexpected. An old Russian lady, with a thick accent, replied to my questions. Was it really a beginners class, I wanted to know, a true beginners class, not an advanced or middle beginners? "Yes, dahling," she assured me, and the cheerful voice and incredible accent drew me in.

I had found the real thing!

The school was in a storefront on a heavily trafficked thoroughfare. It was a tiny, rundown place with flimsy plasterboard partitions between the studio, front waiting room, and dressing room—the sparest of spaces —at the back. There was nothing elegant about it. The walls were a faded cream, and the floors were never polished quite highly enough. There was barely room enough to accommodate all the adults who crowded in. The whole place had a tired, worn, impoverished air. The record player was so ancient that the music strained to reach us over the intrusive mechanical din of a dull needle skimming the surface of scratched, dusty records.

The teacher—Madame she was called—was indeed a former Russian ballerina who had grown old and corpulent, with a huge, tightly girded stomach. She wore her white hair in a thick, teased beehive, and a large cross dangled at her neck. In the mornings, she faithfully worshipped at a nearby Russian Orthodox church and nearly always came late to class.

Her helper and supplementary instructress was a young woman named Anna, a thin, tight-limbed girl, with sharp features, elbows that protruded like the lethal corners of a metal cabinet, knobby knees, and a long, pointed nose. She had never had the slightest hope of being a ballerina but managed to maintain her connection to the dance because she proved so useful to Madame. She fetched and carried, did the books, taught the children, chauffeured Madame, and performed countless other chores with total dedication. One could see that she longed to be Madame's daughter, that she adored the old woman. But she was no more, in her idol's eye, than a needed servant, a weary Cinderella who swept the floor, Windexed the mirrors, and cleaned out the bathroom.

Though sad and pathetic, Anna and Madame were cloaked in the enchantment of ballet. The art rescued its failed artists, and it rescued us, for there was always something charming about those classes. I've been told since that everything she taught us was wrong, but for an hour and a half, three times a week, Madame made us feel like dancers. During those classes, I became light and graceful and basked in the sibilant French sounds, the filmy transparency of the nylon skirts that fluttered around my body, the satin richness of the toe shoes I was finally allowed to don for five or ten excruciating minutes during each class.

When I moved to the East from California, I regretted losing Madame. The classes I took in other cities were far more technically sound, but the teachers were harsh practitioners of the art. In Boston, I took lessons from a former dancer whose adult classes were filled with women like myself—secretaries, clerks, lawyers, would-be doctors —who would never be professionals. You would not have known that from the class. If I made the mistake of impeding someone's view of herself in the mirror, she glanced at me in fury. And when I enthusiastically took a place at the front of the class, I was told that this was a place of honor, and I was moved into a back row. The competitive atmosphere took the joy out of class for me. Without that make-believe ease Madame had created, ballet simply lost most of its illusions.

It shed whatever illusions remained when I did a story on ballet for *Geo* magazine. In 1979, after ABT dancers had taken a historic step in challenging their company and refusing to accept the terms of their new contract, they were locked out of their studios by ABT management. *Geo* asked me to do a story on the changes going on in the ballet world. To approach ballet as a labor story was a novel idea. Yet, it wasn't until I began to talk to dancers that I became truly excited about the project. There was something about them that drew me in immediately. It was more than their art, their stamina, their technical skill and grace. It was their timidity and lack of confidence. During my very first interview, with Kristine Soleri, an active member of the ABT negotiating team during the lockout, this aura of helplessness was unmistakable. Kri described the dancers' rebellion against their company with a mixture of pride and incredulousness. The dancers had acted with great aggressiveness, and their protest had shaken the entire ballet world. They had scored an enormous victory for themselves and for dancers across the nation. Yet Soleri spoke as though the lockout had been led by strangers, as though she could not quite believe that she and the dancers she worked with had actually managed to win such a historic fight.

Somehow, in the course of their training and their careers, these men and women lose part of themselves, and even an experience as powerful as the ABT lockout does not fully allow them to reclaim their sense of self.

As I began to talk to more and more dancers, the extent of their loss of self became apparent. I learned that dancers must sacrifice any semblance of a social or emotional life if they are to advance in a fiercely competitive and overcrowded field; that dancers are often injured because of undue pressure to perform when they are ill or exhausted or already suffering from a minor injury; that anorexia nervosa, a psychological disorder in which young girls starve themselves, sometimes to death, because they perceive themselves as fat when, in fact, they are not, is a prevalent problem among female dancers. And I found that dancers have terrible difficulty facing the real world once they leave the world of dance. I discovered that there was as much anguish as art in ballet, and that the anguish was created by the ballet establishment; it was not inherent in the art.

I could see the anguish in the dancers' bodies, starved of flesh, contour, and health. I could hear it in their voices, the dejected tone, the sense of isolation that was manifest when they asked me how other dancers felt—those who had quit or who were going to retire. Here was a group of people who had achieved the best their chosen career had to offer. They were not just hopefuls; they were students in elite schools or professionals working in major companies, practicing an art they loved. Yet in all the traveling I've done and people I've met, I don't think I have ever come across such a group of unhappy people, for finally what has been stolen from them is not only their power but their enjoyment of their art.

I began to feel a sense of outrage. It is hard not to feel it, hard to watch young students who look like skeletons dance across the floor while parents, teachers, and observers sit measuring technique, so mesmerized by the prospects of future glamour and glory that they are oblivious to the simple fact that these aren't just dancers, they're children, abused children, who are so thin they can barely make it through the day.

It is hard to listen to a male student at the School of American Ballet who is often downcast and depressed because he is burdened with cares no youngster should have to contend with. At sixteen, he faces major surgery for a chronic injury and is engulfed by worries bred by the fierce competition that inhibits his ability to trust fellow students at ballet school. It is hard to listen to the self-chastisement rampant among students and company dancers. Harder still to see a young woman I became friends with decide finally to quit ballet. She felt exuberant about the world that awaited her; I shared her delight. Then she discovered, after she'd quit ABT, that her body had taken so much punishment over the years that a quarter of her knee had disintegrated. She can never dance again, and she can barely even walk.

Some dancers are heartening—the ones who are struggling to find a new way to deal with the pressures and demands of the dance. Some have answers, like Frank Smith, an ABT soloist who suddenly discovered during the ABT lockout of 1979 that he could lead, as well as follow. Smith has concrete suggestions for improvements, which he continued to struggle to realize during last fall's round of negotiations with ABT management. The system, he believes, can be changed. If dancers act, they can alter scheduling practices, challenge an unwieldy company repertoire, and fight for security, respect, and better pay.

Some only have questions. "How do you find the world?" asks Michelle Benash of ABT. "How do you maintain that incredible dedication to dance, a dedication you can't do without, and yet still build friendships, have love relationships, not wrap yourself in the tight little cocoon of ballet?" "How do you grow up," wonders Solange MacArthur, "when you've put yourself on hold for so long? When you're twenty-eight and you're sitting in a college classroom full of eighteen year olds, and you feel like a child because they have had so much more experience in the world? How do you escape the burden of expectations placed upon you by parents, teachers, and fans?"

I talked one morning with Gelsey Kirkland, one of ballet's greatest stars and, in a sense, one of ballet's greatest casualties. She is so talented that onstage she becomes—this woman of no great beauty—the most delicate fawn. You would think she would have confidence in herself. But she is so fearful at an interview that she feels she has nothing of value to say. And she is a woman of astonishing insight.

With great eloquence, she told me of her own dilemma. "How do you find the self you packed away when you were a child?" she asked herself. "How do you cultivate a new self without discarding the skills and talents you've acquired, which are both your joy and your pain?" Like all people who want to change, she was questioning how to purge herself of the bad without excising the good as well.

The dilemmas of dancers are so resonant, their relationships to their art, their teachers, and their families so rich, that to write just an article was not enough. So I decided to write this book.

—Suzanne Gordon, July 1982

OFF BALANCE

The precision is exquisite. At first the stage is empty—a midnight blue grotto filled only with the dolorous sounds of music. Then, on a ramp at the edge of the stage, the first dancer appears, a shimmering white apparition moving slowly to the languorous steps— *arabesque*, *plié*, *cambré*, *port de bras*—legs float backward, knees bend gently, torsos arch, arms encircle. As soon as this dancer glides forward, another appears, and then another. Each is a replica of the one who preceded her and the one who will follow. Their pale, thin torsos are wrapped in white tutus, which flair out at the waist in layer upon layer of fine white net. Diaphanous veils of white chiffon trace the curve of their arms and billow softly as they move. With an attenuated grace, they form an incandescent chain that slowly undulates back and forth across the stage.

So captivated is the audience by this slow procession that time seems to be suspended, as it is in the fairy tales and romances performed throughout this summer season of the American Ballet Theatre in New York. The hall is enshrouded in the eternal silence the dancers evoke, so that the audience not only sees them glide as one but almost hears them breathe as one. Then, as the last dancer appears on stage, the corps de ballet—the body of the ballet—turns, forming a perfect rectangle, to complete this remarkable variation from Act II, the Kingdom of the Shades, of Marius Petipa's ballet *La Bayadère*.

As the corps turns, the house explodes in bravos and applause. Accolades like this abound throughout the performance. When the

3

entire piece ends, stagehands part the heavy gold curtains so Natalia Makarova, the legendary Russian prima ballerina, and Anthony Dowell, Britain's *premier danseur*, can step forward to the edge of the stage, where cheering fans crowd round the orchestra pit to greet them. Despite the dancers' obvious pleasure at the audience's response, there is never a breech of courtly etiquette. Makarova curtsies to the crowd and then to Dowell. Plucking a stem from a huge bouquet of roses, she offers it to her partner, who graciously receives this memento and kisses her hand. They accept the wild appreciation of the audience like two lovers leisurely promenading through a magnificently tended castle garden, stopping to snip an occasional bud, smiling beneficently, whispering in one another's ear; they are secure in the knowledge that nothing can ever mar the perfection of the scene. Finally, when the applause has spent itself, Makarova and Dowell curtsy, bow, and retreat for the evening.

Members of tonight's audience have been more appreciative than usual. They have witnessed a historic event: the premiere of Makarova's lavish staging of the full-length production of *La Bayadère*. Over the years, American audiences have become familiar with Act II, the Kingdom of the Shades, but they have never seen the entire production. To bring them the real thing, Ballet Theatre gave Makarova a half-million dollars and free artistic rein. Like a gourmet remembering an extraordinary meal and trying to assemble the exact blend of ingredients, Makarova searched the archives and her Russian memories, and summoned set and costume designers from all over the world to help her reconstruct this piece of history.

PierLuigi Samaritani, the great Italian opera designer, created sets of exquisite oriental splendor. Fountains bubble outside forbidding temples; giant ferns and a dazzling display of flora and fauna climb the pillars of a rajah's garden where dancing girls bask in the sunlight; a huge, impassive Buddha commands the interior of an ominously darkened temple hall whose long, tunneled corridors extend into infinity.

To construct the sets, Makarova did not rely on the Met's skilled craftspeople alone. She entrusted much of the work to Italian set painters, who did the work in Italy and shipped the sets to America. The costumes were custom-made with equal attention to detail. Since no expense was spared, many of the costumes cost up to $1500 each.

The story is as complicated as its accessories and embellishments. The French choreographer Marius Petipa, who created many of the great classics of Russian ballet, based this tale on love and jealousy on a drama by a fourth-century Sanskrit poet. Makarova plays Nikiya, a temple dancer who loves Solor (Anthony Dowell), an Indian warrior. Solor pledges his love to her but later renounces his beloved when he is ordered to marry the local rajah's daughter, Gamsatti. Nikiya and Gamsatti, the two rivals, meet; and the latter, hoping Nikiya will abandon Solor, tries to bribe the dancer with a gift of jewels. When Nikiya refuses, Gamsatti plants a snake in a basket of flowers and offers it to Nikiya, who is stung and dies. In the famous Act II, the distraught Solor seeks solace in opium and dreams that he has journeyed to the afterworld to join his beloved, where together they dance their remorse. In the final act, Solor must marry Gamsatti, but the gods save him from this fate by destroying the entire temple and all who have come to celebrate this evil match.

Tickets for this gala opening cost $100, and everyone who is anyone in the ballet world is in attendance. As is customary, the red plush seats along the orchestra aisles are reserved for critics from *Dance Magazine, Ballet News, The New York Times,* the *New York Post,* and *The New Yorker.* Lucia Chase, founder of American Ballet Theatre, sits next to Oliver Smith, her silver-haired co-director.

During intermissions, New York's most famous teachers stroll through the lobbies of the Met and along the balcony overlooking the

Lincoln Center fountain. Principal dancers from other New York companies are also in the crowd. Aware of their celebrity and its rippling effect, they strut through the throng of fans who are too polite to ask for an autograph but not too polite to gape.

Wealthy ballet patrons are dressed tonight in tuxedos and silk designer originals. Those who are too poor or were too late to get seats mingle with the students from the city's ballet schools who vie for standing room behind the velvet-covered balustrades at the back of the house.

At the end of the performance, a small group of ardent admirers clusters around the stage door, hoping for an autograph or at least a glimpse of the stars. One particularly devoted balletomane, an old man with sallow skin and thin graying hair, has managed to convince the guards to let him wait in the lounge just inside the door. In his baggy gray suit and black bow tie he stands in front of the reception desk as the dancers leave the theater. "You were gorgeous, darling," he tells Kristine Soleri and Michelle Benash, two corps dancers who are among the first to exit. "Marvelous!" he exclaims as Hilda Morales, a soloist, passes. The dancers later tell me that he is a widower who attends each New York performance and who waits faithfully to congratulate the dancers at the stage door. Tonight they indulge him with a smile, a hand proferred for a ritual kiss before they hurry off in a cab to spend the early-morning hours dancing at Xenon's discotheque.

To celebrate the opening of her ballet Makarova has taken over Xenon's. She has traded the mantle of a scorned lover and returned to center stage as the world-renowned superstar. Dressed in a tight red sequined dress, she is escorted by her millionaire husband and encircled by a bevy of admirers. As if saluting the victory of a champion athlete, the male dancers in the company suddenly hoist her to their shoulders and parade her round the room. In the spirit of triumph, she grabs on to one of the many chandeliers and swings across the ceiling —just like in the movies or in a dream.

There is nothing quite like the spell ballet casts. For many of us it begins with *The Nutcracker.* No matter where they are, no matter what part of the country or the world, children gasp with joy and give themselves up to the sorcery when that tiny Nutcracker turns into a dashing young prince; when an ordinary Christmas tree unfurls into an enormous, luminous cascade of branches dotted with twinkling lights and golden candles; when nursery rhyme characters emerge from under the skirts of Mother Goose.

Later on it is *Swan Lake, Giselle, The Sleeping Beauty,* creating a world where women are soft wisps, almost transparent with passion, fluttering and melting in men's arms; where men are strong, gallant cavaliers in gilt-edged velvet doublets and white tights. Heroes whose kiss or vow can break a spell, they are noble, elegant, gracious, and if not always faithful they are, at the very least, eternally repentant.

You can lose yourself in the theater. You can believe in ballet— in the art and in the artists who practice it, for they are not ordinary people with ordinary needs and ordinary desires; they are a breed apart.

In czarist times, ballerinas were the darlings of the aristocracy. Counts and grand dukes and princes showered them with jewels and furs and palaces. The great Russian ballerina Mathilde Kshessinskaya was mistress to Czar Nicholas II, and later married the grand duke André, who built for her the famous palace that Lenin later appropriated for his revolutionary headquarters. Her famous rival ballerina Olga Preobrazhenskaya married into the aristocracy; other dancers amassed fortunes.

Today, only the settings have changed. Margot Fonteyn's autobiography rivals the Sleeping Beauty's. Mink coats, flowers, and compliments mass in her dressing room. Her professional life may involve hard work, but her personal life is a round of fittings at Dior, trips around the world, dinner parties with Hollywood stars, and voyages on Onassis's yachts. She married the son of the president of Panama after a whirlwind courtship, during which he regaled her with diamond bracelets and rooms full of roses.

Makarova is married to a millionaire; her son's godmother is Jacqueline Kennedy Onassis; Mikhail Baryshnikov drives a white Cadillac and has just had a child with a Hollywood starlet; Fernando Bujones is married to the daughter of the president of Brazil. To those of us who lurch awkwardly through glamourless lives, the dancers' easy defiance of the body's limits, coupled with their fairy-tale existence, makes them truly the children of our imagination.

First, however, they are the children of their own imaginations. The young student who opens the popular book on the Royal Ballet School is immediately drawn in by a picture of White Lodge—"the elegant eighteenth-century residence" that is the school's home. Enshrouded in mist, surrounded by a canopy of trees with delicately curved branches and expanses of finely manicured lawns, the school, with its fine, pillared porticoes, is an enticing apparition. Inside White Lodge, earnest young students effortlessly master new skills. Outside class, they romp in wheelbarrows, practice their *développés* while carrying trays from the cafeteria, and happily sew their toe shoes while chattering excitedly with companions. There is only one photo of an injured dancer: It shows a tall boy bracing himself on a pair of canes, smiling cheerfully amidst a crowd of other youngsters.

In one of America's most popular children's books on ballet—Jill Krementz's *A Very Young Dancer*—the budding student becomes a miniature superstar. Stephanie, a student at the School of American Ballet, is awarded the coveted lead in the New York City Ballet's production of *The Nutcracker*. With that role, she is instantly transported into the land of Sugar Plum Fairies and dainty snowflakes.

The great costume designer Madame Karinska fashions a costume especially for her. The busy Mr. Balanchine personally instructs her and fusses over her attire. Backstage, seasoned stars like Patricia McBride and Colleen Neary befriend the baby ballerina.

Add to such books films like *The Red Shoes,* that bittersweet tale of a dancer who is torn between love and dance, and who dies because she cannot make the choice between the two, or *The Turning Point,* with its wonderous tale of a young ballerina's leap to fame; documentaries about dance; images from dance magazines; and performance— and you have the pomise of grace, wealth, and glory—a powerful potion which, combined with the love of dance, casts an irresistible spell.

"Ballet was always a fantasy," American Ballet Theatre's Hilda Morales remembers. "I would be a ballerina and have a tutu and go onstage and dance on my toes. I would find absolute Nirvana in this world of tutus and curtain calls and flowers." Or as Deborah Marks, a former SAB student, says, "I had daydreams of rescuing my parents from attacks of wild Indians by being the beautiful little girl who dances. I would be so beautiful, they would let my family go."

For American Ballet Theatre soloist Victor Barbee, ballet became a fantasy of conquest and glory. When Barbee was sixteen years old, he came to New York for a summer session at the School of American Ballet. The Royal Ballet was making one of its customary appearances at the Met, and a friend insisted there could be no better introduction to professional dance than this.

"We came over and stood on line at seven o'clock in the morning," Barbee, now twenty-seven, recalls. "We waited for five hours and got two standing-room tickets, top row at the back. The dancers came on. That long procession was the most beautiful thing I'd ever seen," he says, his voice hushed, still appreciative of that first memory, even though he had danced a leading solo role in the same ballet only several days before. "At the end of the first section, the corps got a ten-minute standing ovation. Then Rudolf [Nureyev] and Margot

[Fonteyn] came out and danced the house down, and between every variation there was applause and bravos. Rudolf was phenomenal, and Margot was beautiful, and the ballet took an hour just to get through that Shades section. I thought, 'This goes on every night.' I thought, 'Every performance is like this.' I thought, 'It's great, and all the dancers are great, and it's beautiful, and people tear the house down.' "

That is what dancers and the public see from their seats in the orchestra or the balcony. Once dancers leave the audience and move behind the curtain, their experience is somewhat different. They pay a high price on their way to the standing ovations and the bouquets of roses. First of all, they must make tremendous financial sacrifices. When Europeans and Russians first brought ballet to America in the thirties and forties, it was not well received. Dancers learned that if they wanted to dance, they could not expect financial security. They would have to dance for the reward of doing what they loved and the great satisfaction of building something—a new art and an audience that would appreciate it. These earlier sacrifices have paid off. Over the past decade there has been an unprecedented ballet boom. In 1968 only about 1 million Americans went to the ballet. Last year, the estimated ballet audience in the United States had surpassed 20 million people—7 million more than attended NFL games—and millions more watch televised ballet performances. Far from being an obscure art, ballet has become so accepted a part of our culture that it is now used in advertisements selling everything from panty hose to public television. Yet despite this new interest in the art and despite the millions of dollars spent on it, the ordinary dancer's lot has not improved. In some ways it appears to be getting worse.

Apart from superstars like Baryshnikov and Makarova, dancers earn astonishingly little. Soloists and members of the corps de ballet—the essence of any ballet performance—earn less than the musicians who accompany them and the stagehands who move their props. Unlike a professional musician, who may experience years of frustration, rejection, and penury before winning a seat with a top-flight orchestra but who is then assured a decent living and many years of rewarding work, dancers have no job security, receive little or no pension, and have careers that end early—at age thirty or thirty-five.

Until recently, ballet audiences have been unaware of these conditions because dancers have silently accepted their plight. In the fall of 1979, however, a group of dancers in the American Ballet Theatre decided that their union, the American Guild of Musical Artists (AGMA), was not bargaining effectively with ABT management and its sophisticated lawyers. Hardly a querulous group, ABT dancers hired a combative labor lawyer and began to negotiate with uncharacteristic assertiveness. Management refused to meet the dancers' demands, locked them out of their studios for ten weeks, and canceled the fall season. The dancers took their cause to the public, picketing, leafleting, giving benefit performances, and appearing on radio and television. Although the lockout focused on the problems of underpaid corps dancers and soloists, some superstar dancers like Gelsey Kirkland and Martine van Hamel lent their time and prestige to protest wages and poor working conditions.

During the lockout, fans learned that dancers in the nation's top star company earned woefully little. A member of the corps who had trained for twelve to fifteen years earned a starting salary of only $250 a week. Older corps dancers and soloists were not doing much better. Yet, all had to pay for food and housing in the nation's most expensive city. Dancers got no vacation pay; were guaranteed only a thirty-six–week work year; could be fired at a moment's notice; and when on tour in major American cities, had to pay for both hotel and meals from the $30 per diem their companies allotted them.

The lockout proved to be a truly historic event. "For the first time," Gelsey Kirkland observes, "dancers had found their voices." By the time they settled the strike, with a much-improved contract, their complaints were echoing through the dance world. In smaller nonunion companies, like Pittsburgh Ballet Theatre, dancers fought to join AGMA; and in other already unionized companies, they began to adopt a more militant negotiating stance. Even New York City Ballet dancers, famed for their almost robotlike allegiance to Balanchine, initiated strike talks.

Important as it was, the ABT lockout only hinted at the extent of dancers' problems. These do not begin when a dancer joins a major company. Most parents send their children off to elite ballet schools like the School of American Ballet, assuming that teachers and administrators will ensure their well-being. On the contrary, in the process of turning out superb technical dancers, these schools impose such stern discipline on students—in most cases, very young children—that they often jeopardize their health, both physical and mental.

Dancers in schools and companies are subject to a growing number of injuries. Although some of these injuries are the inevitable result of the strenuous demands that ballet places upon the human body, others stem from policies of large ballet companies and the schools that annually provide them with a new crop of dancers. Many injuries occur when teachers and choreographers, like football coaches, encourage dancers to perform when they are tired or slightly injured. This turns acute aches into chronic pains. Dancing on a strained knee can grind the kneecap down until it eventually disintegrates. Leaping across hard floors with an acute case of tendonitis can create a chronic inflammation. Jumping over and over again, night after night, day after day, can produce stress fractures and injuries to joints that later turn into arthritic conditions. And feet trapped into the prison of toe shoes become painfully calloused and swollen and may also become arthritic.

Heavy performance schedules and ballet's new reliance on athletic tricks increase the risk of injury. In America, dancers often perform eight times a week during a ballet season. When added to daily class and rehearsal, this kind of work load is not only exhausting; it can be crippling. Many of the ballets now performed, furthermore, depend heavily on what is known as tricks, intricate athletic dance movements and lifts that excite the audience but place enormous strain on the dancer's instrument: his or her body. More and more injuries result, and they persist even after dancers stop dancing.

Injuries are also induced by another of ballet's little-known hazards, one that puts female dancers at risk. Choreographers and company directors—almost always male—mold ballet's young women to an ideal of the feminine that equates beauty and grace with excessive thinness. With heightening competition, this emphasis on thinness often becomes an obsession. Students in many ballet schools will do anything to get into a company; many believe they will attract attention and respect if they are almost skeletal.

Nor does the pressure to be abnormally thin end when the dancers are accepted into a professional company. There they will be encouraged to conform to what is known as the ballet look—the thin, breastless, hipless, long-limbed shape American choreographers and companies prefer. In an effort to fend off a "weight problem," some of these dancers develop one of the least graceful and most serious psychosomatic disorders, anorexia nervosa. A disorder that afflicts affluent, adolescent and pre-adolescent girls, anorexia has been called "the relentless pursuit of excessive thinness." Anorectics are not uninterested in food; on the contrary, they are obsessed by food. Because they have a disturbed body image and believe, no matter how thin they are, that they are fat, they refuse to eat and begin to starve themselves. Many young women who exhibit anorectic behavior merely engage in bizarre eating practices (vomiting, using laxatives to cheat calories), which can damage their health. But for others the consequences are more serious; the mortality rate among anorectics is 15 to 17 percent. And anorexia and injury are inextricably interconnected. Malnourished bodies cannot withstand the strain ballet imposes in them.

Ballet training is not only a long and painful discipline of the body; it is a discipline of the spirit as well. Dancers are deliberately schooled in obedience and deference. At a time when most adolescents are learning to stand on their own, dancers remain wholly identified with their teachers. Because many mothers and fathers become completely absorbed in their children's careers, many female dancers, and some male dancers, never learn to separate their own identities from the identities of their parents. Thus, the ballet mother has become a stock figure in the life and the literature of dance.

Dancers learn to master the art of dance, but not the art of life. They are often lonely young men and women who are terrified to go out on a date or who shudder at the prospect of socializing with non-dancers. Others say they are afraid of the world because they have been told where to be, what to do, and how to think for so long that they do not know how to fend for themselves. Many young women, trained to detest fat, begin to hate their bodies and cannot bear looking at themselves in the mirror. Comparing her art to mine, Heléne Alexopolous, a beautiful New York City Ballet dancer, says, "*You* don't use your body as an instrument; *you* don't look in the mirror and hate your body so much that you want to cry."

These problems become even more serious when dancers retire. More than an untimely end to an all-too-short career, retirement means that they must suddenly face a bewildering outside world. At thirty or thirty-five, they rarely have more than a high school diploma; they have no marketable professional skills; and they have few social or emotional recourses in a world they left when they were nine or ten. What do they do? What becomes of them?

People who come in contact with dancers frequently describe them as charming, selfless, cooperative people who are touchingly helpless and incapable of dealing with the realities of life. To the outsider who lives in a conflict-filled world where angry, pushy, sometimes offensive people are the norm, the dancer seems wise to have preserved such childlike innocence. What we fail to realize is that no choice was made. From the very moment they enter the career of ballet, dancers are programmed in diffidence. For ballet is more than art, more than business; it is a closed world where those in authority have almost total control over every aspect of the dancer's life.

Behind the intricate and beautiful choreography we see onstage is an even more forceful yet subtle choreography of power.

At about ten-fifteen in the morning—Monday through Saturday—students of the School of American Ballet arrive at a long, low building on West Sixty-sixth Street in New York. They enter the building through heavy smoke-glass doors with imposing brass fixtures. A reception desk stands in the middle of the lobby; a receptionist and guard scan the faces of the girls and boys on their way to the elevators. All of the students, even the youngest, have a certain look. The girls wear their hair long, in braids or pulled up into the classic ballet bun—tight little pin cushions on top of their small heads. The boys are, without exception, clean-shaven. All walk with their feet jutting off at a 45 degree angle: the ballet "duck walk." Their posture is erect, heads high on their long slim necks; the boys slim-hipped with muscular arms. At the third floor, they exit and pass through two glass doors that mark the entrance to the School of American Ballet—Balanchine's school. Narrow rust-colored corridors, decorated with a series of eighteenth-century architectural etchings, lead to the dressing rooms, where they change for class.

The majority of these dancers trace their careers to a parent who had an interest, or even a passion, for dance. Many parents are eager to interest their children in ballet because they believe it will teach them art and grace. Ballet, with its combination of the musical, theatrical, and decorative arts, has become part of the urban and suburban ritual of after-school lessons. "It's like horseback riding and music lessons," says Mrs. Sarah Harcourt*, mother of a fifteen-year-old student at the San Francisco Ballet School. "It can't hurt, and it gives them a little grace and a little poise."

Other parents think it is important to give a child's life focus, which is just what ballet does. "I like kids to do something, to learn something," one Boston ballet mother explains. "I don't like kids sitting around watching TV all day. This way my daughter comes home late and has to do her homework; on weekends she misses out on a lot of other things, but at least she's busy."

Concern for a child's cultural and emotional welfare seems to motivate most parents.

Ballet's conventions and discipline can make a child feel somewhat in charge of his or her life. This can be a great advantage to teenagers, who worry about school and sex and separating from their families, who feel they will soon have to guide their own lives but who have no idea what path to follow. Dancers do not have to grapple with these problems. They live in a world where they receive constant direction, a world where the barre is never far from their grasp. In her autobiography, Dame Margot Fonteyn sums up how invaluable such programming can be:

People often ask if the discipline of my career is not irksome. On the contrary, I have found it an extraordinary advantage to have a rigid timetable prescribed for almost every day of the year. The necessity of going to class is not only healthy in itself—for the amount of compulsory exercise is far more than anyone would do voluntarily, just to keep fit—it is also therapeutic in times of emotional stress. No matter how often one attends a ballet class, one must still maintain a particular degree of concentration, for each class is different from all others, and the concentrating for an hour

---

* Some of the people I interviewed requested that I use pseudonymous names when quoting them. Pseudonyms are indicated by an asterisk after their first appearance only.

or more on the manipulation of one's limbs relieves and refreshes a mind that may be overengrossed in emotional problems.

Yet when ballet mothers talk at greater length, they often reveal another motive for their commitment to a child's career in ballet. Many of them are willing to spend hours chauffering their children to and from class because they once wanted to be dancers themselves. Their children have reawakened their own youthful fantasies. Alice Oebon, the mother of a child at the Houston Ballet Academy, explains that "from the time I was a little girl, almost as long ago as I can remember, I've been very much in love with ballet. I had some ballet as a child, but it was only a transient thing. I didn't get to study in depth because when I was about ten years old we moved from the city to the country, where there were no ballet lessons. My father was a revenue officer—he was an alcohol and tobacco tax agent—and he chased bootleggers in the mountains of North Carolina. I couldn't take ballet anymore."

While most ballet mothers pin their hopes and dreams on the burgeoning talent of a daughter, some encourage their sons to dance. Angela Faranzano, for example, had always anticipated the day when she could lead her daughter to the barre. Unfortunately, she had sons, not daughters, but she took her eight-year-old to SAB, even though her in-laws objected to a boy ballet dancer.

A less common path to ballet is via pediatrics. A family doctor who notices a potential orthopedic problem may prescribe the perfect remedy: ballet. Van Tania Pelzer, a seventeen-year-old student at San Francisco, attributes her career to weak knees. Vane Vest, a principal dancer at San Francisco, was asthmatic as a child and could not engage in sports. Ballet, with its slow strengthening of the body, was recommended.

Many boys and girls get their first glimpse of ballet when they traipse after an older sibling. Often their brother or sister abandons dance, but they continue. "There was no plan to it," says Mrs. Rosen*, a hard-working divorced mother whose eleven-year-old daughter, Rachel*, studies at the School of American Ballet, "Logistically, I couldn't have one kid going to one place and another to another. So both my daughters took ballet. Rachel liked it, and I thought, 'That's good, the kid likes ballet, she'll be graceful.'" When Rachel's sister quit, Rachel persisted. "Suddenly," her mother says, "she got intensely interested in dance. She read the book about the Royal Ballet School about twenty times, and I decided she was serious and had talent so I'd take her to SAB for an audition. She got in."

The administrative and teaching staff of SAB is headed by the brisk and studiously aloof Russian-born Associate Director, Nathalie Gleboff (Madame Gleboff to the students). Her teaching staff includes several other Russian notables, the foremost of whom is Alexandra Danilova, a seventy-six-year-old vestige of Russia's imperial past. Danilova was a great ballerina who, with Balanchine, left Russia and joined Diaghilev in France. Other Russians on the fourteen-member teaching staff are Andrei Kramarevsky, Helene Dudin, and Antonina Tumkovsky. One of the non-Russians, Stanley Williams, a favored teacher of male dancers, was trained in Denmark, at the Royal Danish Ballet. The youngest of the teachers is Suki Schorer, a former principal dancer with New York City Ballet. NYCB stars like Suzanne Farrell and Jean-Pierre Bonnefous also teach at SAB.

George Balanchine, whose appearances at SAB are rarer and rarer, is SAB's most famous celebrity, followed by Lincoln Kirstein, the wealthy heir to a Boston mercantile fortune who discovered George Balanchine in Paris in the 1930s and brought him to America. Kirstein's figure contrasts strikingly with those of the frail waifs and handsome boys who fill the school's corridors. He is a gawky hulk of a man, with balding gray hair and wire-rim glasses, usually dressed in a somber double-breasted suit, its buttons straining over his chest.

The students, most of them in their mid-teens, arrive in time for a ten-thirty class. Today Stanley Williams teaches the advanced girls, and dancers from the New York City Ballet attend. Suzanne Farrell and other lesser-known company dancers take their places at the barre. Accustomed to their presence, the students nonetheless become a bit more tense and jittery. Models to be emulated, the NYCB dancers are also competitors for the teacher's attention.

Seventeen-year-old Jane Cooper* and eighteen-year-old Regina Gray,* two advanced students, are early arrivals. Jane, a New Yorker, has been at SAB since she was eight. Regina, a judge's daughter from the Midwest, came when she was sixteen. Both live in the same Upper West Side apartment building, where Jane shares a small, one-bedroom apartment with a dancer in City Ballet, and Regina has a tiny studio.

The two girls install themselves at a good spot in front of the large studio mirror. For both, this year is critical. Their aim is to become apprentices in New York City Ballet. Apprentices are provisionally accepted into the company and have a chance to dance in the corps de ballet, the lowest rung on the hierarchically structured ballet ladder. If they prove themselves able to cope with the rigors of professional dance, they will then be accepted as full members of the corps. From there, they can work themselves up to a soloist position, where they will be allowed to dance first small, then more demanding, solos. Finally, if they are extremely talented and extremely lucky, they may become what every young student dreams of becoming: a principal dancer.

If Regina and Jane are not chosen to be apprentices, they must find other options. Although they hope that the capricious Mr. Blanchine will choose them over someone else, the chances are slight that either will make it into NYCB. Thirty students in advanced classes are contenders for a limited number of openings. "The number we take into the company each year varies," Madame Gleboff explains. "It's usually between one and two. Or if we have a splendid year, the company might take eight or nine. But that's very unusual. This year we took eight people into the company because there were other considerations. The company was going on tour, and we were concerned there might be a high rate of injury. If you expect to lose people due to injuries, you need to have replacements."

SAB enrolls about 425 students each year; the company has, on the average, about 100 dancers and a few openings through attrition. Consequently, the company cannot possibly accommodate more than a fraction of the students its school trains. Other companies and schools have a similar ratio of openings to available students. ABT has nearly 100 dancers; and until 1981, its school had 150 students. (The ABT School has since cut back its program to 15 students.) But students vying to make it into ABT have to compete not only with each other but with professional dancers from regional companies who want to move into the big time, and with dancers from major international companies who want to dance in New York. In regional companies, there are perhaps 200 students in upper-division classes. But regional companies are even smaller than those in New York and have from 30 to 50 dancers and perhaps one or two openings a year—openings for which dancers from other regional companies and schools may compete. So at all schools, a large number of students wait anxiously for the unlikely to occur.

For Jane, the chances of being accepted into "the company" are almost nil. Neither ethereal nor statuesque, she is thin but not excessively so. She feels that her looks as well as her seniority at SAB damage her odds. She sees herself as a faded ingénue who has exhausted her store of attention. "They're so used to me, they don't even notice me," she says sadly. "I'm just one of the hangers-on."

Regina, on the other hand, could possibly make it. Sparrow thin with jet-black hair and having a small face with sharp, diminuitive features, she is so much the image of the ballerina that she has posed for a number of Danskin ads promoting ballet products. In two weeks, she will dance in the school's annual Workshop Performance, when critics, directors, and scouts from other companies crowd into the Julliard Theater to watch Balanchine's future stars. Nonetheless, she is formulating contingency plans and, with Jane, will spend her spring afternoons lining up in audition halls to try out for various national companies.

One weekday afternoon, Jane, Regina, and I take the bus downtown to the Joffrey Studios, where the girls will audition for Pennsylvania Ballet. On the way downtown, Jane frets about the wisdom of the journey. She has been accepted at the Pennsylvania school's summer session and feels that during her summer visit Ben Harkavy (then director of the company) will have a chance to familiarize himself with her style and perhaps offer her a job. Here, in a contest with hundreds of other girls, she does not feel she has a chance. If she is not chosen, the director will remember her failure and hold it against her. On the other hand, he may offer her a job, in which case she will score a double victory. She vacillates all the way down to the Village. When we walk into the studios and see how many dancers—at least two hundred of them—have crushed into the small lounge and dressing rooms, Jane instantly opts out.

Regina pushes forward to change, and then squeezes in next to several other SAB students. They huddle together in a corner improvising résumés. Instructions on how to write up professional experience is apparently not part of SAB's curriculum. The girls do not even have paper or pencils with which to write, so they dart into the Joffrey's office and beg scraps of paper. Using each other's backs for tabletops, they hastily scribble down a short history of summer jobs and guest appearances.

They are then given numbers, and about a hundred women and ten men file into a large studio, while the crowd in the hallway peers in. The first test is a series of ballet walks across the floor. Harkavy,

Pennsylvania's portly, bald director, stands to one side. "Thank you," he tells about thirty dancers whom he rejects instantly. They are in shock: After having studied for years, they do not even get a chance to dance but are rejected after a stroll across the studio floor.

Those who remain perform standard class exercises. With each *plié* and *tendu* Harkarvy pares the group down. While almost all the boys—a handful to begin with—make it through the audition, if not into the company, only a few girls remain for final selection. Those who are chosen are ecstatic. Yet their reward is uncertain: Harkarvy will not make his final selection until he has conducted auditions all around the country.

Going out into the world of job hunting and auditioning is a sobering experience. Regina did not even make it through an entire audition for the Pennsylvania Ballet. At least in class at SAB, Regina and Jane are two of thirty and have a chance of being recognized. Each class becomes a mini-audition and each exercise a struggle to improve.

In Williams's ten-thirty class, on the side of the room opposite Regina and Jane, a tall, frail girl studies herself in the mirror. She is Stacey Conners,* a fawnlike sixteen-year-old who is also at a critical juncture in her career. Since she was six, she and her mother have pursued their mutual fantasy of ballet stardom. They came to New York from Florida; and after ten years of dreams and expenses, their money, patience, and hope are about to run out. Although Stacey is only sixteen, Balanchine, who has been selecting younger and younger apprentices, passed Stacey over this year, and she had not been given lead roles in SAB's Workshop Performance. Her mother obsesses about her chances for success, and she had filled her daughter with her fears. When Stacey comes into class, she immediately surveys her rivals until she picks out her chief competitor, Darci Kistler.†

† Darci is now a principal dancer with NYCB.

Balanchine's chosen one, fifteen-year-old Darci is already a company apprentice and will dance Odette in *Swan Lake* at this year's Workshop. The queen of the class, she knows other girls envy her, and she seems to bask in their jealousy. Her rivals whisper about her in private. So intent is she on ballet, they tell me, that she is almost hypnotized when she dances. Once, when she was dancing, the pianist stopped abruptly and she did not notice: She just kept on dancing to the rhythm in her head. Sometimes she gets so carried away that she is unaware that her partner is not there to catch her: She's been known to leap into a boy's arms and land instead on the floor. The girls gasp in horror, but it is horror tinged with rivalrous glee. "We may not be as good as she is," they say, "but at least we don't act like zombies."

At exactly ten-thirty, Williams signals the pianist, and all stand at attention to begin the ninety-minute review. It is an unchanging routine, developed to build strength while simultaneously warming up cold muscles so that as little strain as possible is placed on the body. Also to avoid strain and to keep their muscles warm, the company dancers wear a variety of sweat pants, leg warmers, socks rolled down around the ankles, plastic balloonlike pants, and sweaters. Students look practically naked in their pale-pink leotards. (Each class has its own colors distinguishing one level from the next.) They are not allowed to wear warmup clothes that might conceal either their bodies or their mistakes.

The class begins, as ballet classes do everywhere, with *pliés* at the barre, a long wooden railing that extends around the perimeter of the room. *Pliés*, a variant of the deep knee bend, begin in first position, where the heels of the two feet touch and the feet swivel out in one parallel line. Then there is second position, a wide version of first; then fourth, where one leg is about a foot in front of the other; and then fifth, where the two feet touch, heel in front of toe, toe in front of heel.

Pliés build toward more vigorous motions. Starting in first position, dancers do a series of *tendus*, short movements in which the foot brushes the floor as it moves first to the front, then to the side, and then to the back, without leaving the floor. *Frappés*, or beats, are like *tendus* but are more brusque thrusts, and the foot lifts slightly off the floor. In *ronds de jambe*, the foot passes through each stage of the *tendu*, moving to the front, the side, the back, and then returning to the front as it forms a semi-circular arc around the standing leg. In *développés*, *attitudes*, and *arabesques*, the leg is lifted and extended above the waist. Then dancers execute *grands battements*, or can-can kicks.

From the barre, where muscles are slowly warmed up, the dancers move to the center of the studio. First they perform slow combinations of steps, called adagio, which combine the patterns of the barre but test balance and strength. Livelier combinations follow. Finally, when their bodies are truly warm, dancers gather at one corner and, leaping, turning, and jumping according to instructions, they crisscross the floor.

All these movements, whether fast or slow, at the barre or in the center of the room, must be executed with total precision and grace. The hip is a well-oiled joint and the leg swivels out and up, forward and back, while the body remains erect. The body never sags or collapses but is held on an invisible axis. When you *plié* down, teachers explain, you must pretend that your head is held on a string that pulls you up to the ceiling so that you do not fold in on yourself. When you come up, you must press your heels into the ground; as you rise, a countervailing tension should keep your body from springing up and losing its central grip. The arms are always smooth and fluid, delicately arced, as if you are encircling an enormous beach ball.

To study and correct themselves, the dancers gaze intently at their image in the mirrors that surround them. From an early age, they have developed a scrupulous dependence upon these mirrors, an indispensable feature of any ballet studio. An almost painful fascination, this self-scrutiny is hardly narcissistic because it holds so little pleasure. Yet one understands why dancers are so often considered hopeless narcissists, so absorbed in their own images that they do not connect, not even when they dance together. One of the oddest experiences I've had was watching Natalia Makarova and Alexander Godunov rehearse a lyrical, romantic pas de deux to the strains of Tchaikovsky. I imagined them melting into one another, yet for these two dancers, merging was hardly the order of the afternoon. Coupling to the music, they stared past each other, through each other, over each other, straining for a glimpse in the mirror, making this lyrical dance an almost comic parody.

If the dancers in this class scrutinize themselves with stern intensity, they are scrutinized with even greater rigor by Williams, who stalks the room. Inserting a hand between a dancer's knees, he invites the hips to rotate farther and extend the turnout. Prodding a dancer's behind, he persuades her to tuck it quickly under her hips. He goes up to another dancer and quietly but firmly plants one hand on her stomach and another at the base of her spine. At his touch, she instantly pulls her stomach muscles in and straightens her back.

Approaching his students, Williams rarely jokes or laughs but delivers a series of brief and pointed corrections. At times, his voice bristles with irritation as he barks a harsh reprimand. This tone is not unusual. Ballet is not congenial ground for the progressive educator who believes in building students' egos before delivering criticism. SAB is strictly from the Old School, and teachers are unbending disciplinarians who rarely compliment students. Praise, they feel, is not what steels the dancers; only hard work and acceptance of criticism can accomplish that. "The attitude is very negative," Regina comments. "If you don't have the perfect body or if you can't catch steps quickly enough, the teachers immediately knock you down. They'll say, 'You have bad feet, they're so ugly'; or 'Can't you lift your leg higher, what's wrong with you?' It's always what's wrong, never what's right."

Students can infer praise if they make it from one level to the next, are given roles in recitals and workshops, and finally, of course, are accepted into the company itself. So central is criticism to the ballet experience that it becomes, perversely, a compliment. If a teacher bothers to recognize a student and stops to inform her of her faults, it is because he feels that there is hope and that the student is worthy of his time and attention. In this system, even anger is a kind of gift; dancers worry if they are not chastised. They know that many teachers communicate only with prized students and neglect those they feel are unworthy.

This morning Jane Cooper is yearning for attention. Yesterday, she was awarded the ultimate prize: a teacher's offhand remark that she was showing progress in her elevation. Two compliments in the course of two days would be too much to expect. But any attention would be welcome. Over and over again, however, Williams passes her by without so much as a glance. On her face, the expectant smile has frozen into an anxious grin. "They say my dancing is too introverted, that I don't sparkle enough, smile enough," she anguishes. "But I get so nervous. They emphasize technique so much, it's hard to think about smiling and projecting." All she can project for the next thirty minutes is despair. She is certain that when the students leave class and compare notes, she will have nothing to contribute.

At noon, the girls scurry off. Jane, downcast and depressed, and Regina, not entirely displeased with her performance, rush home to take a quick nap. Stacey and others hurry to their dressing room to change before walking the six blocks to Professional Children's School. The school and SAB form the closest thing to America's version of White Lodge or Vagaonova Institute—the schools that train dancers for England's Royal Ballet and Russia's Kirov Ballet, respectively. Other professional children—aspiring dancers, actors, or musicians—also attend PCS, scheduling their schoolwork around outside lessons.

Sixty-three SAB students go to PCS. Others who are able to negotiate a flexible schedule go to public or private schools in New York. Still others take correspondence courses, following lesson plans they receive in the mail. They send in homework, papers, and tests, and receive grades and comments from their anonymous teachers. The burden of heavy class and rehearsal schedules, the expense of private school tuition, and the desire to get school over with as quickly and painlessly as possible make correspondence appealing to many ballet students. As companies accept younger and younger dancers, this option is becoming increasingly popular.

The education offered by PCS is far superior to that of the correspondence courses. SAB students go to school early in the morning, leave for ballet class two hours later, and return to resume their studies at PCS before an afternoon pointe class or partnering session. "While ballet dancers are in many ways model students," says Betsey Purinton, the school's admissions director, "they do not always share the intellectual curiosity of our acting students. Grades are very important to them, but there is little initiative to go beyond the classroom expectations. When you've got four hours of dance classes a day, plus a workshop to rehearse, you simply don't have the time to do more than what's required. For most of the ballet students, dance is the number one priority."

Students are so involved with the romance of ballet that they can think of little else. "You feel so special here; you feel just like a princess," says eighteen-year-old Lesley Clifford, a student at SAB. "I just feel that the only thing I really care about is being in that company [NYCB] and being near Mr. Balanchine. It's just so special to be close to him, just to be near him and be associated with him."

It is hard to fault adolescents like Lesley for their luminous fantasies. As students they are just beginning to live these out and subsequently fail to reality check. SAB teachers and staff don't actively tell students that they should *not* consider other companies, but they rarely direct students to those companies. They rarely say to a student, "You should go see San Francisco Ballet. You might do well there." The School of American Ballet receives funding from private and federal donors all over the country because its mandate is to train dancers for the nation's ballet companies, as well as City Ballet. But the reverence with which students view NYCB and Balanchine, and the lack of attention given to the options outside of NYCB, creates a NYCB-or-die mentality. Although the school regularly informs students about openings at other companies, there is little attempt to match what the staff and teachers know about a student's background and personality with what they know about a company's reputation and ambience.

The ballet schools are even less realistic about financial reward, rarely teaching their students that they will need to earn a decent living so they can pay their rent, finance their vacations, or save up for retirement. Many schools teach students the exact opposite, that art and money do not mix. Lesley Clifford says that once when Balanchine was making a rare appearance in an advanced girls class where some City Ballet dancers were also attending, "he turned to us and said, 'Don't ever lose your drive. You know, it's strange: Once girls get money and they can buy things, they tend to relax. The apprentices don't have money yet,' he said, pointing to some obsessed young women practicing nearby, 'so they have this drive. But the girls with money, no,' he said, shaking his head. 'They lost it.'"

Art is spirit, innocence, purity. Money, on the other hand, represents the crasser, sullied aspects of life. If you want to transcend this earth, you must sacrifice, and the greatest sacrifice is financial security. Not surprisingly, when we discuss the ABT lockout, Lesley is aghast. She cannot understand how dancers could actually stop dancing, even for a moment, much less ten weeks. "At this point, I can't even think about money. I'm sure once I reach a certain age, maybe I'll feel the way those dancers felt," she muses. "I guess I just can't think about these things now. Of course, I worry about paying the bills, but I can't help but feel I have my parents to support me, and I know they'd help out even if I were working for a company."

Lesley is part of a long tradition. In Russia and Europe, young dancers were companions to rich matrons who provided them, when they were novices, with extra money to take lessons, get coaching, buy clothes, and pay the rent. Today's young dancers turn to their parents.. No one seems to feel that female dancers need to worry about making a living. When their demanding career is over, they are expected to find financial security in a husband.

Male dancers, like most young men everywhere, are expected to support a wife and a family—or, at the very least, themselves. Their parents expect them to make a living; and unless the family is very wealthy, the parents do not often offer to make extra funds available. Once male dancers leave school, they tend to be on their own. They must support themselves with their dancing, earn their own living, and perhaps support a family—after they retire. Male dancers are thus more apt to complain about low wages and to pay closer attention to what they will do if they do not become ballet masters, teachers, or choreographers. Finding a career that will be as rewarding as ballet is not easy, since almost all other professional careers require a graduate education, and most dancers have never even been to college. "I think a lot about what I'm going to do when I quit," a young student at SAB tells me. "I'd like to become an architect. But that will be really hard. It would mean four years of college and then three more years of grad school. If I quit at thirty-five, I wouldn't be able to make a living till I was in my forties. That seems incredible. For now, I just have to concentrate on dancing; I'll worry about what happens afterward."

Boys may be slightly more realistic than girls, but they too are desperate to get through class and into the company. These immediate worries tend to preclude any real attempt to plan for the future. Their paramount concern is with the here and now.

After Williams dismisses his ten-thirty girls class, he begins to prepare for his noon class of advanced boys. Boys who have completed their morning's courses at PCS or who have spent the morning working at a variety of part-time jobs gather at SAB. Williams takes up his perennial vigil over a class that also has its allotment of celebrities. Baryshnikov, who has spent the year dancing with New York City Ballet, and Peter Martins, who will most likely be Balanchine's successor, take prominent places at the barre and lead the boys in leaps and turns across the floor. Casting challenging glances at each other, the two superstars engage in friendly competitive exercises.

Alex Harkin*, Jefferson Baum, and Evan Connell regard them with envy. These students are sixteen, nineteen, and twenty, respectively. Jefferson has been studying dance since he was seventeen. Although his mother was a dancer, she did not encourage him to follow in her footsteps. She felt, in fact, that dance was not sufficiently lucrative for her son, and Jefferson decided, on his own, to give up college, as well as track, to enroll in the North Carolina School of the Arts. Alex Harkin began dancing with his sister when he was eight. Tall, solemn, and dark-haired, he is the kind of good-looking boy high school girls whisper about in study hall, and the kind who would be vaguely embarrassed by their attentions. Of the three young men, he has the most seniority at SAB, having come to the school three years earlier from a professional ballet school be began attending at age ten.

The oldest of the three, Evan Connell is a mild-mannered blond who lights up when he speaks about his career. A former piano major at a Philadelphia high school, he started dancing after a teacher suggested he try ballet. There, in class, he found a home and a direction. "You're not supposed to take any responsibility in America before you go to college," he explains. "Then you're supposed to get out and decide what you want to do and do it. When I started taking class, it seemed really good to me to have a sense of what I was going to do when I was still young, to feel I was doing something important."

Coming to New York, the center of the ballet world, has only increased Evan's sense of possibility. "The whole world looks to New York as the place where it's happening in ballet," he says, explaining why it was that he passed up the security of a job with Pennsylvania Ballet to pursue a far less certain dream: being accepted into New York City Ballet. "There's no place like New York. I mean, in Pennsylvania you can't go just anywhere to take class because, there *is* no other place to take class. But here, you can take class with the greatest teachers in the world. And every night, there are seventeen different companies performing. And you see the greatest dancers in the world. They come to class. Like Peter Martins, he was in class today. I know it's a risk, but I'm going to stick around because you never know what the company's going to be like in two years. I mean, Balanchine could die, and who knows what would happen."

Alex is less sanguine but no less determined than his classmates. He knows that the presence of a Martins or a Baryshnikov is not just a blessing; it is an obstacle as well. Not only do these superstars rob needy students of a teacher's attention, but they are symbols of the competition men who now enter dance must cope with.

Before the great deluge of male superstars that swept America in the sixties and seventies, ballet was primarily a woman's career. In the nineteenth century, male dancers were considered no more than appendages of the ballerinas they partnered. They were referred to as *porteurs*, men who carried women. At the turn of the century, a few legendary male dancers like Vaslav Nijinsky, captured audiences' imagination and allegiance. But these dancers were exceptions. Even so, the role of male dancers was far less taxing than it is today; technical demands were not as exhausting; and there was far less competition among male dancers in the late sixties and seventies.

When Nureyev and Baryshnikov made the cover of major newsmagazines and starred in feature films, they catapulted the male dancer into the limelight. Whatever their private sexual proclivities, these two men were personalities of stature to be envied rather than mocked. With such respectable idols to identify with, more and more boys have found ballet an attractive profession. A shortage of male students still exists in younger grades, but Alex and his fellow classmates find it increasingly difficult both to compete in school and to get into companies. Frank Smith, an ABT soloist who was lucky enough to get his start when male dancers were far more scarce, says quite simply, "A lot of us wouldn't be dancing here today if we'd started later." Or as Alex puts it, "Boys may be in demand in smaller regional companies, but in big companies, it's very competitive and it's getting harder and harder."

Competition is still far less intense among the boys than among the girls. Although a few boys start their careers before the age of twelve—because of parental enthusiasm for the art or, because, like NYCB's Christopher d'Amboise or ABT's Raymond Serrano, their parents were dancers—early starters among the men are the exception, not the rule. The widespread public association between ballet and feminine grace leads girls directly to ballet but takes boys away from it.

Most male dancers start when they are in their early or even late teens. Their interest is usually spurred by attending a ballet performance or seeing a national company perform on television or in the movies. As a child, NYCB apprentice David Keary had supplemented his regimen of after-school sports with tap dancing lessons. When he was fourteen, Gelsey Kirkland and Edward Villella came to his hometown of Jackson, Mississippi. "It really transformed my life," Keary remarks. "I was astounded. Up until that time I'd done athletics, but I could see that this was what I wanted to do." His musically oriented parents did not object, so he studied locally and finally went on to the SAB.

ABT's Victor Barbee literally wandered into a ballet class when he was fourteen. He had originally planned to study acting and had applied to the North Carolina School of the Arts. To his disappointment, the school's drama program did not accept students who had not yet entered high school. They did, however, accept younger students for their dance program.

"I had no ballet training," twenty-seven-year-old Barbee says in a soft, southern voice, "and I thought it was a bizarre idea. But I'd played baseball when I was young, so I had a lot of stretch. 'Okay, I'll give it a whirl,' I thought. My mother and I went out and bought a pair of tights and a tee shirt, and I went to this audition. They lined us up and asked us how long we'd been dancing. The first guy was twenty-five and said he'd been dancing for fifteen years; the next boy was twelve, and he'd been dancing for three years; the next had danced for five years. I was starting to panic. I thought, 'God! They've gotten me into something here that I can't handle.' Then they asked me how long I'd been dancing, and I had to admit this was the first time I'd ever even been in leotards. Then they asked me where my ballet shoes were, and I said I didn't get ballet shoes because if I didn't get accepted I'd never use them again and they cost $12 a pair and we couldn't afford to pay that just for one day."

Barbee tried his best to imitate the steps assigned the other boys. He turned out, pointed his feet, jumped . . . and then crashed to the floor. "Hallelujah!" he thought. "I'm out of it, and they'll let me go." But two weeks later, a letter arrived at his home: He'd been accepted. The school recommended he try to make up for lost time in their summer session. He politely replied that he couldn't accept their advice because "I had baseball that summer, and I was committed to the team. I said I'd come when school started, and they accepted me anyway."

Hearing these stories, a female dancer, who has to begin her career by age nine or ten, might feel that boys, as usual, can get away with anything. If a fifteen- or sixteen-year-old girl tried to enter a professional school, she would be turned away in an instant; a particularly kind teacher might suggest modern dance. Boys, however, can embark on their ballet careers later, not only because there is a shortage of good male dancers, but because of the very concrete physical realities that rule ballet. If they show musical aptitude, coordination, and have well-proportioned bodies, their physical and muscular structure will enable them to catch up. For women, there simply is no catching up.

Ballet's fundamental physical requirement is a 180 degree turnout; that is, the feet swivel out from the hips, the heels touch, and the result is first position, from which all other ballet positions flow. To the untutored eye, turnout seems only a matter of twisting the feet and ankles. It is, in fact, the result of a gradual rotation in the muscles of the thigh and of actual structural changes in the bones of the hip. Dr. William Liebler, an orthopedic surgeon at Lenox Hill Hospital in New York who specializes in sports medicine and who has treated thousands of ballet dancers, explains: "Early training is essential if a dancer's bones are to be malleable enough to allow the femur bone in the thigh to actually twist in its socket." If that doesn't happen, dancers will "cheat" with their turnout: they'll twist their knees rather than their thighs. This will prove disastrous. The knee is a hinge, constructed to move backward and forward rather than sideways, and such cheating causes severe strain on the knee ligaments, leading to chronic tendonitis, arthritis, and eventually to the end of a dancer's career.

Because women are not naturally as muscular as men, they must begin training early on so that they can develop the muscular strength to support ballet technique. An early start also enables them to build strong legs, which will sustain the terrific strain of pointe work. Ballerinas make standing on one foot look the simplest feat. It is not. Pointe shoes, with their stiff construction, are only a minor aid. The entire body, especially the strengthened stomach muscles and steeled legs, carry the dancer's weight. The would-be ballerina's ascension must be a gradual process. If a girl goes on pointe too early—say, before age ten—she can completely compromise her career: Her toe joints will be permanently damaged, and she may suffer from arthritis. If she starts too late, she will fail to develop the necessary strength to go on toe. Optimally, male dancers should also begin class early. But choreographers, who must adapt to the shortage of male dancers, will work with what they can get. Nonetheless, boys do their share of jockeying for attention. "When you're outside New York, things are different," Alex Harkin says. "The whole world isn't watching you. It's more relaxed. You can work better, you're under less pressure. Here, it's for keeps, and that changes everything. In smaller schools, there isn't so much rivalry between you and your friends. But here, this is the end of the line, and it's either them or you." The competition, Alex continues, can become almost unbearable. "It seems that every day it's do or die, and sometimes I think it's just too much. Sometimes I think it's better to be a big fish in a little pond than a little fish in a big pond. But until something very concrete tells me I can't, I'm going to keep slugging away."

What Alex objects to most about SAB is that competition is not a contest between equals. Politics, not talent, he says, is the determining factor. "I guess everything you do in life is political," he concludes with weary resignation. "I mean, if you're super, they can't ignore you. But if you're pretty even with other people, then it all depends on who likes whom." He hesitates before explaining exactly what he means, looking around anxiously to see if anyone is watching. "I mean, it all comes down to whether you kiss behind or not," adding, as if I might not have grasped his point, "I mean, if you kiss ass."

According to Alex, such "political" behavior takes a variety of forms. Sometimes it just means getting to know teachers, being extra friendly, saying hello, and asking, at the beginning of the day, how a teacher feels. Sometimes it means more. "I guess it might help if you're gay. Most of the teachers and choreographers are gay. And the gay guys get more attention from certain gay male teachers. It's very frustrating because you know how good you are and you know what you could be doing, but certain people don't know you and don't pay attention to you."

To the SAB students, competition is no friendly exercise. It is a constant and corrosive acid that erodes their self-esteem. They may have felt special when they were the stars of their local ballet schools —indispensable advertisements of a teacher's skill and judgment—but once they arrived in the big city they realized that they were only one among many talented, successful young people who showed great promise. Students like Jefferson and Alex and Evan can recapture that feeling of uniqueness when they compare themselves to the kids who were left behind; but when they glance at one another and compare themselves to other professionals, their pride evaporates.

If the boys suffer from competition, the girls suffer far more. What is a major problem for boys becomes a central obsession for girls. "You can see it in their eyes," Alex says, "when they look at each other. Or when you're partnering them. I guess it's just that they're together so much, in such tight quarters, they get on each other's nerves."

The competition among young women is palpable. You can read it on their faces, in their dancing, and most visibly in their relationships with one another. This furious rivalry is on display in Suki Schorer's pointe class, a class for advanced women students to which Jane and Regina have returned after lunch. To the casual observer, Schorer's class might seem the very picture of balletic harmony. From windows that wrap around the upper third of the classroom's high walls, sunlight streams across the enormous studio floor. Outside, dozens of Upper West Side skyscrapers form a pleasant backdrop.

Suki Schorer, whose thin brown hair is pulled back into a ponytail, wears a filmy baby-pink nylon ballet skirt over her leotard and tights. She is a plumper, shorter version of the dancers who eddy around her. Standing in the center of the room, she shouts corrections above the music. "And position, and position," she instructs. "Up, up," she says, launching herself on demi-toe to illustrate. "When you *relevé*, your arms should help," she says, letting her arms float gently upward. "Place your foot as you start out." She directs this comment at a figure speeding past her. "No, no, don't bring your head too far back," she tells another. "You should make a pretty pose in the *développé*, with your face, head, arms, body. No, no," she spies a dancer who has gotten it wrong again. "Don't do this," she parodies an awkward gesture, jerking forward grotesquely, like a bag lady who has inadvertently wandered into a congregation of princesses.

Stacey Conners is one of the girls who cannot seem to get it right. As she sets off from the corner of the room, she seems as graceful as a Greek statue come to life. Arriving in the center, she loses her grip on both the sequences and the technique. After the third try she grimaces; and while the other girls continue, she withdraws to the back of the room and goes over the steps, again and again. First she *pliés*, then her feet and arms accompany her in a series of steps. Then she halts. Wincing, she marks the steps again, trying to commit them to her reluctant memory. She has stopped following the class, and is trying to master the variation, but no matter how hard she works, there is no improvement. She seems almost hypnotized by her own failure, so distracted that when I approach her at the end of class, she does not even recognize me.

The constant war that Stacey wages against herself and her companions has transformed her life. During one long interview, she confesses that at SAB, she feels she is swimming in shark-infested waters. Her teachers are not her helpers but her judges. Should she confide in them, she is certain that they will use her weaknesses against her when it comes to decide who is fit enough to survive. "You basically can't go to anyone for help here," she says. "Some people would, but I wouldn't. You could go to ask advice for a technical problem but not a personal one. It would be good if there were somebody not involved in ballet that you could go to," she adds wistfully, "but there isn't."

Competitive feelings also inhibit students' relationships with each other. "There's a lot of rivalry," says Kathleen Hanrahan,* an advanced SAB student. "There are some people who would do anything to get a rival out of the way." Some students do overcome their suspicions and form fast friendships, but Stacey Conners is not one of them. Certain that, given the opportunity, even the most loyal friends will steal a place at the barre, a role, or a teacher's affections, she says, "I try not to have too much social interaction with dancers. I find I get too snappy around them. The girls are so competitive. You try to block it out because it hurts you. But it's still there, and it affects you."

Competition, she feels, also poisons her relationships with her teachers. "The other day," she recounts, "I got a compliment from a teacher, which I very much appreciated. But the very first thing that hit my mind was that she wanted me to think I had improved so much that I would stop working. Then one of the girls she liked better than me could get ahead. That wasn't fair. I know it. It was all in my mind. But you find yourself thinking things that are completely untrue, and you keep putting yourself down."

At the School of American Ballet, as well as at most other ballet academies, rivalry goes beyond competition for technical proficiency. Students also compete about their weight. Because the ballet look idealizes the thin-hipped, flat-chested figure, young dancers feel that they will be favored if they are thin. If they want to get ahead of their classmates, it is not enough to dance better; they must also struggle to be thinner. "It's incredible," says Kathleen, who is, herself, almost skeletal. "I mean, there are contests here about who can lose the most weight."

As they lounge in the halls, students exchange tales about their caloric exploits and latest diet discoveries. The preoccupation with food affects even those who are so young and so thin that their worries about gaining weight seem positively ludicrous. As I pass two eleven-year-old students in front of dressing-room mirrors, I overhear yet another conversation about diet. There is not a trace of fat on either of their delicate bodies. Yet the prospect haunts them. Practically in tears, one confesses her latest binge. "God, I got so hungry last night, I snuck downstairs and ate a piece of chicken." "I ate two ice creams this week," her friend groans. "Can you believe it?"

When the older girls arrive in the dressing room to change for class, they strip and scan their figures for bulges or curves. They debate the effectiveness of the banana and Tab diet—a current favorite —versus that of simple fasting. Abstinence is a virtue. "We get pretty neurotic about food," Regina Gray admits. "I fast and I gorge, and then I fast and I gorge. If nothing's happening I say let's go out and munch. I won't eat anything for three days because I feel guilty. Some people will go out and eat ten doughnuts and two quarts of ice cream and a Hershey bar. Or we'll go out and eat a pint of ice cream or a huge Chinese dinner. Or come home and make a batch of cookies and eat them all. Then we feel bad, and we won't eat at all. This is a thing with SAB. I mean, if you look at European dancers, they have women's bodies, a bust and a butt, but at SAB they think there's something wrong with you if you're not ninety pounds. In fact, the teachers will announce in class if you've gained any weight, so you get pretty paranoid about it."

The competition to control their bodies has a more immediately pernicious effect on dancers. Because injuries are considered a sign of weakness and because they force a student to take time off, students who are afraid to lose their place in line conceal injuries. Dance, in and of itself, strains the body. In the course of a month, students twist ankles, pull muscles, tear ligaments, develop tendonitis or serious foot or knee injuries that may require surgery. Feet imprisoned in tight toe shoes suffer from painful bunions, calluses, and corns. Dr. William Liebler says, "You have to see them to believe them."

As I watch an afternoon pointe class at SAB, a girl sits with me, following the movements of her fellow students. She rolls and rerolls an Ace bandage in one hand while massaging a swollen ankle with the other. She twisted it a few days earlier and probably will not be able to dance on it for a week or two.

Lynn Mueller, an eighteen-year-old student, walks in during class and stands by the door. This has been her fifth week "out," as it is called in ballet lingo. To be out is the worst thing that can happen to a dancer. Lynn fell out when she hurt her leg in class. Instead of taking it easy, she pushed herself, tried to "dance through her injury," the phrase dancers commonly use to refer to dancing with a serious physical problem. It did not help. Finally, she accepted the fact that she would have to stay home and nurse her leg. This was no welcome recuperation.

Students like Lynn worry that their classmates will get ahead of them, that they themselves will have dropped not only out of their teacher's sight but out of mind as well. Furthermore, they worry that teachers will think them poor risks because they have succumbed to their bodies rather than vanquishing them. This is why Lynn and her downcast companions who have admitted their injuries are exceptions rather than the rule. Taking time off to heal properly is not, in the dancer's unwritten code, accepted practice; hiding injuries, dancing on them until they become so painful that they can no longer be tolerated, is. As Regina Gray says, "Everybody's dancing on injuries at the moment because it's annual Workshop time. You feel that if you take a month off, you're not going to get into Workshop and that whole bit. It's very difficult to make yourself take off even a week. When you get injured at the school, they also start to look at you as a weakling, someone whose resistance is low and who isn't going to make it. So naturally you don't want to tell them you're injured."

These problems are not unique to the School of American Ballet. The dilemmas students contend with there and at other New York schools are merely heightened versions of what students experience at most elite ballet schools. Take the San Francisco Ballet School. In many ways, it appears to be as different from SAB as San Francisco is from New York. The company that it feeds takes its inspiration from a rich amalgam of styles and sources. Director Lew Christensen, a member of one of America's most famous dance families, was a *premier danseur* with Balanchine. Michael Smuin, San Francisco Ballet's other director, worked on Broadway and with the American Ballet Theatre. The company includes dancers from a variety of ethnic backgounds—two Hungarians, a Russian, an Englishman, and a Columbian.

The school and company are located in the Sunset district of the city, out toward the ocean, past San Francisco's stately old Victorian houses. Golden Gate Park divides the city; and on the east side, a series of small, low, Spanish-style row houses edge their way up the Sunset's gently sloping hills. The school has turned two small, two-story houses into studio and office space, which it shares with the company.

At first glance, the school looks like a relaxed place to study. But students told me of the same problems that plague their New York counterparts. One afternoon when I came to watch their class, students Diana Adams,* Joyce Atkinson,* and Erica Harcourt* got an unexpected but dreaded surprise. Instead of a teacher discussing introductory melodies with the school pianist, a large scale dominated the room. During the year they had had a series of "weigh-ins," during which their teacher recorded their weight. A gained pound or two could be a major obstacle blocking their advancement to the next level or into the company. The weigh-ins are never announced beforehand. To warn students in advance, say teachers and the company director, Richard Cammack, a former ABT soloist, would defeat their purpose. Forewarned is forestarved. Given prior notice, students would fast for several days, thus weighing in at a lighter than normal rate.

Joyce and Diana feel their chests constrict when they line up with other girls—so many so much thinner—to await their turn. Each girl gets on the scales hoping the teacher will leave the heavy lead weights at the left side of the scale. "One hundred and eight, one ten, one fifteen," she notes. Girls turn crimson, particularly if their weight exceeds 110. Even the eleven-year-olds who weigh fifty or sixty pounds gasp in horror when their weight is recorded.

On days like today, seventeen-year-old Diana Adams wishes she had gone to college. "It's humiliating. They used to tell us a week ahead when they were going to do it, and people would go out and starve themselves. This one girl fainted right in front of the scales because she hadn't eaten for a whole week. Now they don't tell us in advance. But it's awful. It makes me mad because I feel like no one needs to tell me whether I'm heavy or not because I know. I see myself every day in front of the mirror, and I know whether or not I need to lose weight."

What attracted her to ballet, when she was ten, was that special feeling it gave her. "I loved to dance because I could do what I wanted." But after three years at San Francisco Ballet School, she has learned some of its accessory rituals. Competition, for one, interferes with her relationships with her friends. "It's really weird," she reflects, "but when you get into the advanced class, something clicks. You suddenly realize you have one year to make it, and all this competition comes in. It's doubly hard because you're competing with your friends.

We've all known each other since we were twelve, and it's hard when someone else makes it. With my best friends, it's almost a race to see who's going to be an apprentice first."

When she first arrived in San Francisco, at fourteen, Diana discovered that her roommate was a closet anorectic, a girl who took ballet's weight strictures so seriously that she vomited everything she ate, and at 5 feet 2 inches weighed only seventy-four pounds. "It was a horrible experience," Diana says. "I knew that every time she ate something, she would go into the bathroom and turn on the faucet and shower and do her thing. She was sneaky too. She'd eat food in a bag, like a drunk. Then she'd throw up. I had two years of that. I finally found out she'd been doing that for five years. She'd even been to the hospital once and almost died. But the thing was, I didn't know what to do. All of a sudden I had to be so grownup and responsible. I confronted her, and then my other roommate and I talked to her. But she kept on doing it. I mean, she could have *died*."

Just as the school is doing little to help Diana's roommate or others like her, it takes minimal responsibility for students' injuries. "Right now I have very bad shin splints and bad bunions," Diana complains. "They're really inflamed. But there's no way I could take off because it's *Nutcracker*, and I'm afraid they'll put someone else in my part. . . . If you have an injury they don't want to bother with you. Michael Smuin can't tolerate an injured dancer. If he's doing class and you can't jump because you're injured, you feel he's kind of disgusted, that he doesn't want to waste time on you."

This does not make it easy for dancers to deal with physical problems. "I don't know what I'd do if I were really badly injured," she says. "I'd go crazy. If I have a vacation, after a couple of days I want to take class. I mean, I don't know what to do with myself. I don't have any social life or any friends. I don't have time. I have class at nine-thirty in the morning, and then I rehearse all day. I spend my free day doing household duties. There's no chance to meet anybody. I don't have friends outside ballet. Sometimes I wonder how I'm going to manage to meet other people. Because you live with ballet people all week, and then suddenly you're a couple of years older and you find you haven't done anything with your life except ballet." Student dancers, like professionals, study six days a week. As they advance, they must do schoolwork, as well as take two or three classes a day. At the most advanced levels, they often dance in company productions; added to their normal course work are extra rehearsals and performances. This leaves little time for socializing, since any free hours are spent running errands, sewing toe shoes, or catching up on needed rest.

As ballet students grow older, their social horizons become even more limited; and their most faithful companion is fatigue—the constant, searing exhaustion that crowds out any other sensation at the end of the day. "When you're so tired, it's hard to think about going out and seeing friends," Michelle Benash says, recalling her student days. "You may be lonely and want company, but you just don't have the energy to lead two lives. Plus you're afraid to do what normal people do when they go out. I used to be afraid to go out because when people get together they usually go out and eat, and I was always afraid to eat because I might get fat."

As teachers are so fond of remarking, a truly satisfying and varied personal life may be an impossibility, something students and professionals must relinquish until their careers are over. Even a modest social life seems impossible not only because of the constraints on dancers' energy, but because of constraints on their social will. In the world of ballet, dancers are often discouraged from engaging in any activity that might draw their attention away from dance. Romantic attachments, friends, and family indicate a diminishing ardor.

From their first classes on, students are treated to balletic morality plays. The classic ballet movie *The Red Shoes* is a clear warning against romantic entanglements. Dottie Houey, a sixteen-year-old student at the American Ballet Theatre School, was so moved and terrified by Moira Shearer's tragic end that she says she will never think of taking up with a man. "I can't believe what that man did to her!" she exclaims. "He made her choose between him and dance."

Daily reminders at school reinforce these lessons. Any woman can marry and have children, says Balanchine, but only the elite can become ballerinas. If women want to choose the former, they must forgo the latter. And so students are treated to modern tales—like that of the famous NYCB star Suzanne Farrell—of transgression and forgiveness.

Farrell was Balanchine's favorite dancer. In fact, he was said to have been in love with her. But she fell in love with and married another City Ballet dancer, Paul Mejia. Mejia was also a Balanchine favorite, but Balanchine seems not to have blessed their union. Suddenly Mejia started losing roles, and he and Farrell were forced to leave the company to dance with Maurice Béjart. Some years later, Balanchine forgave her, and she returned to City Ballet.

Farrell's case is in some ways paradigmatic. "When we were in the company," a former NYCB dancer says, "we knew Balanchine didn't like his women dancers to have outside relationships. Several dancers hid the fact that they were engaged or married for up to a year so Balanchine wouldn't find out." More recently, Kyra Nichols, one of Mr. B.'s current favorites, told a dance magazine reporter that she "was a little bit afraid to tell him [Balanchine] that she was about to marry another City Ballet star, Daniel Duell. "I didn't know how he was going to react," she said. "But, he [Balanchine] was most benevolent about it," her husband rejoined in the article.

Male dancers have far greater latitude where sex is concerned, but even they are taught that ballet is a jealous and demanding lover, and that they will have to temper outside involvements. "If you want to go out at night, you must worry about how you'll feel in the morning," says City Ballet's Robert Maiorano. "And if you want to fall in love, you worry that you're cheating ballet. You have to approach ballet with the innocence of a child and never question it. That's what's expected of you." Abstinence does not seem to be a requirement, however. And one simply does not find twenty- or twenty-five-year-old male dancers who have never gone out on a date or who have never had any sexual experience, as is the case of many female dancers.

Late one Friday afternoon in the fall of 1981, about a year after our first interview, I meet Alex Harkin as he is walking home from SAB. Alex looks very troubled, and I suggest a cup of coffee. We sit talking in a quiet coffee shop across from Lincoln Center. In the past year, he tells me, he has gotten a different perspective on dance. An injury has forced him to take time off, and he has had a chance to look more critically at the school and his classmates. And what he sees is disturbing. The competition among the boys has intensified considerably since we last met. The school staff has recently instituted a special class for boys whom it considers "company material"; and they, too, Alex says, are troubled by the constant contest they wage with one another. "It's really sad to see," he tells me. "They're not growing up socially. There's so much turbulence in their heads. One guy in that class, he's starting to get so tense that you can see it in his body. It just won't work right. But he has no perspective. In that place," as he refers, with scorn and bitterness, to SAB, "You just get tunnel vision. You get hypercritical and narcissistic."

Ironically, Alex's injuries and a part-time job have given him some perspective on the ballet world by teaching him that there is more to life than *entrechats* and *doubles tours*. "You're forced to deal with other people. You meet people your own age. You learn that there's another world out there." Which is something girls—and now some of the boys—never learn. "All they do is concentrate on ballet. They live with their mothers; they get an apartment two blocks from the school; and all they do is go zip, zip," he gestures. "It's so abnormal, the existence they lead. I mean, you don't want kids to have sex when they're real young. But these girls never go out at all." Alex has found a girlfriend at work. His friends who live their lives in school, he says, are not as fortunate.

When Roger Wehrlie, a twenty-two-year-old SAB student, came to this country from Europe, he was surprised to discover that American ballet students all seemed to suffer from the tunnel vision Alex described. "In Europe," explains Roger, six feet tall, with long, light-brown hair and a classically handsome face, "girls weren't loose. But they knew what a guy was. They had dates. When I came here I found out they didn't even go out on dates, not even once. I wondered, was this possible? What does that girl do when she is dancing a pas de deux and has to show love for her partner? She doesn't even know what she's doing. They give up everything. I can't understand it. I don't think it's so bad in Europe."

The fact that so many girls are interested only in ballet makes them unappealing to those male dancers who want to take the girl, not the ballerina, out on a date or home to bed. "A lot of girls just aren't that interesting," Roger says, echoing the sentiments of other male students. "I would rather go out with someone who isn't so obsessed with ballet. I just can't hear about *tendus* all day long. It makes me crazy. I mean, is that all there is to life?"

What puzzles Roger, as well as professional dancers who look back on their early training, is the asexuality of the ballet world. The students at SAB and other elite schools are developing adolescents. The ballet world, where men and women dance together in the patterns of sexual intimacy, would seem to raise all the issues of burgeoning sexuality. Boys say that they do feel the initial stirrings of sexual curiosity about girls or about each other. Girls, on the other hand, say they are afraid of any sexual feeling lest it get out of control and ruin their careers. "It's very asexual at school," Regina Gray comments.

"You're brought up not to think about sex. You're brought up to turn off, not on."

With over thirty thousand ballet schools in America, thousands of ballet students vie for one of the few places in the country's ten or twenty top ballet academies. They regard Stacey Conners, Jane Cooper, Regina Gray, and their classmates, as well as students at other professional training institutes, with envy. These dancers form a privileged caste, expected by less fortunate students to radiate contentment and security. Were the rejects to have a more intimate view of their rivals, they would be surprised to find that these "lucky ones" are a group of gravely troubled dancers who are hypercritical of their own accomplishments and insecure about their futures.

After years of training, they have learned that advancement does not depend solely on talent, creativity, technique, or a willingness to play by the rules. For there is only one hard and fast rule in ballet: A truly great, a stunningly bold dancer will probably be recognized, nurtured, and pushed ahead; a dancer who is not great but just one of hundreds of good, competent dancers—the kind, the Royal Ballet School book reminds us, that companies all over the world depend upon—may or may not succeed.

Much to their dismay, these dancers are judged as racehorses rather than as artists. Their physical characteristics often determine their future. In any given year a company might focus on tall dancers, ignoring short dancers who are superb technicians; the next year, the same company may search for short dancers and reject taller contenders. One director may be unable to tolerate men with short legs and muscular torsos; another may fancy just the opposite. One may not favor breasts; another might find the occasional womanly body inoffensive; yet a third may deem mature ballerinas—those twenty or older—to be too "matronly" and may send off scouts to recruit fifteen- or sixteen-year-olds.

Any student who has reached the upper levels at SAB is technically competent to join the company. Therefore, artistic decisions are often a matter of whim. Of late, both Balanchine and Baryshnikov have developed a taste for young ballerinas, "baby ballerinas," as they are known in the trade. Grumbling New York City Ballet dancers bemoan the fact that they can no longer get a good role if they are over twenty-five. Across the street at ABT, Baryshnikov is weeding out the twenty-five-, twenty-six-, and twenty-seven-year-old dancers who have been working for years to refine their technique and replacing them with new stock just out of the ballet academy cradle.

And no one can predict if or when this predilection will change. One day that "something special" a choreographer seeks might be "stage presence," another day it will be blond hair and blue eyes; another day a long neck or perfect feet. "No one really understands why people are taken into the company," Lynn Mueller says of NYCB. "Sometimes you don't get in because Mr. B. has seen people too much and gets tired of them. But then some kids stick around and finally get in. Sometimes he'll take a beautiful tall girl, or he might like someone's face and try to make her a dancer. It's hard to deal with because you never know what you're doing wrong."

"The rules are bent for talent," says a former SAB staff member. "Kids have been expelled from the school and then taken back because Balanchine thought they were talented. It's frustrating for kids who are less talented because they get away with less." This lack of clear direction means that kids just "hang around," hoping and praying that some "mysterious" something will light upon them.

Listening to the litany of these dancers' complaints, one wonders why they do not simply turn heel and leave. They are certainly young enough, bright enough, to develop other skills and interests. Most are from affluent families and could become well-paid professionals in other fields. But most stay because they are truly in love with dance and because they believe they will make it. "I'm just so optimistic,"

Lesley Clifford sighs. "I can't think about anything else. Look what I'm doing. Look what I'm giving to the audience and creating." Lesley, who at 5 feet 9 inches, is so tall she would find it difficult to gain a place in almost any major ballet company in America, is oblivious of the need to feed her soul with more attainable dreams.

Love of the art is not the only force that motivates these dancers. Many unhappy students do not leave their elite schools because they are afraid to admit defeat, afraid they will no longer be "special" if they do quit. Valerie Marshall, a seventeen-year-old former SAB student, says she had to overcome terrible feelings of weakness before deciding to leave SAB. "Your whole hometown is behind you. But you know what the reality is in New York, you know there's a very small chance you're going to be a star, but you have to live up to all these expectations.

"At school there are all these people who are so much better than you. But you just can't tell that to people back home. So you talk yourself into thinking that you love ballet. One day I realized I didn't love it anymore. I wasn't dying to perform. I was only thirteen years old when I made the decision to dance. That's pretty young. And as I got older, I started thinking: What am I going to do when I'm thirty years old? I'll be in the same place. That's when I started thinking about all the things I wanted to do. And the minute I realized I could get out, I felt really happy and free."

Deborah Marks decided to leave ballet when she was eighteen. "In spite of the fact that I got all A's in school," she says, "I was like a lot of other dancers. I performed well, but I had no connection to my schoolwork. I never had a sense of myself. In ballet, you're just not allowed to have any individuality. So when I left, I felt stranded, shattered. I have never gotten over that sense of failure, that inability to really commit myself to anything because I've given up dancing." Deborah says she regrets that she was like an addict, a person who had an all-or-nothing attitude about ballet. "There's a snobbism about it. I was in New York, so I looked down on regional companies. I could have danced outside New York. I would have enjoyed dancing or teaching children," she says with sorrow, because she could not, when she was young, conceive of other options. "I only wish there were someplace else that kids could get that sense of dance without getting all this fucked-up stuff as well," she concludes.

Female dancers seem to have a harder time separating themselves from the dance than do male dancers. Girls who abandon themselves to ballet often lose an important part of their identity as they immerse themselves in the dance world; boys who choose ballet themselves often assert themselves through dance. Ironically, America's prejudice against male dancers has had some hidden advantages. Few male dancers are confused about who wanted them to dance: they or their mothers. "Boys are more dedicated and determined because they know it's going to be harder," says Clare Duncan, director of the Houston Ballet Academy. "But they're more adult as well. They know why they want to dance. They've chosen it themselves." When they do master their bodies, they are affirming themselves, not living out someone else's fantasy. "You ask a girl why she wants to dance, and she says she doesn't know," Duncan adds. "It's because Mummie's brought her to school. That's why female dancers are so often so physically and emotionally immature."

Talking to teenaged dancers, I was struck by how alone they are with their problems. They suffer from injuries, from a preoccupation with dieting, from social isolation, and from a complete inability to put their lives in perspective. Where are the adults in their world? My conversation with Nathalie Gleboff helped me understand why so many of these students feel so alone. Dressed in a serviceable tweed skirt and a white cotton blouse buttoned at the neck, this seasoned woman is a study in politeness and good breeding. In a world of eccentric artists, Gleboff, with her short, gray-streaked brown hair and low-heeled pumps, is stability incarnate. She greets me in the hall and escorts me into her office, where she courteously responds to all my questions, getting up, on occasion, to pick up a brochure from an efficiently organized shelf nearby. During our conversation, a stream of visitors comes to her door. With a wordless nod toward me, she quickly indicates that she is occupied.

According to her philosophy, each of SAB's 425 students is a special case that needs careful evaluating. "The criteria for evaluations are less strict in the children's division," Gleboff explains. "But in the advanced division, students are judged as to their professional potential. In those classes a teacher may feel a dancer doesn't have enough talent or has a problem with his or her body. The student may have a wonderful body and not have great talent for dancing, or he or she may have talent but a body not suited for ballet."

Although Madame Gleboff insists that there is no such thing as an ideal dancer's body, certain traits are essential: a well-proportioned, flexible, coordinated body; a good turnout; and a good arch. "A student must also have good training and superior talent. A student must be musical, must be a hard worker, must have dedication and intelligence, and must be able to handle the discipline, because classes are extremely disciplined and quite structured." They must also be so self-motivated that they will continue to push themselves even when there is no one to supervise them. "When they finish here we do not give them a degree, because our philosophy is that we are just the first step in their career. At no point has a dancer achieved all there is to achieve, nor can he or she remain on a plateau. Dancers have to go on achieving throughout their lives."

But first students must survive the elimination process to which they are subjected at SAB. Teachers are on the lookout for the child who has lost interest in ballet, who has emotional problems, or whose parents are pushing too hard without heeding their child's wishes. The staff cannot afford to coddle a student who gains too much weight, is unable to master difficult technique, or is too frequently injured. "When we deal with students who injure themselves too often," she says, "their bodies may not be capable of sustaining this type of work."

This suggests that the school does not make a policy of intervention to ensure that a child is emotionally and physically healthy. Once the children become advanced students, at age thirteen or fourteen, they are on their own. The school provides a list of families, apartments, and residences where out-of-town kids can live, and that is about it. There are no staff guidance counselors, no friendly housemothers, no psychologists to give advice to a confused adolescent. Teachers are generous with their technical advice, but most of them are Russian or European, from a sterner era, and somewhat forbidding.

Nonintervention seems to be the school's response to most personal difficulties. Injuries, Gleboff admits, are the worst physical problem students cope with. The company provides them with a fine orthopedist, Dr. William Hamilton, who comes to the school once a week. But his ministrations have little effect if students return to class too quickly. Although the school is aware that dancers tend to return to class far too soon after an injury, there is no real effort to keep a child out as long as the healing process demands. "We cannot tell a student, 'Well, you can't dance for the next two weeks,'" says Gleboff. "That's a function of the doctor, and obviously it's a function of the parents."

Nor does SAB tend to intervene when a child has emotional problems. That, too, is the parents' burden. "If it's a serious problem," Gleboff says, "we would communicate with the parents. The final decision is up to them." In 1980, Vivian Diller, a psychologist in New York, spoke with Gleboff about the problems of young dancers and offered to counsel them. But Diller's proposal was rejected. "In 1980, I talked with Madame Gleboff about helping students in SAB. I wanted to give workshops or groups on how to adjust to being a working person before you're really an adult, about how to cope with leaving home and family, about how to deal with the rules of being a dancer, about weight and nutrition," Diller recounts. "Mrs. Gleboff was not interested. If a dancer at SAB has an emotional problem, the staff tends to send the child home to her family. It seems as though they don't feel any responsibility to deal with these kids' emotional difficulties.

"I told Mrs. Gleboff that such an attitude might be all well and good but that sometimes dancers who know they'll be sent home if they have problems will be more likely to hide what's wrong. By the time someone finds out about it, the problem has become much more serious." Diller feels that SAB, and the dance school establishment's attitude, is neither helpful nor productive. "Most organizations or schools do take some responsibility for their students' problems. They don't send them home, they send them to school counselors. But in ballet, it's like they're being punished because they have problems. Instead of helping the dancers, it appears to these young kids that they're being chastised."

Children are also painfully isolated when the school informs them that they are not New York City Ballet material. At a certain point, when a student has hung around for years hoping to make it into the company, the school suggests that he or she try to get into another professional company. They do little to help disappointed students accept reality; they merely dismiss them.

Not all ballet schools are as detached as SAB. Some schools work at creating a more relaxed and supportive environment for their students. Passing through the corridors of the Pennsylvania Ballet School, which occupies the same building as the Pennsylvania Ballet, one does not sense the tension that permeates SAB. On the surface, there are many similarities: eternally patient mothers waiting for their daughters to emerge from class; students sobbing on each other's shoulders when they learn they will not dance in this year's *Nutcracker*; ecstatic girls who have gotten a compliment from the school's director Lupe Serrano, a former principal dancer with American Ballet Theatre for seventeen years.

Yet the school is more student-oriented than most. The founder of both school and academy is Barbara Weisberger,† a warm, generous woman whose personality infuses the place with motherly concern and good humor. Students say they feel their teachers are accessible. And indeed, teachers and administrators at Pennsylvania seem to deal with the whole student, the growing child as well as the dancer. The school has a housemother whose job it is to be supportive when a student has personal worries.

The professional dancers after whom these students model themselves are also far more relaxed than dancers in New York. Routinely acclaimed as some of the best in any regional company, they do not seem to live only for ballet. Many are married or live together, and the company does not discourage them from having an outside social life. Ben Harkarvy feels it is part of his job to act as a father figure for his younger dancers. They are not just artists, Harkarvy says; they are kids, and they often need help. He does not shy away from suggesting that a troubled dancer seek psychiatric counseling. In fact, he has told some dancers that if they do not go into therapy, they will be in trouble.

Just as Barbara Weisberger's personality has shaped the Pennsylvania Ballet, so is Clare Duncan's reflected in the more relaxed atmosphere at the Houston Ballet Academy. Duncan, a forty-five-year-old Englishwoman, was a soloist with London Festival Ballet and danced as a principal with London Contemporary Dance Theatre, where she also taught. When she chats with students who seek her advice, her speech is peppered with English endearments. Because

---

† Barbara Weisberger and Benjamin Harkarvy left the Pennsylvania Ballet Company during severe financial difficulties in the winter and summer of 1982. It will be interesting to see if the company can retain its more supportive attitude toward its dancers while struggling to achieve financial viability.

Duncan has danced both modern and ballet, for her ballet is only one form of dance, not *the* form of dance. A tall, robust woman, with ash-blond hair that is turning white, she illustrates her points with broad mimetic gestures and candidly speaks of the many problems with which her students must contend. What she says she wants most is to create healthy dancers, not just good dancers. "This means creating healthy kids," she says. That is not easy in ballet where dancers are always dead tired and unable to imagine life without fatigue. But Duncan does not feel that life and dance should be mutually exclusive. She helps her students by heeding their emotional as well as their technical problems. This desire to build a student's self-esteem is nowhere more apparent than in her way of dealing with those dancers who fail to fulfill their promise.

Duncan tries to soften the negative impact of telling a child he or she may not "make it." "I try to make it as positive an experience as is possible," she says. "I try to get them early, when they're thirteen or fourteen, so there's still a few more years of school and a few more doors can be opened for them." With the aid of a professor from Southern Methodist University, she debriefs her students and reintroduces them to life. "I want them to know they can go to college or into commercial theater. When this woman comes from SMU, she tells them about college and makes it sound like fun. Dancers feel they've failed if they go to college, and you just have to make them understand there is another life out there."

When girls are advised that their bodies have become "too feminine" for the art, it is particularly important to shore up their self-esteem. Duncan cannot change ballet's standards (although thinness in Texas is less excessive than in New York), but she can help girls feel good about themselves. "I don't want to make them feel fat and ugly. I point out to them that their phone is always ringing now, while that little snook over there with the flat chest and no hips, her phone never rings. They have to see that they might not have the ideal physique for ballet, but the ideal physique for ballet is perhaps not the ideal physique for a normal person in this world. They have to learn to love their femininity, not to deny it."

The more compassionate attitudes of Duncan and Weisberger unfortunately are the exceptions. More often ballet school administrators are like SAB's: cool, detached, only mildly interested in the dancers' other needs. Directors of most schools believe that the harshness of the training is necessary, as it equips the future dancer with tools for dealing with the difficult world of professional ballet. They do not object to the ruthless competition in their schools because they insist that competition keeps dancers more alert and productive. Kids have to learn to be on their own at an early age because, in a professional company, no one will pamper them; teachers must discourage rebelliousness or assertiveness because if dancers are too temperamental and aggressive, they will cause trouble when they are accepted into a major company.

By tailoring their training to approximate the harsh realities of the ballet world, Gleboff and others seem to feel they are actually doing their students a favor. True, reality may be difficult, taxing, sometimes even crippling, but that is the world dancers live in. It is not the school's function to transform that world but rather to transform their students so they can adapt to it.

Given such attitudes, it is clear that students cannot turn to teachers and administrators. But why are they unable to turn to their parents? The ballet world is well stocked with mothers, and an occasional father, who wait in attendance on the child's every need. If their children are unhappy, why don't parents intervene as they would in ordinary schools? Why don't they question the policies and practices that are so damaging?

Most parents do not act for a number of reasons. First of all, many of them have no idea what their children are going through.

Many children are afraid to confide their miseries because they do not want to disappoint their parents as much as they have disappointed themselves. This is not an unfounded fear. Clare Duncan reports that when students are told they will not make it into companies, their parents are often the ones who take the news "badly." One girl said to her, "I'd like to go to college, but Dad's put so much money into my ballet classes I don't want to tell him that."

And if kids do speak up, their mothers may be afraid to complain to the school for fear of jeopardizing their children's chances for advancement. Rachel Rosen's mother, a forty-eight-year-old partner at a large New York law firm, is one of those women who feel torn between their desire to do their maternal duty and their fear of endangering their daughters' future success. SAB's minimal concern for its pupils' emotional well-being is a considerable source of disturbance to Rachel's mother. "The thing I worry about," she says, "is that they don't encourage a love of dancing. I think their highest priority is to find someone with great turnout or amazing extension. They're not looking for someone with a passion for dance. They're looking for a body they can mold, a body with certain characteristics, like a racehorse. The person gets lost inside the physical qualities."

Mrs. Rosen says she never knows what she will find when she picks Rachel up after school. Some days, Rachel is elated; most days, though, she is in tears. Yet Mrs. Rosen dares not complain. Even as we talk, the knowledge that I have promised to change her name and certain salient facts about her and her daughter does not seem to ease her worries. Rachel becomes increasingly nervous as she and her mother detail SAB's many drawbacks. Like spies who fear their cover will be blown, they keep asking, "Are you *sure* they won't find out it's us?" Mrs. Rosen's anxiety astonishes her, for it does not fit her image of the combative mother who fights to protect her daughter. "Look," she says angrily, "when my kid gets mistreated at public school, I go dashing into that school and collar the teacher and say, 'What the hell are you doing to my daughter?' It's happened to Rachel at different times, and I've had battles. But I don't do that at SAB. The dread that I and most parents have is that if I go to a teacher and say, 'How dare you humiliate my daughter?' the school would just say, 'Fuck you.' Parents are afraid to run the risk because SAB is the only good professional school in the city. So the school has a free hand and can do anything. They criticize in nasty ways. On the orders of George Balanchine, they won't let kids go anywhere else to dance except maybe in *Nutcracker*. They make them starve themselves, and we sit helplessly by because we're terrified to make a peep."

Mothers all over the country share Mrs. Rosen's fear of expressing their complaints. Sarah Harcourt does not like what she sees her daughter experiencing at San Francisco Ballet School. "It seems like a very cold world, so much of it just crushing and devastating to these kids. When Erica was fourteen, she said she didn't think she was doing well, and I mentioned a teacher who had liked her. She said, 'Yes, but she liked me when I was young and thin, and now I'm old and fat.' She was fourteen and weighed one hundred and seven pounds. You hate to see that happen."

Nonetheless, Mrs. Harcourt insists she would never discuss such reservations with the school administration. "It's better to keep your mouth shut. I've seen mothers go in with legitimate questions or complaints. They're not really invasive ballet mothers at all. And they suffer for it through their child. If a parent goes to the administration in good faith, like you would in an academic school, the child is going to pay for it later on. So people learn not to talk out." Whether or not Mrs. Harcourt's fears of repercussions from the school administration are valid, her anxiety governs her attitude to her child's welfare.

Harcourt and Rosen are not parents of poor or disadvantaged pupils. Nor are they immigrant parents who have failed to master a foreign tongue and who are intimidated by people who "belong." Rather, they are affluent women who, under any other circumstances, would fight for their daughters. But when it comes to ballet, they suddenly become the most diffident and obedient of observers.

Fear is not, however, the only reason why parents fail to object to their children's mistreatment at the hands of severe autocratic teachers. Fascination accounts for some measure of their silence. Some parents, particularly mothers, are so mesmerized by the promise of their child's future glory that they feel any sacrifice is justified. These mothers are the classic ballet mothers. They are a staple of ballet life, and the complex interaction between them and their daughters helps determine what happens to many young dancers—both in schools and in their professional lives.

It costs about $78,000—the equivalent of a college degree and at least part of a masters—to produce a dancer. For a child of six or seven, parents must spend about $400 a year for lessons, plus $30 for shoes, $60 for tights and leotards, and $30 for dance slippers. As the child grows, the sums grow too. From a class once a week when she is six, the budding dancer moves to daily classes when she is ten or eleven. Then the annual bill may come to $900 for classes, $110 for pointe shoes, $90 for tights and leotards, and $40 for leg warmers.

By the time a child reaches thirteen or fourteen, the price has escalated still more. A professional student takes more than eight classes a week at an elite school and attends summer sessions. Since none of the nation's top professional schools—the School of American Ballet, the American Ballet Theatre School, or the schools that feed regional companies like Houston, Boston, San Francisco, and Pennsylvania—provide either a general education or room and board, if a child is not a local resident, either a parent must move with her away from home, or the child must live with a family or in a special residence. Thus, added to tuition is the cost of an apartment or room and board. And, because very few public schools will accommodate the demanding dance student's schedule, many out-of-town, or even in-town, students attend private schools.

A family can count on paying about $1030 for ballet school tuition, $600 for summer courses, $3000 or more for private school tuition, $5425 for room and board, and $600 for transportation for visits home. And, of course, on top of that are the usual fees for tights, shoes, slippers, leotards, and leg warmers. Some of this financial strain is relieved if the child receives a scholarship. The School of American Ballet has two hundred scholarship students who are awarded their tuition plus $900 toward private schooling at Professional Children's School in New York. Students at most schools can purchase pointe shoes at a discount from a selection of company rejects, though not all can find the right pair of shoes in a company shoe room. SAB is the only school that contributes to the price of room and board for its students, and no school provides pocket money or travel allowances for visits home.

Not surprisingly, then, most of the boys and girls who pursue their dreams in one of the nation's thirty thousand ballet schools come from middle- or upper-middle-class families. Ballet is an expensive undertaking. In addition to financial support, there is, however, another form of parental support that ballet demands. As Arlene Croce states in her book *Afterimages*, "The dancers . . . are generally too young to know what they're getting into at the age when they have to get into it. . . . Ballet mamas are the great realists of the business."

Caroline Houy is a plump, affable, forty-year-old southerner with brightly painted lips and short, highly teased and lacquered brown hair. Alabama percolates through her voice as she guides me across the small New York apartment she shares with her two teenage daughters. She has lived in this high-rise complex across the street from Lincoln Center for a year now, her second year in Manhattan. Before that, she and her two daughters—Dottie, a sixteen-year-old aspiring ballerina, and fourteen-year-old Caroline, who waits patiently for her voice to mature so she can begin opera lessons—lived in cramped quarters in the Hotel Alcott on West Seventy-second Street. Pointing out the features of her new home, with its crowded kitchen, its compact and sparsely furnished living room, and an abbreviated rectangle of a bedroom that just barely accommodates three narrow beds, Caroline

Houy is clearly delighted to be living in such grandeur. Her original New York lodgings in the residential hotel contained a kitchen that was so tiny that it had room only for a small sink, a half-fridge, and a hot plate. "It's amazing what you can get used to," she says.

On the wall of the dining room is a commemorative collection of pictures like those displayed by politicians and restaurateurs in which various celebrities and the collector are caught in fleeting poses of friendship. Caroline Houy's collection includes glossies of ballet stars, as well as photographs of her children in theatrical costumes and tutus.

Unlike many ballet mothers, Caroline Houy tells her story with great candor. There is no syrupy southern sweetness in this former Birmingham matron. Uninhibited by the presence of her fourteen-year-old daughter, Mrs. Houy talks of her marriage, her relationship with her parents, and her life in the South before ballet.

It was a life of affluence and comfort. Before she married, she was a stewardess, but she was happy to trade in her uniform for marriage. Her husband was a football trainer working for pro teams like the Dallas Cowboys and the Atlanta Falcons. In both those cities the family lived in large homes and fraternized with football celebrities. Mr. Houy eventually left the sports world and took a job with Caroline Houy's father in the family business in Birmingham. She has always regretted his taking that step. "I didn't like everyone knowing my business," she says.

Caroline Houy felt condemned to a life of frustration and suffocation in her hometown. "In Birmingham everything is the same," she comments. "Everybody conforms. You have to dress to go to the grocery store. You see all your mother's friends. I thought my life had ended in Birmingham. I was just buried alive. All I did was spend money and give volunteer parties—patrons parties for the ballet—just to stay busy."

Her daughter's ballet career was Caroline's way out. When

Dottie was fourteen, she was offered a scholarship at the American Ballet Theatre School in New York. Mrs. Houy says she was forced to choose between living apart from her husband or sending her daughter to New York alone. Her decision was to go with Dottie. "She may never do anything with ballet," she says in determined tones, "but I hope she does. Still, I never want a child of mine to look back and say, 'Mama, why didn't you have guts enough to give me my chance?' This way I'll know she had her chance."

Guts was what it took. No one in Mrs. Houy's family supported her decision. "The family was in total disagreement with me," she acknowledges calmly before giving vent to the full weight of her bitterness. "In fact, I fought heaven and earth to come here. My mother always understood. But my father didn't and was wholly against it and fought me every step of the way."

Her husband also objected to her decision, and Mrs. Houy held a garage sale to pay for the plane fare to New York. Although her husband finally agreed to pay her rent, he had hoped that her determination would be transitory, she explains. "I don't think he bargained on my enjoying it so much."

New York, however, has given Mrs. Houy a taste for urban life and culture. "This is a whole world I would never have seen," she says exuberantly. "I have a lot of friends and acquaintances—ushers at the Met, people at the grocery store. Sometimes it's hard, but once you get used to it you really enjoy the challenge. You get standing-room tickets at the Met, you meet friends backstage. People here are so much nicer than they are down south," she says, countering New York's bad press. "They really care about each other."

On a strict budget, Mrs. Houy admits that life is not easy. But she brightens considerably when she talks of her return to the world of work. She positively delights in describing how her friends from Birmingham would react if she checked their hats at Alfredo's restaurant on New York's elegant Central Park South or served them a croissant at the Essex House's patisserie, or ushered them down the aisle of the Met or sold them a book at her current place of employment, The Ballet Shop, across from Lincoln Center.

More than adventure, Caroline Houy has found something unexpected in New York. "I had been told I didn't have sense enough or drive enough to do anything with my life," she recalls. "I never thought I could manage money or anything else. There've been times when I've been down to ten dollars, and that's kind of scary, but here we are today," she says, pointing proudly to her home and to her wall of photographic trophies. "Here in New York, you can do anything, be anything, and nobody cares. It's been an experience because I finally found out I was worth something."

Caroline Houy's story explains a great deal about ballet mothers and what drives them. These women, like stage mothers, have become comic figures in theater lore. Almost any ballet novel includes the obligatory caricature of a woman so driven by her own frustrated ambition that she has become a predator on her daughter's talent. The fictional ballet mother shamelessly pesters teachers and directors, cattily tries to demean her daughter's competitors, and will do anything to get attention through her daughter's career. In *Mirrors*, a recent novel about a ballerina's trials and tribulations, a vicious ballet mother actually forces her daughter to bed down with a lecherous choreographer in order to get a coveted role.

In real life, some of the mothers of America's most renowned dancers have achieved their own brand of acclaim. The mother of former NYCB principal dancer Violette Verdy, who is now director of the Boston Ballet, is one of the most famous ballet mothers. "Mama" Verdy, as she was fondly called, not only lived with her daughter, she accompanied her when Violette danced with Roland Petit in France. Her job was to tend to her daughter and care for other "motherless" girls, making sure they were protected from men who swarmed around impressionable young ballerinas.

When Violette joined City Ballet, "Mama" Verdy moved with her, and the two shared an apartment in New York. In New York, Violette's mother occupied herself with SAB students who boarded in her spacious apartment, which became a noted balletic home-away-from-home for many young students. Mrs. Verdy now lives in Paris, but she has been replaced by a new generation of ballet mothers. To mothers of aspiring ballerinas, these women are models of maternal success. They are proof that despite a child's age or status, her mother will always hold an integral place in her life and career.

Contrary to the common stereotype of the ballet mother, Caroline Houy—and many women like her—is not moved solely by ambition. What drew her away from home, and to her daughter's career, was the simple desire for freedom. Caroline Houy was born in the wrong time and the wrong place, was trapped by conventional expectations, and had neither the internal nor external supports necessary to legitimize goals of her own. Like Mrs. Houy, most ballet mothers have done the socially correct thing: gotten married and had children. But it has not brought them fulfillment. Caught in a net of obligation, they have been unable to search for a different sort of life.

This syndrome of discontent is particularly pronounced among women who come from the most comfortable backgrounds. Margot Fonteyn's mother, for example, was the wife of a well-to-do London businessman. They traveled round the world together, and were waited on by countless servants. She had plenty of leisure time and the means to enjoy it. But once her husband's career took the family from England to the Orient, her idle existence became oppressive. "With the company house came a boy, a cook, a coolie, an amah, and several relatives," Fonteyn says in her autobiography. "My mother had always enjoyed cooking, but with so many servants, she would have 'lost face' had she lifted a finger to do anything herself in the house. So, with time on her hands, my mother looked for a dancing teacher."

What a relief it must have been to accompany Margot to classes, and what a relief, when it became apparent that Margot had the makings of a great dancer, to find an excuse to leave Shanghai and return to England, where she could share her daughter's life and career. There, in London, the two lived together until Fonteyn married in her mid-thirties—not an unusual arrangement for ballet dancers, who often live with their parents until they are well into their twenties or early thirties.

Had Caroline Houy deserted and divorced her husband, there would have been little to boast of in her new life in New York. Scrimping, saving, and hatchecking would not have seemed such a great adventure if she were just another in the swarms of struggling single women in the city. Dottie's career, on the other hand, has allowed her to get away from home without severing family ties and suffering the resulting social isolation. Mrs. Houy lives away from home, but she has a permanent safety net under her: Her husband pays the rent, the bills, tuition, class costs, and the price of visits home; and her daughter leads her into a world where she can socialize with ballet and opera stars.

While I talk with Mrs. Houy, her daughter Caroline puzzles over a homework assignment in the dining alcove. A sturdy, pudgy girl with straight blond hair framing a plain but amiable face, she nods in agreement when her mother asks her to second an opinion or provide forgotten details for a particular anecdote. Without openly acknowledging the fact, her parents have essentially separated, and Caroline has stayed with her mother, which means that she has had to leave Birmingham and travel to New York. Her sister's career has cost her her father, grandparents, and schoolmates in Birmingham, and she has also been deprived of ordinary school life. Her mother, unwilling to send her into the jungle of New York's public schools and unable to afford private education, has arranged for her to do high school on correspondence.

She works by herself at the dining-room table, reading, writing, doing homework, taking tests, sending the results in to some anonymous grader who sends back comments and scores. Alone all day, she waits for her mother and sister to return. "Caroline has really been a brick," her mother admits, "because she loves her home and naturally loves her daddy. A lot of people shake their heads when they hear she's on correspondence. But I think her education is fantastic up here. Caroline works round the clock. There are no holidays on correspondence. They're workaholics," she beams, "and it's great."

When Dottie, a tall, slender, fair-haired girl, returns from class about an hour after I arrive, she nestles in near her mother to join the discussion. Clearly she has chosen sides. "My father," she announces with acerbity, "tries to make me feel guilty. Like when my birthday comes, he says, 'It's the second time I haven't been with you on your birthday.' It makes me feel so bad," she says. "I get so down. Last year, he asked me when I was going to come back home, and I had to say that I'm not."

Mrs. Houy hurriedly informs me that the children visit their father, and both he and their grandparents have made the trip north. The family still hopes the prodigal wife and her daughters will recant and come home, but the three Houy women have become increasingly estranged from Birmingham; and when they do go down for a visit, they feel they are straying into alien territory. "I didn't even bother to call my friends when I was back home," Dottie observes, "because they don't understand why I'm here. All they talk about is sororities and rush, and I don't know about all that."

I ask what would happen if Dottie decided to go to college rather than to dance. Mrs. Houy is appalled at the thought. She reflects a moment and then candidly answers, "It would be awful tough. If

Dottie didn't want ballet and decided to go back to Birmingham, I selfishly wouldn't like it because I've enjoyed myself. But I'd do what I'd have to do."

Like the dancers who avoid thinking about the potential problems in a ballet career, Mrs. Houy rarely thinks about the possibility of Dottie's failure. She prefers instead to create a permanent place for herself in Dottie's future. "I'd like to be like Beverly Sills's mother or Cynthia Harvey's mother. Cynthia Harvey has this wonderful relationship with her mother. I'd keep working," she interjects, lest she appear too much to dominate her daughter's life. "I'd have friends and enjoy going to the opera and ballet. I'd stay out of the way and not bother anybody. But I'd be there."

The ballet mother's departure from home is usually not the beginning of emotional and physical separation from family and friends; rather, it is the end. In most cases, ballet mothers (and their daughters) have spent years disengaging from their routines and commitments. When Rebecca Wilson,* now a soloist with ABT, was six, her mother took her to her first ballet class in her hometown of Lee, Massachusetts. As Rebecca made progress, her mother increased her class schedule to twice a week; and then, as Rebecca showed real promise, she began going every day. Eventually, she outgrew local schools and her mother enrolled her in the Boston Ballet School about a hundred miles from Lee. For two years, Rebecca's mother made the four-hour round-trip drive six days a week. To get to class on time, Rebecca had to leave public school early in the afternoon; when the public school system refused to excuse her early, she was transferred to a more flexible private school.

Every weekday morning Mrs. Wilson woke her daughter at six in the morning, drove her to private school, returned to collect her in the late afternoon, drove to her ballet school in Boston, waited for her class to end at eight o'clock, and drove back to Lee. Mother and daughter went to bed at midnight. This rigorous schedule became the centerpiece of the family's life. Mr. Wilson, an accountant who owned his own firm, often helped with the driving and even installed a special desk and lamp in the back seat of the car so Rebecca could do her homework. Given the demands on their time and energy, neither Rebecca nor her parents saw much of their friends in Lee.

At thirteen, Rebecca was accepted at SAB, and she and her mother moved to New York, where Mr. Wilson visited them on weekends. The break from a quiet life in a small, provincial city was not difficult for Mrs. Wilson. After years of attending to every detail of her daughter's involvement in ballet, she no longer had a life of her own, no longer even had friends of her own. The most difficult moment came not when Mrs. Wilson left her hometown for New York but when her daughter decided that she was old enough to live alone in the city. Then Mrs. Wilson had to return to the life she had left.

Like their daughters, ballet mothers wean themselves from a more balanced life. They may work at menial jobs or make friends in an apartment building, but they rarely seek out and form attachments to other ballet mothers. Unlike parents whose children go to ordinary schools, whose common concerns unite them in school-related activities, the ambitions of ballet mothers are a barrier to forming friendships; and the competitiveness of the average ballet academy exacerbates those ambitions.

On any given day, you can see this dynamic at work. A group of mothers assembles outside their daughters' class. When class lets out, they anxiously await the day's verdict. Some girls are in tears; others are beaming. These mad swings between highs and lows affect the mothers as much as their daughters. They have come to understand that their daughter's success depends on another girl's failure; and they are concerned, solely, with that success.

In any competitive school, you would be likely to find the same preoccupation with a child's achievements. But in most schools, parent organizations allow mothers to worry about common concerns as well as individual advancement. Giving parents a voice in the running of a school not only improves conditions for all students but helps temper competitive drives so that mothers are free to form relationships with other parents.

In ballet schools no such organizations exist. Schools consider parents irritating pests and try to defend themselves against their interference. Having absorbed this negative image of themselves, fearing to hear the constant, catty comparisons between their daughter and someone else's, ballet mothers avoid one another rather than uniting around shared preoccupations and issues. This means that ballet mothers often experience considerable loneliness. Nevertheless, when they compare their new lives with their lives back home, even the tedium and loneliness usually seem preferable.

Sarah Harcourt appears hopelessly out of place and isolated in her rented San Francisco apartment. She is a worn woman, with tightly knotted brown hair streaked with gray, and a haggard face that seems wrinkled by hardship rather than age. Her package of cigarettes lies close by her side. As soon as it is empty, she excuses herself to replenish her supply. Between puffs, she coughs. When she is not holding a cigarette, she is toying with the plastic-wrapped package. She has emphysema, she tells me almost apologetically when a particularly bad coughing spell interrupts our conversation. But as soon as she regains her composure, she inhales again.

Before she came to San Francisco a year ago Mrs. Harcourt worked with her husband in their small grocery store in California. She spent her days serving customers, doing the books, raising three daughters and a son. The older three children are now out of the house, she explains, and she can focus her attention on her youngest, Erica, who is fifteen. (Erica is far younger than the other children, which is why Sarah, unlike many other ballet mothers, is in her mid-fifties.)

For some years Erica's blossoming talent as a dancer has been one of her mother's only joys. "I always enjoyed her classes," she reports in a tired, low voice. "I think a mother always enjoys it when she sees her children enjoying something, when they take pride in themselves and their accomplishments."

Otherwise, Mrs. Harcourt seems to have lead a fairly cheerless life. She talks with an obligatory display of pride about the grandchildren who live in the same town or the next town over, and points to several photos exhibited on a fake wooden side table with a tall, ornate white-and-gilt lamp. But they do not appear to have compensated for the unhappy childhood she herself had. When she was only eight, she developed anorexia nervosa, and her parents shipped her off to an institution that was supposed to cure her. "I know all about anorexia," she says. "Nobody diagnosed it then, but I know what it is when you see food and you vomit. At an institution where they were supposedly doing me good, I was punished for not eating, and then punished for vomiting. One of the punishments, other than cleaning the plate and being served another one, was that you had to spend an hour in bed on Saturday for every meal you didn't finish. So other kids would laugh at you. But they finally had to let me out of bed because there weren't enough hours on Saturday for all the meals I missed."

After recovering from anorexia—by herself, not with the help of the institution—she encountered other traumas. At home, she had to watch over a retarded sister and help her mother with family chores, secretly hoping that once she was old enough she could go to college. But this dream was unfulfilled. "When I was making a decision in high school about whether to go to college," she continues her tale, "it was the end of the Depression and it wasn't possible. There just wasn't any money available." She minimizes her disappointment. "I didn't blame anyone, but I decided that with my own children, it was best to be prepared. If you get your chance, fine; if you don't, that's the way the cookie crumbles."

Mrs. Harcourt's fate was marriage, which seems only to have heaped more burdens upon her. She raised four children and also cared for her mother during a twenty-year illness.

Two years ago, when she decided to leave home for a summer so Erica could enroll in San Francisco's summer program, she discovered that Erica's career was an unexpected respite from family obligations. "The first summer we came, I looked forward to it. And the two summers we were here, I thoroughly enjoyed it," she explains with palpable relief. "She was still a little girl then, and we could enjoy things together."

After Erica's second summer at the school, she was asked to attend the school's main program, and Mrs. Harcourt insisted that her daughter take advantage of this opportunity. Her family did not take the news well. "I have many obligations. I've been sort of the wheel-horse for everybody all my life, and they feel I'm sort of letting them drift now. I tried to assure everybody that my priorities were straight and that I wasn't abandoning them for a thirteen-year-old, that if anything happened I'd come home immediately and Erica would have to take second place."

Although Mrs. Harcourt justifies her flight in terms of her daughter's needs, it seems clear that what led her to San Francisco was her own overwhelming desire to escape. She has not, however, thrown herself into the life of the city. San Francisco is not, for her, the kaleidoscope of entertainment and excitement New York is for Caroline Houey. While her daughter goes to a local private school, she stays home to clean, or to run errands, always making sure she is at home to greet Erica after school. The two then ride the bus to the San Francisco Ballet School, and Mrs. Harcourt returns home. Several hours later she goes back to the school to pick up her daughter. During off-hours, she occasionally visits a friend in the building, but like so many ballet mothers, she studiously avoids other mothers at the ballet school.

Worry appears to be her most faithful companion. She is apprehensive both about Erica's choice of career and about her own role in encouraging that career. On the one hand, she wants to help her daughter; on the other, she does not want to foster unrealistic hopes. "I've tried to warn her that there are other kinds of dance and other areas to fall back on. I know she'll be tempted to quit school when the company starts using her for parts. And I've told her to finish high school no matter how long it takes. But I can already feel her resisting."

While she has tried to persuade her daughter to provide herself with other options, Mrs. Harcourt seems to have none of her own. Even the time she has to enjoy her daughter's companionship is limited. The day is not far off when Erica will no longer need a mother to come home to, when she can stay in San Francisco alone. Then it will be time to return to the life she has put on hold.

Mrs. Harcourt's case may seem to be an extreme example of frustration and discontent, yet her story and the reality it reveals are typical. Like Mrs. Harcourt, almost all ballet mothers insist that their home lives are in fine shape. Without a strong marriage, they ask, how could they leave home and pursue this dream of glory? If you talk with these women long enough, however, you begin to pick up hints that things at home are not what they might appear to be. Fearful of an open rupture with their husbands and families, they may be picking an acceptable course of ostensible self-sacrifice, which actually frees them from an unacceptable situation.

Loretta Strizak is a blond fifty-year-old whose two daughters, Carol and Barbara, studied at the School of American Ballet. In her late teens Mrs. Strizak worked as a professional figure skater, but she quit when she married. She then had five children, three boys and two girls. While the boys played football and baseball, Mrs. Strizak took her girls to ballet class at a local school near her suburban New Jersey home. At thirteen Carol became a full-time student at SAB and enrolled in Professional Children's School. In the morning, Mrs. Strizak drove Carol to school in Manhattan, raced back to New Jersey to complete her household chores, and went back to New York to pick Carol up in the evening. It looked like this frenzied routine would end when Carol, at fifteen, decided to share an apartment with another ballet student. But then Mrs. Strizak's second daughter, Barbara, got into SAB. Mrs. Strizak decided to move into New York, where she shared an apartment with her daughters, took a job at J.C. Penney's, and helped pay the rent by taking in other SAB students as boarders.

One spring afternoon I talked with her in the New York apartment where she still lives (her daughters, now eighteen and twenty-five, have moved to Maryland to dance with the Baltimore Ballet). After tracing the outlines of her daughters' dancing careers and her own commuting career, she describes her decision to leave her family as an unfortunate sacrifice she had to make. "I just couldn't do it anymore," she sighs, as if still exhausted by the very thought of so much driving. "I was totally worn-out, completely drained. My eyes were getting bad, I was getting nervous about driving. I just had to move into town." Because her older boys were college age when she moved to New York, she felt she could keep the family and her marriage together by returning home on weekends. On the surface, it appears to have been a valiant gesture, motivated by a mother's desire to put her children before herself. But as we continue talking, Mrs. Strizak reveals that her husband was a traveling salesman who was rarely home. Even when her daughters were old enough to take care of themselves, Mrs. Strizak did not return to New Jersey. Over the years, she had built a far more satisfying life in New York and was reluctant to leave it. "I don't know what I want to do with my life right now," she muses.

"My plans are up in the air. I wouldn't want to quit working. I'm used to being here."

The same themes are repeated in Carol Goza's story. A lanky, redheaded Texan, Mrs. Goza accompanied her twelve-year-old daughter Tracy to New York so she could protect her from the perils of the city. She left a seven-year-old daughter and her husband back home. The move so strained the family's budget that Mrs. Goza rented a bed to another SAB student, and back in Texas her husband rented out the family house and moved in with Mrs. Goza's parents, who looked after their grandchild in her mother's absence. Carol Goza staunchly maintains that her family's ability to withstand separation is a mark of its strength, and that absence is a mark of intimacy. "It takes all of us, my husband and my parents, working together to do this," she asserts, only later revealing that her life in Texas was somewhat dull. "At home," she recounts, "if you don't work—and," she adds hastily, "most husbands don't want their wives working—you sit around and watch TV and then you clean the house in an hour and watch the soap operas and get up and cook supper. And that's about the extent of it, unless you go out at night." Nonetheless, she still emphasizes how much she has sacrificed; lowering her voice she expresses scorn for women who are "too cowardly" to risk their marriages for their children. "Most women wouldn't even go for a couple of years. They feel they just can't leave. Mainly because of their husbands. They feel they'll stray if they go away from home. My husband isn't like that," she reports with satisfaction. "He says, well, she's talented and this is where she has to be and it's only going to be a couple of years."

"A couple of years" often stretches into a lifetime, however. Once Margot Fonteyn and her mother moved to England, Margot's father gradually disappeared from the narrative. A sentence or two, scattered through the three-hundred-page book, allude to infrequent visits. But these became rarer and rarer. Before and during World War

Two Fonteyn's mother and father, the dancer casually mentions, were actually separated for ten years.

The separation that may relieve the disappointment of a dull life and unsatisfactory marriage for a ballet mother takes its toll on other family members. Like parents of a child who is ill, handicapped, emotionally disturbed, or retarded, ballet parents often expend so much energy caring for the needs of the special child that their other children are slighted. Exhausted mothers who come home after hours of commuting have little energy for the child who just wants help with a math problem or wants a mother to listen to tales of troubles at school. "The problem right now," says Alice Oebon, a ballet mother in Houston whose nondancing daughter is left alone for hours at a time, "is that her sister's ballet classes really cost her. It takes my time away from her. She has had to be pretty independent and on her own."

Time with a parent is not the only thing nondancing siblings forfeit. They suffer financially as well. If the family is not wealthy, the expenses incurred in training the dancer are so heavy that there is little left over to provide other children with piano lessons or summer camp. The siblings' contribution to the dancer's progress is learning to do without.

The most damaging effects of this mother-daughter syndrome, however, are often on the dancer herself. Ballet mothers spend all their time trying to protect their daughters and to support their careers. They frequently envelop these children in a web of suffocating closeness, which, ironically, poses other problems for the child. In many of the relationships between ballet mothers and their daughters, the parent and child are practically fused. They are in what psychiatrists call symbiotic relationships. For the child, such closeness does not encourage eventual independence but ties her so fully to her mother that she is often unable to develop the sense of self that is a prerequisite to an autonomous life.

■ ■ ■

On a bright fall day, Ellen Conners* spends the morning in her nondescript split-level suburban house twenty miles outside Baltimore, Maryland. Her husband, a salesman, has gone off to work, and her only daughter, Stacey, a ballet student at SAB, is dancing with Natalia Makarova's temporary company of student dancers recruited for a four-week stint in New York. Mrs. Conners is spending a wistful morning, her thoughts far from the provincial town where she lives and the suburban kitchen where she lingers over her morning coffee. She is a woman hemmed in by her environment, thwarted in her ambitions; her life is relieved only by the dreams she has for her daughter's future.

She wanders through her home like a visitor. The compact split-level is clean and tidy, but not welcoming. The neutral walls and carpets, the old settees, and the dark mahogany furnishings are somewhat lifeless. The only hints of spirit are the paintings of beautiful ballerinas (her own work, she tells me proudly) exhibited all over the house. Dancers twirl in the basement, pose in hallways, leap up the stairwells. In the master bedroom, with its frilly white nylon curtains and bedspread, a painting of a long-limbed ballerina, the image of Mrs. Conners's daughter, hangs over the bed.

Mrs. Conners is a small, slender woman with straight brown hair curled up at the ends. She is dressed in wine-red slacks and a matching turtleneck sweater. I am a bit startled when I meet her, for her daughter Stacey is a delicate, beautiful, sixteen-year-old, and Mrs. Conners seems both too stern and too old to have produced this gossamer beauty. When we settle into chairs on the back porch to begin our conversation, I am tempted to ask her why she had a child so late in life, but Ellen Conners's summary reveals that she is, in fact, only forty years old. I find I can set aside my agenda of questions as we talk. The barest hint of interest in her daughter's career triggers a well-rehearsed tape. Speaking in a high, harsh voice with a thick Florida accent, she is so absorbed in her recitation that even when I try to stop her to clarify dates, places, and personalities, she cannot quite come to grips with my presence.

Because she is so preoccupied by her own recasting of events, we do not begin at the beginning, with her daughter's first class and pointe shoes. Mrs. Conners is worried about the here and now, with yesterday and the day before. During a recent performance in New York with Makarova's company, Stacey's toe shoe came off onstage. According to Mrs. Conners, this unfortunate accident infuriated Makarova. Her company had not been well received by the critics, and her dreams of having her own permanent troop were dashed. "The company directors were angry at Stacey and wouldn't let her dance for nearly a week," Mrs. Conners explains angrily. "I thought they handled it very badly. They wouldn't speak to her in class. They blamed their problems on Stacey. My husband and I tried to explain to her that they acted that way because of the reviews, not because of her. But it nearly destroyed her, and she lost all her confidence."

It was a terrible setback to the plan Ellen Conners had begun drawing up ten years ago when Stacey's talent exerted its charms on her first ballet teachers in Florida. "They were just crazy about her," Mrs. Conners recalls. Their response, of course, confirmed her own opinion that Stacey—with her smooth, pale skin, perfect ballerina profile, slim hips, and fine, long limbs—was all a ballerina should be. "She was," Mrs. Conners tells me, "the image of Suzanne Farrell."

After Stacey's initial training in Florida, Mrs. Conners packed up and took her daughter to SAB. "When Stacey came to New York she was twelve years old," her mother reminisces. "Our whole goal was for her to be a star. 'If you can't be a star or the best, forget it; and get into something else, because ballet doesn't pay enough.' We always held on to that, and we always believed that."

Unfortunately, when Stacey appeared in his school, Balanchine did not immediately discern either this star quality or the Farrell resemblance. "I don't understand why Balanchine hasn't already used her," Mrs. Conners frets. "The day before yesterday, two other dancers were put into the company. And yet Stacey isn't even an apprentice. It's beyond my comprehension. I keep trying to comfort myself with the thought that the reason Stacey isn't an apprentice is that, let's face it, Balanchine hasn't really looked at her. He's had a cataract operation," she says, trying to justify the master's indifference. "Maybe now he'll actually be able to see."

The conversation ebbs for a moment as she pauses to sift through the evidence, like a neutral party weighing Stacey's guilt or innocence. While she is considering her daughter's future, I think of my visit to Stacey's room at The Swiss Town House on West Sixty-seventh Street in New York. She was lucky to have found a room at this popular women's hostel, one of the few like it in the city, which houses about fifty budding dancers, models, and actresses. It is not, however, a welcoming retreat. The house was once a fine Upper West Side brownstone, but hundreds of anonymous residents have driven it into a state of permanent decline. Downstairs is a dismal hall, a large untenanted parlor filled with straight-backed chairs and old-fashioned horsehair settees. A receptionist monitors the switchboard. Breakfast and dinner are included in the price of room and board, but Stacey rarely mingles with other girls over meals because she cannot eat the starchy institutional food provided. Up three flights of carpeted stairs, tattered and worn, is her room—a tiny cubicle painted a drab blue, with a narrow bed, a desk, and dresser. One window offers a faint glimmer of light and a view of the soot-encrusted brick wall of a neighboring building.

Stacey's room is decorated with posters of David Bowie: David Bowie playing the guitar, David Bowie as The Man Who Fell to Earth, David Bowie in an advertisement for the Broadway play *The Elephant Man*. Amidst the treasure trove of Bowieana is one reminder that Stacey is a dancer—a ballet calendar with City Ballet's Helgi Tomasson as dancer of the month.

Stacey is such a dedicated young dancer that it's somewhat surprising and refreshing to find that underneath is a normal teenager with normal adolescent fantasies. "I met him once, real quickly, as I stood around the stage door after his play. I wrote him a letter," she says wistfully. "If only I could figure out some way to really get to know him," she puzzles. "I mean, all I want to do is talk with him for a couple of hours."

Stacey's life is dominated by dance. In her meager spare time, she works at The Swiss Town House switchboard to make some extra money or sews the pointe shoes that are collected in a large heap in a corner of the room. As we talk, she pulls out several pairs of gleaming satin shoes, clips the pink satin ribbons off a worn-out pair, and prepares to sew them on to a fresh pair of slippers. At night, she does her homework and waits for a call from her mother.

"My mother has always helped me," she says. "A lot of drive really came from my mother. I pushed myself, but it wasn't quite me who wanted to be a dancer. It was my mother who wanted me to be a dancer. That is, until I came to SAB; then it was me." Upon her arrival, Stacey says, she had a sudden burst of certainty: this was it, her career, her life. That momentary certitude may have saved her from her doubts, but it has not saved her from herself. "I get very upset if I can't do a step, if things go wrong," she says, picking at her swollen, raw cuticles. "I want it all right now. It's hard; you have to have a lot of drive as a dancer. It's hard to control it. I go to class every day, and I just kill myself doing one step. Sometimes I get upset and start to cry in class. It's because I feel I have to make it when I'm young. I'm competing against myself, against that girl in the mirror."

That girl in the mirror has had to become a one-dimensional person. Schoolwork intrigues her, and she says that if she does not succeed in ballet, she would like to become a biologist. As quickly as the thought crosses her mind, she grabs it and tucks it safely out of sight. "My mother wouldn't like that," she explains fearfully, as if her mother is a permanent lodger in the tiny room. "Sometimes I feel she's watching me. I mean, she's always asking me if I like my schoolwork and when I say yes, I can tell she's worried that I might like something better than ballet. And I do like my schoolwork. I enjoy it," she asserts fiercely but retreats just as hastily. "But I want to be a dancer. I'd never quit. Never."

Stacey, it seems, is a product of her coach's game plan. For that is Mrs. Conners's view of the maternal relationship. Like a trainer or coach or ballet master, she is concerned only with short-term victories. "If you're a mother, you can't make their lives for them," she recounts her philosophy. "But sometimes, if you make someone really angry, then they can do it for themselves. I've made Stacey so angry in her life that I know she could take a knife and just kill me. Because she'd be trying to do *entrechat six* and she'd get frustrated. So I'd say, 'Well, why don't you just quit? You'll save money, agony, and time.' Then I can hear in her mind, 'Well, I'll show you.' That's what I've done with Stacey all her life. It's like coaches with football players: that's what you do, you make them angry.

"But you never praise them," Mrs. Conners warns solemnly. "My god, you're never satisfied. I hope I'm never satisfied. And if I am, I hope she never knows it. I watched her in New York in Chopin one night, and I just cried. I thought, 'Oh god, is that really Stacey?' But when she came out and came over to me, I said, 'Oh yeah,' "—she mimics the studied indifference she displayed—" 'I liked that; that was all right.' "

It is a chilling monologue. Mrs. Conners says she has stripped her emotions of all maternal feeling because this is best for Stacey. Having led an unproductive life herself, she has determined not to let that be her daughter's fate. "You can do anything you want with a kid. Anything," she says passionately, her voice rising with her expectations. "You can make them a Dr. Dooley or a Suzanne Farrell. Why, they can even be president of the United States. Some people will settle for less," she asserts with disdain, "but I won't."

As swiftly as the passions swells, it recedes. Describing the price her daughter has paid to fulfill her mother's dreams, Ellen Conners once again becomes the detached clinical programmer interested only in results. In matter-of-fact tones, she admits that Stacey has suffered because her talent has separated her from her peers and has made her classmates into rivals rather than allies. "From the first day when she went to ballet class and everyone raved about her, she was alienated and hated by every child there. And I mean really." Mrs. Conners leans toward me and confides, as though she were talking about someone else's child. "The child was warped that day, and she's been warped ever since. She was unhappy because the kids wouldn't want to go across the room with her, the kids were being mean to her. She still has a problem with friends. She really does. I keep telling her it's a shame she can't find a good friend who has nothing to do with ballet because it's so competitive that you can't really be good friends with anyone there."

But Stacey has not found such a friend. Her only friend is her mother. Stacey's father occasionally drifts into the conversation, just as he occasionally drifts into his daughter's life. He is the man who pays the bills. But he, like most ballet fathers, appears to have no more than a walk-on role in this drama where the dancer and her mother dominate the action. The mother is writer, director, and producer, as well as one of the stars in this three-act play. We are now watching Act II, in which Stacey, the student, struggles for acceptance. Act III, the conclusion, is well rehearsed. Its ending is even happier than one would have expected. "You don't think Stacey's being a star is going to be the end," Ellen Conners reveals. "Once she's a big star, she's going to be queen of England. What I'm saying is that there are no limits. There really are none. You can dream about whatever you want."

She is so committed to that dream that she cannot imagine any other future, any other ending. Failure is not something she can adjust to or something she, as a mother, ought to help her daughter face. To her, dancing with City Ballet is life; not to dance is death. "When I'm really depressed," she says bleakly, "I feel like both of us should walk out and throw ourselves in front of a truck. Me and Stacey, we'll just die together in front of a truck, hand in hand, together."

Mrs. Conners's vision of maternal protection is an extreme case, but the ballet world is full of such ambiguous and interdependent relationships. They function on the premise that the young dancers have chosen to accept the stern discipline their training requires. Mothers rush to assure me that their children willingly skip birthday parties on Saturday afternoons, sleepover dates, football games, dating, and college. "I always asked her if she wanted to go to parties," echo Mrs. Houy, Mrs. Harcourt, and Mrs. Conners, "but she always said she'd rather not miss class." If the child chose freely, why should we worry? They are, after all, only getting what they want. These children, however, have spent all their lives with their mothers. They have observed their mother's sacrifices and they realize how much their parents want them to dance. If a child feels she will hurt her mother by choosing against dance, she will be reluctant, as Houston Ballet Academy's Clare Duncan points out, not to make the "right choice."

When I asked Sarah Harcourt's daughter whether she and her mother ever argued, she said, "Me and my mom, we've had lots of disagreements. We love each other so much that we get too close or something. My mom, she lives for me. Whatever my dream is, it's her dream and that's why she's up here with me. But if I do anything wrong, she says, 'Oh, you've ruined my life.' She lives for me and so it's really hard if I hurt her."

The class is in Studio Three, a large windowless room, on Level C, one of the Metropolitan Opera House's many sub-basements. A huge, vividly colored canvas covers one wall with a Chagall-like scene: an orchestra of butterflies playing to a full hall. The wall opposite is hung with mirrors; and portable barres, which look like equestrian jumping posts, are scattered across the floor.

Worn and exhausted after having performed until eleven o'clock the previous evening, ABT dancers straggle in late the next morning. Their fatigue, they know, is irrelevant; nothing—neither exhaustion nor performing nor touring—interrupts the ritual of daily class. When they are doing their annual eight-week stint at the Met, class is held there; when they are rehearsing, it is at the ABT studios; and while they are on tour, they congregate at any one of a dozen or more theaters across the country.

Today, the room is only half-full; when they are in New York, many company dancers prefer to attend class at a favored teacher's studio. At eleven, Madame Sulamith Messerer, one of ABT's recent Russian defectors, calls the class to order, and the pianist begins with a slow, melancholy prelude. Messerer, a small woman with black hair, speaks little English and addresses the class in French. At times even that language fails her, and she gesticulates in an elaborate pantomime that dancers who have trained with teachers of many different nationalities have little trouble deciphering.

About fifteen minutes after the class has begun, Alexander Godunov comes in. Godunov, with his long, shaggy blond hair and thick, muscular body, wears a worn green sweater, green leotards, and moth-eaten leg warmers; he looks more like a rock star than a classical dancer. Taking a place at an empty barre in the corner of the room, he runs through a series of *pliés*. His solitary position seems deliberate, a symbol of his initial estrangement from his colleagues. This year is Godunov's first. The superstar-defector is in an alien land, far from his wife and friends, and is unaccustomed to both the American style of life and American dance.

A former Bolshoi star, he was trained in the art of the grand gesture. In performance, he sometimes pauses after completing a difficult variation, waiting, as Bolshoi stars commonly do, for the audience's warm response. But the audiences are tepid; many critics, unimpressed; many fellow dancers, unsympathetic and often hostile. To them, he is proof of ABT's commitment to a star system studded with Russian or foreign luminaries, a system, they feel, that deprives them (as well as all American-trained dancers) of the chance to advance. "Not good enough," they call him behind his back, meaning that he is not worth the $150,000 salary ABT is rumored to be paying him.

ABT's other Russian superstar, Natalia Makarova, is also in class. Dressed in camel-colored tights and leotards, with a matching sweater draped casually around her shoulders, she focuses intently upon her image in the mirror. During a pause, she may exchange friendly looks or comments with her colleagues; they, however, are ever mindful of her caste and its privileges. "Natasha" is the only dancer in the entire company with short hair, a deviation permitted only those of star rank. In class, she is also the only dancer with a personal attendant; Dina Makarova, another Russian, serves as Natasha's personal photographer, secretary, and all-round assistant.

Makarova has a clear view of herself in the studio mirrors. The ABT public-relations staffer sitting next to me has seen the dancers exercise over and over again, but each time is like the first. "Look at them," she murmurs, her one lapse in formality toward the visiting reporter. "Look what they can do." In spite of the fact that on my own I recently spent three weeks with the company in Washington, someone from the ABT staff is almost always present to escort me around the Met. New York is where the royal treasure is stored. Here, I must be closely watched. It is so suspicious, this careful chaperoning, that when I get up to go to the bathroom, my staff escort jumps up with me to inquire anxiously where I am going. Reassured, she relaxes and continues watching the class.

At noon, the class is over and the dancers rush back to their dressing rooms. Other corps members and soloists who have attended outside classes join them. Kristine Soleri arrives with a sackful of deli salads, carrots, celery, juice, and fruit. This is her day's ration, for she will be at the Met through lunch, dinner, and far into the night.

I join Kri as she proceeds into the soloists' and corps members' dressing room behind the Met stage. The dressing room consists of a lounge area, with sofa and chairs, bathrooms equipped with washing machines and showers, dressing tables, and an adjacent wardrobe room. The costumes hanging there are a preview of the next week's performance schedule. White tutus from *Swan Lake* dangle from the ceiling; orange and red and black Spanish dancers' costumes from *Don Quixote* hang on one rack; and a far corner of the room is dedicated to *La Bayadère*.

As we go by, soloist Hilda Morales is engaged in a heated debate with coach Elena Tchernichova, another of the Russians on staff. With some difficulty, Hilda is holding up a Spanish dancer's costume. "It's so heavy, I can't dance in it," she complains. "Look, who needs all this lace?" she asks in exasperation, lifting up the skirts to reveal cascading layers of heavy lace petticoats. Hilda wants Tchernichova to intervene with ABT's management. She realizes, she says, that famous designers must be humored, but doesn't management understand that a dancer's ability to perform in a particular costume should take precedence over design? Tchernichova nods sympathetically. "I know, I fight about it," she says soothingly in Russianized English. Then she shrugs and indicates there is little that can be done. The costumes are here, and they must be danced in. Hilda looks miserable and heaves the dress back on the rack.

Kri and I continue down a narrow corridor where long tables flank the wall. Before each performance they are laden with headgear and accessories. Finally, she reaches the dressing-room area: A large square is set aside for corps dancers to the right, and to the left is a smaller soloists' area. Each dancer has an aluminum locker, dressing table, and mirror. The tables are a jumble of powder and makeup boxes, Band-Aid cartons, knick-knacks, cards from well-wishers, and good-luck charms. Boxes of fabric softener, bottles of cleaning fluid for toe shoes, and cannisters of Fabulon Floor Wax, used to harden pointe shoes to make them last longer, cover the shelves.

Setting down her groceries, Kri hangs her clothes up and dons her work uniform. Today, it is a navy-blue leotard, black tights, and a tee shirt proclaiming her PROPERTY OF ABT. She adds a beige crocheted shawl, which she winds round her waist, and pulls on a pair of hand-knitted purple-, pink-, and white-striped leg warmers decorated with embroidered flowers. Like all the other dancers, she wears something distinctive—a sweater draped around the shoulders, a colorful shawl, a scarf wound round the head—to vary the monotony of the regimental uniform: leotard, tights, and leg warmers. These personal touches in their daily livery offer a rare opportunity for dancers to express their individuality; they have a harder time defying the physical homogenization ballet imposes.

Ballet companies are rigid hierarchies. They take their conventions, spirit, and dramatic sustenance not from the democratic culture that now shelters them in America, but from the rituals and patronage of the court. Ballet has always been the aristocrat's art. Born in the chateaux of the kings and queens of France, ballet traveled over the centuries through Italy to the palaces of the czars of Russia. Ballet's nomenclature is borrowed from the French, and its social structure is borrowed from monarchy. The relationship between the student and the teacher, or between the professional dancer and the company director, involves the same stylized deference, the same obedient attentiveness, that a courtier showed a monarch.

The ballet monarch is the choreographer or artistic director. Under him are the *prima ballerina assoluta* and the *premier danseur*. Then come principal dancers, soloists, and, at the very bottom, the corps.

Most classical ballets depend on corps work, in which forty or fifty men and/or women are arranged in formal, static tableaux. Ballet's classics are odes to romantic sentimentality and to the romantic vision of women. As Roger Copeland explains in an article on women in modern dance, ballet began to "idealize the image of the disembodied woman" and the passive woman in the nineteenth century. George Balanchine's dictum that "the ballet is a purely female thing; it is a woman—a garden of beautiful flowers, and the man is the gardener"† captures the essence of romanticism. Women had become buds to be planted, clipped, and arranged by the male imagination.

Like the discreet borders in a formal garden, corps dancers are not supposed to stand out. Heights, weights, hairstyle, costume, and makeup are standardized. The classic book *Life at the Royal Ballet School* explains the essential requirements of the corps dancer:

The girls especially have to be of a rather uniform physical type. It is not quite so necessary for star dancers precisely to fit this mold. However, one of the School's main tasks is to train girls, at least at the beginning of their

† Roger Copeland, "Why Women Dominate Modern Dance," *The New York Times*, Arts and Leisure, April 18, 1982.

careers, to be useful members of The Royal Ballet's superb corps de ballet, not too tall, not too short—and not too temperamental—someone who will fit in in every way.†

The mold female dancers must fit is a peculiar idealization of the feminine. Onstage, ballerinas appear to be perfect women: delicate, graceful, slender, yet well rounded and well proportioned. Like so much on stage, this is no more than an illusion. The first time I went into a dressing room after a performance, I found row upon row of bare-chested women at their dressing tables removing makeup. They were alarmingly frail and curiously defeminized. Collar bones jutted out at the neck, shoulder blades pierced the skin, each rib was clearly articulated, and arms seemed no more than brittle twigs. Occasionally, the pattern was broken by a woman with small but well-rounded breasts and curved hips. But most of these young women looked more like pre-pubescent girls. The ballet aesthetic seems to eradicate all marks of the feminine.

Women are supposed to be placid, passive, and cooperative. This applies not only to their conduct, but to their appearance. Combined with the ballet bun, the smooth, pale skin, the short jackets worn over tight jeans—calling attention to the long, tapering legs—this surface layer of sweetness seems to be one of the identifying marks of the ballerina. By her expression, you can be certain which of the wait-resses in an Upper West Side café is a dancer, which an actress or a singer. You can identify as a dancer, almost without fail, the girl walking to the subway or waiting for a bus as a ballet dancer.

That most dancers must cultivate conformity rather than original-ity is clear when you observe the rare dancer who is, in fact, a great beauty—a dancer like Pennsylvania Ballet's Robin Preiss. Her jet-black hair frames a sculpted face with strong, high cheekbones and a prominent nose (the kind young girls despair of and grown women

† Camilla Jessel, *Life at the Royal Ballet School* (New York: Methuen, 1979), p. 16.

come to appreciate). She has the flashy presence of a gypsy or flamenco dancer. In ballets like José Limón's *The Moor's Pavane* or in comic spoofs, Preiss is at her best. Classical ballets suit her less well. When Preiss takes her place as a soloist in *Swan Lake*, standing in a line of maidens who all seem to look alike, her distinctiveness mars the symmetry of the classical line.

Preiss' looks do not compromise her career because she has worked, for the most part, outside New York, either in Israel or Philadelphia. Were she to enter a New York company, she might be obliged to accommodate herself to the New York look. Regional companies seem to tolerate a wider range of physical features. Pennsylvania Ballet welcomes dancers who do not, to their sorrow, fit the New York mold. Preiss is one of these, and so is Cynthia Powers.* A fine technician with great dramatic flare and feeling, Powers was trained at the School of American Ballet and had hoped to dance with NYCB. At puberty, however, her body began to betray her. "I could never dance in New York," she says looking down at a rather moderate-sized chest, "so I came here." Other Pennsylvania Ballet dancers are slender but not emaciated. The same is true of dancers in regional troops like Houston, San Francisco, and Pittsburgh. All of these companies boast at least a handful of dancers who actually look like women.

There is also a standardized look for men in ballet, but the standard is far less rigid and unnatural. Most of them are of medium height. Occasionally, a very tall dancer, like Michael Owen or Alexander Godunov, or a very short dancer, like Baryshnikov, breaks the pattern. With the rare exception of a Nureyev or a Martins, most of them have only average good looks. An unwritten code regulates their appearance: Beards, mustaches, or very long hair are rarely permitted (except for the privilege extended to a star like Godunov); and those dancers who are losing their hair use toupees during performance.

Male dancers tend to have lean hips and broad torsos. Unlike weight lifters, whose muscles bulge along their arms, chests, and thighs, male dancers have muscles that are long-sanded arcs, and their costumes highlight the masculine. The finely pronounced mound always appears in prominent relief under tight leotards. "In ballet they like men who are well built and well hung," one ballet observer says bluntly, "and they like women who look like little boys."

The dancers' working day and working life are as rigidly circumscribed as the ballet look. In all companies the work load is a taxing struggle. But in New York, the challenges are multiplied, the competition stiffer, and the work a complex and multifaceted test of endurance that strains dancers' bodies and draws on all their emotional resources.

After they have assembled at the Met for a day's work, ABT's corps members and soloists spend each afternoon juggling rehearsals. The daily schedule is so tightly packed that they must constantly check the mimeographed sheets posted by the stage door to remind themselves where they are supposed to be and when. I look at a typical listing. From noon to twelve-thirty is a rehearsal of *At Midnight*; from twelve-forty-five to one-fifteen, *Don Q.*; from one to one-thirty, *Concert Waltzes*; from one-fifteen to one-forty-five, *La Bayadère*; and between two and five there will be run-throughs of *Billy the Kid*, *Fall River Legend*, *Rodeo*, *Swan Lake*, and *Voluntaries*.

Major rehearsals are held onstage. Kri Soleri, Michelle Benash, Michael Owen, Frank Smith, and a score of others gather to rehearse the evening's performance of *Swan Lake*. At the bottom rung of the ballet ladder, corps dancers will rehearse and perform variations in which masses of dancers form a backdrop for soloists and principals, who parade their individual talents and accomplishments. Favored soloists will have a chance to dance alone or with a partner before principals return to dominate the stage. When they are waiting to go on, dancers sew pointe shoes, read or do warmup exercises. The wings are littered with dance bags, sweaters, scarves, paperback books, and ubiquitous cans of diet soda. Battered toe shoes lie in heaps, their fine satin finishes scuffed and bruised. In various corners, tired dancers push aside the debris and stretch out for a nap, using their ballet bags as pillows. Others slip out to the canteen for coffee or a yogurt.

After an hour's rehearsal onstage, the dancers disband and scatter in different directions. Some return to their dressing rooms for a quick break; others hurry down to the ABT studios on West Sixty-first Street, where more rehearsals take place. Still others descend to the rehearsal studios on Level C, where, in Studio Three, about twenty dancers labor over the one-act ballet *Billy the Kid*. Four women start the first steps of a Mexican dance, then stop, huddle around a television to watch a tape of a previous performance, and then go back to the center to continue the rehearsal.

In another studio I watch Godunov and Makarova run through a pas de deux from *Swan Lake*. When these two Russians work together, the drama is not only in the dance but in the debate. In the middle of a tender, languid variation, the two dancers suddenly split asunder. Prince and Swan begin to chatter furiously in Russian. Godunov advances, goes over a few steps, halts, turns to Makarova with a challenging look. Undaunted, she repeats the same steps with a slightly different cast, stops, plants herself in front of him, and snaps something incomprehensible. What is happening? I ask. "Oh," someone explains, "just the usual. They're arguing about the relative merits of the Kirov versus the Bolshoi version of *Swan Lake*."

Not far away, at the Sixty-first Street studios, Cynthia Gregory and Fernando Bujones rehearse a different scene from *Swan Lake*. Students peer through a window overlooking the large, bare room. One of ABT's conductors, a ballet mistress, and I watch from within. As soon as the pianist begins, Gregory's arms go limp, her body shivers and trembles. Dressed only in her practice togs—white long-sleeved leotard, black tights, filmy black nylon practice skirt, and a black scarf wound round her head—the ballerina transforms herself into Odette, half-woman/half-swan, caught, frightened, torn between longing and terror. Bujones, in thrall to the magic, swells with aristocratic passion, and the two complete the entire act without a pause or an error. It is a miraculous moment. There are only three of us watching; but like the exuberant audience of a packed house, we spontaneously rise to our feet with applause. The two dancers bow to us, then to each other, wipe the sweat off their streaming faces, and hurry off to change.

Gregory, Bujones, van Hamel, Makarova, Bissell, Dowell—principals at ABT—perform only once or twice a week and have fewer daily rehearsals. Corps dancers and soloists, who perform almost every night, spend four or five hours a day rehearsing. During the day, they not only attend rehearsals for parts they will dance or understudy, but fill every break and free hour with a rehearsal to learn the part of another understudy or refine steps or polish the myriad dramatic gestures that will add richness to an otherwise routine performance. Everywhere dancers are practicing in corners, or sitting and watching colleagues rehearse.

Today, soloist Lisa de Ribere has two free hours in the afternoon. Instead of resting or going shopping, she attends a rehearsal of *La Bayadère* so she can absorb the part of Garmsatti. At first the twenty-six-year-old soloist, with long, sandy-brown hair cut with a blunt fringe, is friendly but a tiny bit aloof, polite but reserved. Beneath that reserve she approaches the world with more curiosity than most dancers and considers her chosen career with a critical intelligence that distinguishes her from other ballet workaholics. Curiosity and distance notwithstanding, Lisa plays by the rules.

For nine years, from age sixteen to age twenty-five, she spent her days and nights in the corps of City Ballet, hoping Balanchine would notice and promote her. He never did. When Baryshnikov, who had been dancing with City Ballet, was made artistic director of ABT, he encouraged Lisa to audition for the company. According to ballet's rules of etiquette, when a dancer in one company wishes to work for another, she discreetly lets that be known; then she is invited to attend company class rather than having to attend a huge, cattle-call audition.

After vacillating about the wisdom of her decision, Lisa walked down Broadway one morning to take ABT company class. She gambled and won: Lucia Chase offered her a corps contract, followed a few months later by a soloist contract. Now she works constantly so as to be ready to step into an important new role if someone is injured or sick, or if an artistic director decides he would like to see her dance in the spotlight.

While Lisa rehearses in a basement studio, Kri Soleri steals an extra minute onstage to go over the steps of a variation of *Swan Lake*. It is late afternoon. The stage has been stripped of its layers of scenery. The receding wings, in their blackness, form a cavern against which she appears—a solitary figure, scoring the air with her arms and legs, and then bending over delicately like a willow bowed to the ground. Still later she will try to find a few minutes to review variations from *Swan Lake*. I watch her dance in the women's lounge a few hours before the curtain rises. Wardrobe mistresses sewing steadily in the costume room next-door watch her, too. Humming the music quietly to herself, she marks steps. Completely oblivious to two of her coworkers napping nearby, she remains intent on her private agenda. She is like those obsessed, self-absorbed souls who mutter to themselves as they walk down a crowded city street.

By five or five-thirty, as the dancers retreat to their dressing rooms, the Met seems enveloped in a haze of exhaustion. Watching the dancers, knowing how much energy they have already spent dancing in rehearsals all day, one wonders how these dazed, depleted bodies will be able to perform in just two or three hours' time. Yet by six-thirty, the fog has lifted, and the men's and women's dressing rooms are alive with activity. Dancers troop in and out of the costume rooms, sit at their tables applying makeup, and engage in peculiar and arcane pre-performance rituals. In the men's dressing rooms, several dancers plug in their heating pads and warm up aching muscles as they transform themselves into handsome young aristocrats for *Swan Lake*'s first act. In the women's dressing room, a soloist unfurls a role of plastic wrap and begins winding it around her calf. Over this she wraps a heating pad. It is a trick dancers have learned to make the heat treatment more effective. Immediately before the curtain goes up, women will begin painting their toes with Benzodent, a Novocaine-like preparation that dulls the pain of performing in pointe shoes.

At every dressing table, young men and women apply the evening's veneer. Each ballet has a different look and a different cosmetic recipe. Tonight is a "white night." The women's faces, arms, and torsos must be coated with white body makeup and base. A light dusting of rouge is added; then the hair is parted in the middle and coiled in a bun at the base of the neck.

This particular cosmetic preparation reflects more profound prejudices that inform the hiring policies of most ballet companies, for if there is a standardized ballet look, there is also a standardized ballet color: white. In a famous interview in *Vogue* magazine, Balanchine once remarked that the color of a ballerina's skin should match that of a peeled apple. And so it does. There are almost no black or Hispanic dancers in major companies, and few Orientals.

The prejudice against black dancers is the most prevalent. Last year, Augustus Van Heerden, a South African dancer with the Boston Ballet, quit the company, alleging racial discrimination. Despite the fact that he had been elevated to principal dancer, Van Heerden said he was never chosen to dance star roles like Siegfried in *Swan Lake* or Albrecht in *Giselle*. Although he later returned to the company, the ensuing debate highlighted the black dancer's problems. Just as blacks are not chosen to play opposite whites in major films (unless, of course, the film explicitly deals with interracial coupling), blacks and whites do not couple on the ballet stage. Since there are rarely two black principals—one male and one female—in the same company, black dancers are passed over. And then there is the intractable problem of the color of their flesh. How can a black woman dance *Swan Lake*? some in the ballet world ask. What happens when she must play both the White Swan and the Black Swan?

In ballets like *Swan Lake*, *La Bayadère*, and particularly in *Giselle*, a ghostly pallor is the desired effect. In *Don Quixote*, on the other hand, dancers must look robust, earthy, and sensual—a look achieved entirely with makeup. Like refined southern belles always carefully shaded from the sun, dancers never have tans. In fact, tans are expressly forbidden in most companies. City Ballet dancers in Saratoga for a summer season at the Performing Arts Center there are often seen sitting around the pool under huge parasols to avoid the slightest exposure to the sun.

Giving emaciated ballet dancers a look of earthy sexuality is also a matter of artifice. To remedy both cosmetic failings, dancers cover their bodies with dark makeup. Deep crimson rouge is used to create a healthy Mediterranean glow. Huge flashing eyes are produced with shading and liner. And, for the thinnest of the thin, a quick stroke of chocolate pencil between the breasts creates the illusion of cleavage where, in fact, there is nothing but skin and bone.

For special character makeup or an elaborate effect, ABT dancers rely on the skilled ministrations of makeup consultant Leopold Allen, a cheerful man who is also keeper of the company's wigs. Before each performance, he ushers dancers into his small studio, equipped with barbershop chair, huge mirrors, and myriad small containers of makeup. While he transforms the faces of his subjects, he talks and giggles; his studio is an excellent place to pick up company gossip.

A soloist sits in the makeup chair while Leopold adjusts her wig and eye coloring. Alexander (Sasha) Minz, who will dance the role of Don Quixote in this evening's performance, peeps in from the men's dressing room to see if Leopold can take him next, and then sits down to await his turn. As Leopold and the two dancers chat amiably, another soloist storms in. She has spent an hour doing her makeup only to have Charles France, the company's publicity director, send her to Leopold with instructions to "make her face bigger."

Most of the ABT dancers do not care for France. They were appalled when they discovered that Baryshnikov had decided to elevate him from publicity director to artistic co-director, thus making him second-in-command. France, who looks obese, is now a permanent fixture in company life. He hovers about the theater ordering changes in technique, costume, and cosmetics. He has flair, the dancers admit, but still they do not welcome his advice.

An announcement on the backstage PA system interrupts the scene in the makeup room: "Half an hour, please, ladies and gentlemen." The dancers stop joking and gossiping, and Leopold begins to work faster.

In the wings, in transit between reality and illusion, one finds the company in a variety of incongruous poses. Elegantly attired courtiers, whom one would expect to see drinking from gold or silver chalices, hastily gulp down a last swallow of Tab; a dancer carries her pointe shoes over to the heavy stage door and shoves them into the space between the door and the frame, crushing them to loosen them up; a swan smoking a cigarette bends over to stub her butt in an ashtray, exposing a rear end framed in stiff prickly net.

During the entire performance, the area behind the stage is a scene of silent, purposeful activity as stagehands move props into and out of place. Dancers, wearing sweaters, leg warmers, and robes over their costumes, stand and whisper, waiting for their cues.

Onstage, another stream of whispers helps performers get through boring moments when they must stand in regimental rows or when they feign amiable conversation as guests at their prince's birthday ball. What are they talking about? A *danseur* whispers an apology to his partner when he grasps her too zealously during a lift; hopelessly perfectionistic, a soloist finishes a variation and curses herself under her breath; rivals gloat when someone misses a step or leaves out an extra *pirouette* because of fatigue or laziness. For many of the dancers, the staged conversation may, in fact, be masking a rising panic. Sorely underrehearsed, they may be begging an older dancer to coach them through a rough spot.

"I remember the first time I did *Giselle* with ABT," Michelle Benash recounts. "I'd done it five years before with National Ballet and hadn't danced it since. They just threw me on. During the second act people near me talked me through and told me what to do and where to go next. Four years later, when I was the old one in the company, I remember talking three new girls through it at the Met. More often than not, when a dancer is pale during *Swan Lake* or *Giselle*, it's out of fear. She simply doesn't know what she's doing."

But get through it they do, each night, each matinee. It is what dancers and critics refer to as the Ballet Theater miracle, the company's ability to pull together a performance at the very last minute. Not reserved to ABT alone, it happens, in varying degrees, in all ballet companies when an unexpected illness or injury occurs, and an under-rehearsed dancer is given the chance to fill in and prove herself.

When this performance of *Swan Lake* is over, dancers limp and straggle offstage to their dressing rooms. Seated at makeup tables, men and women smear on thick gobs of cold cream and wipe off layers of stage makeup. Fanning out along Broadway, some will stand for ten or twenty minutes waiting for a bus; others, like Kri Soleri, will descend into the subway. The majority live on the Upper West Side and can walk home. Dancers also flock to the restaurants dotting Columbus Avenue and Broadway. There they try to relax after a day of all-consuming physical activity and to circumvent, as well, the sudden feeling of emptiness that often follows a performance. "I so often felt up when performing," says Michelle Benash. She recalls the feeling of elation, that unimaginable high that comes when the dancer and audience are one; when the dancer feels that, with a gesture, a glance, a movement, she has taken two thousand people and made them her own; when she is drawn into the immensity of their appreciation. "Then, in the dressing room, I'd come down. I'd walk home and it would be a very sad time because I gave so much and suddenly the curtain came down and there was nothing. I'd be left going home to an empty apartment."

Even if a friend or lover is waiting in the apartment, even after a whirlpool bath and a hot cup of milk, many dancers say they still find it hard to relax. "When I get home I really can't sleep," a young soloist says. "I just twist and twitch. So I take Excedrin P.M., and that calms me down," she explains, as if doing a television commercial for an aspirin company. Others rely on a pipe of grass or a drink before they go to bed.

On Sundays, their only free day during the six-day week, the pressure may be off, but the pain is not. Drugs can become, if not habit-forming, at least a regular escape. "I'd say for many dancers, using drugs is almost a constant," a male ABT corps member tells me. He explains that on weekends, he "does" Indocin or aspirin to relieve the inflammation in his joints. "People use Indocin or cortisone, Motrin, Butazolidin. You go to the doctor for an injury, and he gives you some stuff. Then when you're on tour, you go to another doctor, tell him you're injured and that this other doctor gave you such and such a medication. They don't check; they just give you more. So you collect the stuff by going from one doctor to the next. Sometimes other dancers who have lots of meds will give you some."

Drugs are a common way to ease the tension, pain, and loneliness of the dance profession. Sex, on the other hand, may at times be more of a burden than a release. Dancers complain that it is hard to make a nondancing partner understand that after a trying performance, they are just not in the mood. Fearful of romantic involvements, many dancers do not have a mate to fend off. Those dancers who would like to have companionship after a performance find it difficult to go out searching for it. "You're too tired to go and look for someone at a bar at eleven o'clock at night," says Michelle bluntly. "And if you're dancing an important role the next day, you wouldn't spend the whole night making love even if you could."

Dancers live in constant fear that the temptation to engage in normal personal relationships will seduce them. "You have to be totally dedicated," Robert Maiorano says. "Once you start saying, 'I want to go out tonight'; once you say, 'Okay, so I'll stay up late and miss class in the morning,' you're automatically putting something ahead of ballet. Interfering with that 100 percent dedication you're trained to have is dangerous because the more you know of life, the more you'll need from it and the more you'll want to subtract from that 100 percent." Young female dancers who do have outside relationships maintain that such "life experiences" enable them to perform well. Art does not exist to serve life; life exists to serve art.

Some dancers do interfere with that 100 percent dedication and marry while they are still performing. At any given time, at least half the young men and women have spouses or lovers, either inside the company or outside. Very few American dancers, however, have children while they are still performing. Competition is so stiff among women that few married dancers dare take time off to start a family. San Francisco Ballet, however, has a different philosophy. Its director, Michael Smuin, who is himself married and the father of one child, actively encourages female dancers to have children, and supports their decision by allowing them to return to the company after they have had a baby and resume their careers where they left off.

While some men refuse to accommodate to a dancer's exigent schedule, others consider ballerinas a good catch. In talking with the husbands of several Houston and New York ballet dancers, I discover that men who would ordinarily feel threatened by a woman with a career welcome having a dancer as a wife. "She has a kind of celebrity status, which is a real plus," the husband of a Houston corps dancer tells me. "I mean, she's not an MBA who's got this big corporate-type career." The young husband, who is a businessman, elaborates: "She doesn't have a job that's going to compete with mine. I don't think I could handle that. I mean, those women are too much like men. But this way she's got a nice career, which won't last forever and which doesn't really interfere with my life."

This young man finds that his wife is both traditional and exotic. "Sally serves me breakfast almost every morning. But if it comes to a dinner party, I do most of the cooking. She thinks she has it great," he says almost conspiratorily, "but I have it better than she does. She still does the laundry and the cleaning, and we get along just fine."

The husband of a principal dancer in another regional company also feels that dancers make almost-perfect mates. A hard-working doctor, he says he enjoys the periods of solitude when his ballerina-wife goes on tour, and he relishes the fact that she brings him all the pluses of a career without any of the minuses. "I like it when she gets her picture in the paper and when I tell people I'm married to a ballet dancer. And I like the fact that her profession is so different from mine, because otherwise I'd feel in competition with her."

Many male dancers find mates inside the company; those who do not want to be "married to ballet" look for women who have different interests. Gay dancers—whom one might expect to pair up with other dancers in their companies—often find internal competition an obstacle to intimacy. This is not the case for heterosexual couples who belong to the same company; when they become romantically involved, competition does not often interfere with their ability to relate to one another, as they become partners, not rivals. "I don't think I could have a successful relationship with a dancer," says a gay dancer from San Francisco Ballet. "Competing for roles could get very nasty."

A dancer at Pennsylvania Ballet says that's why he has not had many successful relationships with men in the ballet world. He also says that it is not so easy to find mates outside ballet either. They may not be rivals for parts, but they are often jealous of their lover's close relationships with other dancers. Speaking of the reasons why his long-term relationship with another young man broke up, this young man explains that his lover could not tolerate the fact that he looked to other dancers for support. "Most people aren't that close with the people they work with. But dancers are very close. And that's hard for lovers to understand. They try to be part of the group, but they aren't, and so they become jealous."

They also become jealous, he says, of the attention paid by members of the audience. "My lover was jealous of the people who saw me dance. People would compliment me and write me letters. I felt his jealousy wasn't fair because I hadn't done anything to provoke it. But it affected our relationship. And yet that was how he and I met. He watched me dance, and after a few years we got to know each other."

For the average dancer, life is not filled with glamour and adventure. Almost all companies spend some part of the year on the road, generally in or near their home states rather than in the romantic capitals of distant lands. Houston Ballet tours the southern states, stopping at Charleston, Lakeland, and West Palm Beach; occasionally the company will venture into Michigan or Illinois. Pittsburgh Ballet and Pennsylvania Ballet visit the small towns of Pennsylvania. Regional companies do not often tour major American cities, though they will occasionally make international appearances; rarely, however, will they perform in cities like Paris or London.

ABT is America's most successful big-city and international dance export. The grande dame of touring, ABT usually spends five or six months each year on the road, performing in the capitals of both

America and Europe. In 1981, they danced in Boston, Milwaukee, Chicago, Washington, Los Angeles, San Francisco, Detroit, and Atlanta. New York City Ballet tours the country less frequently, and Europe about once every two years.

No matter how exciting the tour, dancers are there to work, not to play. "I've toured Europe five times, and I didn't see that much," Michelle Benash says. "I was just too tired to walk around on my day off. You do see some things. But you've got to remember that you've been performing all day every day, and sometimes you just want to sleep on your day off. You're not a tourist; you're a dancer. You have to think of your legs and be aware all the time that you shouldn't tire yourself out walking around because you have to dance the next day."

Touring is also hard on dancers' relationships with friends, spouses, or lovers. "It's very weird," one dancer's husband says. "After years and years of this, you get used to them going away. You even begin to look forward to it. You construct a life of your own that you can slip into; you see friends you haven't seen, go out for a drink, have people over. Sometimes it's even a relief when she leaves because dancers are always so unhappy; there's so much disappointment and struggle and competition in their lives, and you get tired hearing about it over and over again. But then, when she comes back, it's another adjustment. For five or six months, you're single, then suddenly you're married again. It's not easy to do."

On tour, in rehearsal periods, or during the performance season, the six-day work week is standard for most companies. At ABT and City Ballet, free days are regularly scheduled for either a Sunday or Monday, and these do not change. In some companies, like Houston, dancers never know in advance when their free days will be, and when they arrive, the hours are packed with dance-related chores. If Kri Soleri or Michael Owen has two or three hours off during the day, the priorities are to catch a class with a favorite teacher; go to a coaching session to work on an upcoming role; attend a special exercise class where physical therapists help strengthen muscles that are not exercised during class; take a much-needed massage; go to a chiropractor, acupuncturist, nutritionist, or orthopedist, all of which they pay for themselves. In New York, ballet dancers spend more time and money on upkeep than do dancers in regional companies because the cities outside New York simply do not offer a wide range of dance-related services. Thus, dancers in Houston, Philadelphia, or San Francisco have to content themselves with company class and limited outside coaching. Although they complain about the scarcity of ballet services, they also admit that there are benefits: They lead more relaxed, less expensive lives than do New York's dancers.

With so little time and energy left over for extra-professional interests, many dancers quickly develop tunnel vision: Their lives revolve around the ballet stage and the rehearsal studio; the world between home and work becomes a mere passageway. News from the outside may filter in from an occasional glance at a newspaper or magazine, but many dancers simply do not know what is going on outside ballet because they do not have the time or energy to find out. "If you went down to the women's dressing room and asked the girls who Khomeini is," Michelle Benash said at the height of the Iranian hostage crisis, "I bet half of them wouldn't know."

"You get so out of touch with the world," says San Francisco Ballet's Elizabeth Tienken. "You come home and you're tired and you don't want to listen to the news. I think we should all know what's going on in the world, but a lot of us don't, a lot of us block it out. We don't get involved, we don't vote. We say, oh, I don't need to know, I'm a dancer."

To a certain extent, their ignorance is fostered by an art that, unlike most theatrical arts, does not require them to have much contact with the real world. Many actors and actresses may have no compelling interest in current events, history, or psychology, but they must learn about the world if they want to be successful onstage or in films. You cannot act convincingly in *Kramer versus Kramer* if you have not steeped yourself in the conflicts of modern marriage and divorce; you would have a hard time playing a soldier in *The Deerhunter* or *Apocalypse Now* without having spent some time learning about the war in Vietnam; and it would be difficult to play any historical figure without some extensive research into the period in which he or she lived.

Dancers can easily function without such knowledge or experience. Here in America, they do not even know much about the history of ballet—a fact that troubles some of the thoughtful dancers; others merely shrug it off. "Ballet history has no effect on what I'm going to do when I get onstage at eight o'clock tonight," says one of the soloists with New York City Ballet. "I don't know about it and I don't care. Ballet history is only words. If someone tells me that the only thing that's important is what Pavlova looked like onstage, yes, I'll go and watch a film of her, but that's not going to change my style of dancing. My style of dancing is whatever George Balanchine wants me to do."

Generally regarded as the tools of the choreographer, dancers are taught not to participate in the creative process. They empty themselves out and allow the choreographer to fill them up. "In ballet, the dancer isn't really a creator," explains former Boston Ballet dancer Rachel Isadora Maiorano, now an artist and illustrator. "You're there to dance, not to think or suggest, but just to focus. The difference between the dancer and other artists is that in dance, you don't use your experience. You can get by being a superb technician and being entirely unthoughtful."

Taught to obey orders rather than to think for themselves, and encouraged to avoid the outside world, which is either a temptation or a trap, dancers begin to live in a cocoon. "When you get onstage," according to Michelle Benash, "you're living in the world of *Swan*

Lake or *Giselle*. It's almost as though the dreams you had when you were a child are coming true. For a while you can live in that separate world. But it's not part of life; it's an illusion. Pretty soon, it begins to limit you. You start hanging around with dancers because you can't talk to anyone else about anything else. Dancers begin to live exclusively in the theater because they just don't know what to do with themselves when they have an hour off."

In the dark recesses of the ballet theater, where mute monarchs preside—the huge Buddha from *La Bayadère*; the melancholy swan that glides across the stage in *Swan Lake*; *Don Q*.'s windmill, whose arms, like swords, cut all dreams down to size—it would seem that nothing can disturb the rules of chance, fantasy, and fortune. It's only when you leave the theater, for an hour or two in the afternoon, that you are startled to find, in the bustle of the city and the sunlight of Lincoln Center Plaza, that there is indeed a world that exists outside—beyond ballet.

1. CAROLINE AND DOTTIE HOUY, A BALLET MOTHER AND DAUGHTER,
POSE IN FRONT OF THEIR COLLECTION OF CELEBRITY PHOTOGRAPHS IN THE
LIVING ROOM OF THEIR NEW YORK CITY APARTMENT.

2. TRACEY GOZA.

3. ANTONINA TUMKOVSKY TEACHES AN INTERMEDIATE CLASS AT
THE SCHOOL OF AMERICAN BALLET.

4. Tracey Goza, a fourteen-year-old student at the
School of American Ballet, takes a private class with
Robert Denvers, one of New York's most prominent
ballet teachers.

5. The Ballet Look—fluid, graceful, super-thin—is
epitomized by this young dancer in an advanced pointe
class at the School of American Ballet.

6. Four advanced students share a moment of
relaxed camaraderie in the hallway at
the School of American Ballet.

7. Two students at the School of American Ballet practice
partnering between classes.

8. A YOUNG BOY RESTS AFTER A SUCCESSFUL CLASS AT THE
PENNSYLVANIA BALLET SCHOOL.

9. AN INJURED STUDENT AT THE SCHOOL OF AMERICAN BALLET
STUDIES HER CLASSMATES AND WORRIES ABOUT WHAT SHE WILL
HAVE TO DO TO CATCH UP.

10, 11, AND 12. PENNSYLVANIA BALLET DANCERS MAKE UP
BEFORE A PERFORMANCE.

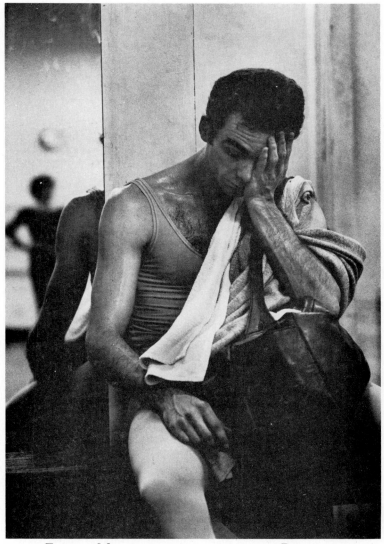

13. EDWARD MYERS, A PRINCIPAL DANCER AT PENNSYLVANIA BALLET, RESTS AFTER A STRENUOUS AFTERNOON CLASS.

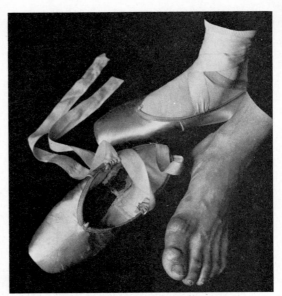

14. "You have to see them
to believe them," says orthopedic
surgeon Dr. William Liebler
about ballerinas' feet.

15. Fanchon Cordell, a member of the corps de ballet of
American Ballet Theatre, spends an evening sewing pointe
shoes in her apartment.

16. A DANCER WORKS ON A VARIATION IN FRONT OF A MIRROR. MIRRORS
ARE AN INDISPENSABLE TOOL FOR SELF-CRITICISM, AND SOMETIMES A
SOURCE OF REASSURANCE.

17. FOR BALLET DANCERS, THE OUTSIDE WORLD OFTEN SEEMS REMOTE
AND INACCESSIBLE.

18. A DANCER EXERCISING AT THE BARRE EXHIBITS THE PREREQUISITE
OF BALLET TECHNIQUE—MUSCULAR STRENGTH.

19. LISA DE RIBERE, A SOLOIST WITH AMERICAN BALLET THEATRE, TAKES PRIVATE CLASSES AT ROBERT DENVERS'S STUDIO WHENEVER ABT IS IN NEW YORK.

20. BENJAMIN HARKAVY, THEN ARTISTIC DIRECTOR OF PENNSYLVANIA BALLET, AND BALLET MISTRESS FIONA FUERSTNER SUPERVISE AN AFTERNOON REHEARSAL.

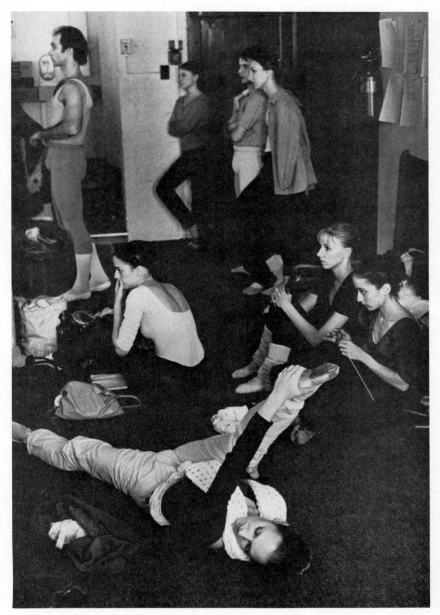

21. WAITING, STRETCHING, KNITTING, CHATTING, AND SURVEYING THE
COMPETITION ARE THE STAPLES OF BACKSTAGE BALLET LIFE.

22. Kristine Soleri of American Ballet
Theatre is an example of a new kind of ballet
dancer—as dedicated to improving the dancer's
lot as she is to her own career.

23. For the first time in history, ballet dancers lead labor,
rather than lag behind: Locked-out American Ballet Theatre
dancers lead the 1982 New York Labor Day Parade.

S *wan Lake* is the quintessential ballet, the most popular and well
known of any of the classics. More than a bittersweet love story, it
is a ballet about ballet, encompassing the nature of sexuality, love,
femininity, masculinity, allegiance, power, and powerlessness in the
ballet world. With a score by Tchaikovsky and choreography by Lev
Ivanov and Marius Petipa, *Swan Lake* was performed for the first time
in St. Petersburg in 1895. For those who are unfamiliar with the story,
it is the tale of a prince who falls in love with a woman trapped inside
the body of a swan.

In the first act, Prince Siegfried is celebrating his twenty-first
birthday. His mother, the queen, interrupts the festivities to present the
prince with a crossbow, his coming of age birthday gift, and to inform
him that he must leave the world of childhood and assume his adult
responsibilities. He must choose a bride the following evening at his
birthday ball, where he will meet some of the fairest princesses in the
land. Siegfried is not at all pleased by this news. He has no desire to
trade the pleasures of adolescence for the obligations of marriage and
adulthood. Taking advantage of his last moments of youth, he sets off
with his friends to hunt a flock of wild swans.

In the next act of the ballet, the hunters come upon the swans as
they gather at the edge of a misty lake. Just as the hunters take aim, a
magnificent plumed creature appears in their midst; she is Odette, the
swan queen. Siegfried is enchanted by her beauty, and learns that she
and all the other swans are not really swans at all but beautiful young

women under the spell of the evil sorcerer, the Baron Von Rothbart. Between the hours of midnight and dawn, they are free to resume their human form, but during the waking hours they are imprisoned in the bodies of swans. Only one power can release her, Odette says, and that is a faithful suitor's pledge of eternal love.

As she explains all this, the evil magician Von Rothbart, dressed in his fantastic cloak of feathers, his pointed talons clawing the air, swoops down to separate the two. Siegfried impulsively tries to kill him, but Odette intervenes. Tied as she is to the sorcerer's fate, his death would bring her own. It is only through love that she can be won, and so the prince pledges his love.

In Act III, Siegfried surveys the great beauties whom his mother has assembled at his birthday ball. Smitten by Odette and determined to be loyal to her, he dismisses them all. Suddenly Von Rothbart appears, accompanied by a dazzling woman in a sparkling black tutu. The very image of Odette, she is Von Rothbart's daughter, Odile. Mimicking Odette, Odile convinces the prince that she is really his beloved; and, breaking his vow to Odette, he proposes to her. Odile and Von Rothbart, triumphant and gloating, reveal their treachery; in despair, Siegfried rushes off into the forest in search of the swan queen.

There, in the last act, he finds Odette, distraught and broken. His unwitting disloyalty has doomed her. Siegfried once again pledges eternal love, and the two cast themselves into the lake. In death, the power of their love destroys Von Rothbart, and the curtain goes down on the tender vision of the lovers, reunited in eternity, gliding across the stage in their swan boat.

Beneath this fairy-tale exterior, *Swan Lake* is a textured allegory of sexuality and power. A dominant male—in this case, the evil sorcerer Von Rothbart—controls a flock of women. Rivals may challenge his hegemony, but, like Siegfried, they are too young and impotent to counter his cunning and magic. The sorcerer is preeminent:

He determines how his women look, feel, and act. Fearful and obedient, they are indeterminate creatures of indeterminate sexuality, adolescents frozen on the border between childhood and adulthood. Although women are the main victims of his magic, his sorcery transforms all men who enter their world. In it, love and sexuality can never be consummated, except in the eternity of death.

It is precisely in the way that power and powerlessness are enacted that *Swan Lake* reflects the contemporary ballet world. In most companies, dancers, like the swans and their consorts, are controlled by choreographers, who are nearly always older men. Balanchine, and other choreographers of his stature, molds the lives of his dancers, both onstage and off. He decides how they are to look, feel, act, and think. He influences their decision whether to marry, whether to have children. He even determines what will become of the dancers when they retire. The burden of the choreographer's sorcery falls mainly on female dancers, but for men and women alike, the result of his hegemony is their own powerlessness. Even as full-grown adults, they are emotionally trapped in an unending childhood.

It is important to understand the peculiar quality of the power choreographers and their companies exercise over dancers. In most professions, particularly in the arts, it is not unusual for people in positions of authority to wield enormous power over young men and women who are willing to do almost anything to get ahead. But what makes ballet special is the fact that abuses of power are institutionalized. They are built into the very structure of a ballet career, because most dancers have never had any experience of autonomy. For students who enter ballet school at an early age, teachers and choreographers become surrogate parents. Admission into a professional company is not a rite of passage into adulthood. No graduation ceremonies mark the dancer's entry into professional life. In fact, schools like SAB scrupulously avoid such ritual events, insisting that a dancer's training is never-ending. Yet dancers are not really different from other professionals, whose education continues though they graduate from school. For dancers this notion of continuous learning is an indefinite continuation of childhood.

A company, then, does not function as an adult community but as an extension of the family. Dancers are asked to conduct themselves as "adults"—to be disciplined enough to work vigorously and forgo outside pleasures—but they are without autonomy, independence, or self-determination. In most companies, grown men and women, accomplished professionals, are commonly referred to as boys and girls. Ballets have "boys" variations and "girls" variations, and commands are shouted out to "the boys" and "the girls." To teachers and directors, even forty-year-old dancers are "kids." In contrast, other professionals working in the same theater—stagehands and musicians, for example—are referred to as ladies and gentlemen.

Dancers all over the country complain about this persistent infantilization. If the problem were just a matter of language, they say, it could be easily remedied. The language is, however, a reflection of deeply ingrained company attitudes. Boys and girls are supposed to be seen and not heard; boys and girls are supposed to be obedient; boys and girls need protection, not autonomy.

"What happens when you're a dancer," says Michelle Benash, "is that you have to lose your personality. Your movement, your style, are dictated to you; you have to give up part of yourself. The company should be grateful to have us as artists. But it isn't that way at all. Their attitude is, 'You're a little kid; if you're good we'll give you this role, and if you're not good you're not going to get it.'"

Another former ABT dancer, Solange MacArthur, tells me that she became aware of just how childlike she had become when she left ballet at age twenty-eight and started her freshman year of college. "I feel very immature," the spare, almost tomboyish woman explains ruefully. "I feel like I've been kept as a child for ten years. I've never had any responsibility in my life." She compares ballet to the army: "You know when kids don't know what to do with their lives, they join the army and somebody tells them what to do all the time. That's what it's like in a ballet company; you never have to think, you always follow orders. It's funny, because people think dancers are so disciplined, so self-motivated. But so are soldiers, and that's what we're like."

Dancers rarely engage in open mutiny, but they do not relish this kind of infantilizing treatment. "If you disagree with something a choreographer says," observes Elizabeth Tienken, "they say you're being rude. You're just not given credit for your expertise. This is one of the most frustrating things about being a dancer. I have a good mind, and I'm an adult. I resent it when people think I can't think on my own, when they tell me what to do every ten seconds. What do they think I do when I go home and lead my own life? Do they think I call someone up and ask them what I should cook for dinner or if I can go to the bathroom?"

Tienken, who is thirty and a mother of a three-year-old child, feels she has proven her ability to take care not only of herself but of her company as well. In 1974, she and four other San Francisco Ballet dancers engineered San Francisco Ballet's rescue from bankruptcy. For years the company had been in serious financial trouble, and management finally decided to "face reality" and terminate the company. "The management and company manager just decided to give up the ship," Tienken relates. "They called us in one afternoon and said, 'Well, kids, this is it.' It was a terrible blow. We were all used to doing what we were told, but not on this one. Five of us got together in someone's apartment and just said, 'Let's do something about this.' And so we did."

As their managers prepared to pack up, the dancers rallied the support of their co-workers, the public, other California artists, and the state legislature. Suddenly, tourists walking the streets of San Francisco were greeted by ballet dancers collecting money on street corners. Shoppers glancing in the window of I. Magnin or Macy's were treated to scenes of ballerinas and their partners dancing pas de deux. "We stood on street corners and did *echappés* for a quarter and *fouet-tés* for two dollars," Tienken recalls, adding that this was one of the happiest periods in her life. "We hopped in a car and went to L.A. and knocked on the doors of movie stars to appeal to them. No one told us to knock on Paul Newman's door; we just did it. We went to parties to get donations; we went to Sacramento and cornered legislators. We had this feeling that nothing could stop us. We loved the company, it was ours, and we would save it."

And save it they did. "Children" who had been taught that they were incapable of acting on their own rescued a company that the adults had abandoned. "It was a terrific feeling," Tienken says. "It gave us an incredible sense of accomplishment."

Unfortunately, Tienken and others say, the glow did not last long. Once the company was again solvent, internal relations returned to the status quo ante. Heart-felt congratulations were delivered by grateful teachers and choreographers, but Michael Smuin and his managers took back the reins of the company and have held them firmly ever since. No matter how resourceful dancers may be, no matter how savvy they prove themselves, their companies continue to see them as children, unable to act as and be treated as adults.

If dancers are treated as children, what kind of surrogate parents do they have? What is the family of ballet really like?

It is a family that abhors independence, financial or otherwise. Given the time, energy, and expense that go into the dancers' early training, rehearsing, and touring, and given the brevity of their careers, one would think that dancers in America's top-flight companies—companies that are to ballet what the Dallas Cowboys or San Francisco 49ers are to professional football—would be well compensated for their labors and talent. They are not.

The average football player starts at $30,000 a year as a rookie and, by the time he has played for four or five years, is earning about $72,000. Symphony musicians earn up to $1000 a week, and stage-hands make over $600 a week. Until 1980, Kri Soleri and her co-workers, experienced corps dancers, earned $285 a week for a six-day week. They are paid by the week rather than the year because they receive no salary during the ten to sixteen weeks each year when the company does not perform or rehearse. Beginning corps dancers earned even less, $235 a week; and a soloist who had been with the company for ten years earned $422 a week.

In other companies, wages fluctuate a bit higher or lower. The New York City Ballet corps dancer started at $250 a week in 1979–1980, while a fifth-year corps dancer earned about $355 a week. At the Pittsburgh Ballet, one of the smaller regional troops, dancers who had been with the company for three years earned only $168 a week in 1980. ABT dancers work a forty-week season; at City Ballet, dancers are guaranteed at least forty weeks of work; and at Pennsylvania Ballet the season is thirty-six weeks long.

For dancers, a long summer hiatus is a distinct drawback of their profession. Some well-known dancers, like Godunov and van Hamel, form touring companies that perform in Europe and America during the off season. Lucky corps dancers or soloists hired for a month's stint earn an additional $10,000. Most dancers are not so fortunate. Since companies do not provide any vacation pay, dancers have to rely on unemployment insurance. (In New York, that is $125 a week.) To supplement that, they may teach in a local or regional school, or they may try to guest in local performances. Even if they do have money set aside for a vacation, many dancers will not take more than two or three weeks off. A month or two away from daily class would make it too difficult for them to get back into shape for the next year's season.

On their meager salaries, dancers must pay for food and housing in some of America's most expensive cities. And they must pay for dance-related extras—the cost of an outside class ($5), a special exercise session ($10 to $15), or a massage ($15 to $25). As Kri Soleri quips, "It costs a lot to keep up the equipment."

During the touring season, most dancers are allotted no more than $30 per diem, which has to cover the cost of a hotel and meals in cities in which it is hard to find a hotel for under $50 a night. To make up the difference, dancers are often forced to dip into their personal savings or to borrow from parents, if they can.

Company contributions to dancers' pension plans come to 5 percent of their gross weekly salary. But to qualify for a pension, dancers must work with one company for ten consecutive years, a rare occurrence in the ballet world. Thus, when thirty- or thirty-five-year-old dancers find themselves jobless, they have no pension and hardly any savings on which to retrain for a new career.

When dancers' benefits are compared to those of musicians and stagehands working at the same performances, it is clear that dancers are not only the lowest paid workers in the ballet world; they are also the least respected. Musicians and stagehands receive far better insurance coverage, as well as generous pensions and paid vacations; and their unions have negotiated much stronger grievance procedures. No musician or stagehand can be arbitrarily dismissed unless there is just cause; that is, unless he or she is drunk, on drugs, or repeatedly absent from rehearsal or performance. If a conductor wants to fire a musician for so-called artistic reasons, the case goes to a jury of the musician's peers. Dancers, on the other hand, are subject to the whim of their company director and, in many cases, can be fired at a moment's notice.

When a company hires a new director, he is free to dismiss dancers who do not suit his fancy, regardless of how long they have been employed. He may change the face of the company, depriving dozens of dancers of their livelihood, and then in several years he may move on. When Baryshnikov took over at ABT, he immediately fired principal dancer Kirk Peterson, who had been with the company for six years, simply because he "didn't like his body." The following year, he fired company veteran Hilda Morales because, at thirty-four, she was "too old." Dancers fear that Baryshnikov, who has been pursuing his own outside interests—in Hollywood and on a variety of international stages—may simply grow tired of ABT and leave. While he is well protected, they are powerless.

The principals at ABT—Baryshnikov, Makarova, Godunov, Bujones, and Gregory—like principles in other companies, have the security accorded the superstar. These men and women absorb the lion's share of the ballet company's annual budget. What is not spent on a ballet production and its accessories (it cost $500,000 to mount *La Bayadère*, and one costume can cost as much as $1500, four times what a dancer earns in a week) is allocated to the salaries of the superstars. A Makarova or Gregory, a Baryshnikov or Nureyev, can earn between $2000 and $10,000 for a single performance. Baryshnikov has earned up to $40,000 a night guesting. This means that in two performances, a superstar can earn more than a corps dancer does in a year. Superstars also are in constant demand for guest appearances with national and international companies. Add to this television appearances and movies, and their incomes can soar into the hundreds of thousands of dollars.

The star system, which creates such great inequalities in pay, is a product of the recent commercialization of ballet. The need to popularize the art and please not only the discriminating but also the untutored ballet goer now governs the way many companies are run. America's lack of governmental support for the arts has created a unique situation. In Europe and Russia, ballet, like most other arts, depends for its financial well-being on generous government subsidies. In America, where we spend very little on the arts (under the Reagan administration cutbacks have significantly reduced even this paltry sum), ballet companies must depend on the vicissitudes of the market.

Ticket sales produce only about half of a ballet company's annual budget; the rest is made up from foundation grants, donations from rich patrons, and corporate contributions. Because ballet has become a cultural product that must be packaged and sold, companies hire publicists and fund raisers who spend their days trying to attract both customers and patrons who will support their product.

Stars are the most reliable way to sell a company. Certain formulas—for example, the stories of Russian defectors—are fool-proof. Consider how much suspense and public interest were created when Godunov defected and the daily papers were filled with gripping accounts of his wife's decision to return to Russia after hours of con-fused negotiations between American and Soviet diplomats huddled around her plane at Kennedy Airport. The drama of Nureyev leaping into the arms of the Paris police or Baryshnikov sprinting down a Canadian street in the dead of night pursued by the KGB is a PR person's dream. The money and attention showered on the Russian dancers are so great, in fact, that American dancers at ABT live in constant fear of a total Russian takeover. "I once had a dream," Kri Soleri reports, "that we came to work one morning, and the whole company was fired because the entire Bolshoi had decided to defect."

In their own way, companies also pander to the ballet public's curiosity about the love lives, domestic spats, personal eccentricities, and emotional problems of prominent dancers. Like movie fans, many ballet goers follow, with great interest, Gelsey Kirkland's anorexia and other emotional problems, a possible budding romance between Fonteyn and Nureyev, or Baryshnikov's affair with Jessica Lange. When pub-licity staffers cannot rely on dramatic events, they hype any interesting extra-curricular accomplishments. The culinary accomplishments of a male Pennsylvania Ballet dancer were recently offered up to women's page editors, who published his store of recipes.

In order to promote ballet among affluent patrons of the art, dancers may also be called upon to socialize for their suppers. During intermissions in Houston, ambitious young dancers stroll into The Green Room, the lounge reserved for wealthy patrons, to mingle with local oil millionaires or real-estate men before preparing for the next act. The Texas company also delivers soloists or principals to lavish parties, sponsored by wealthy women's groups like the Houston Ballet Ambassadresses.

One night in December of 1981, I accompanied ABT soloists Lisa de Ribere and Gregory Osborne to a gala party at Macy's in honor of Baryshnikov and his troop. The entire company was expected to attend and grace this corporate fête. Only an hour after the store had ushered out the last of a throng of late-night Christmas shoppers, invitation-only guests entered the front doors on Sixth Avenue and Thirty-fourth Street into an almost surreal scene.

The illuminated interior was sealed off and heavily guarded. We passed display cases filled with gleaming leather handbags, wallets in alligator and soft leather, silk scarves, and key holders. We deposited our coats at racks positioned between the store aisles and were then escorted down to Macy's Cellar. There a series of boutiques open off a wide interior arcade. Along with celebrities like Peter Martins and Heather Watts, and critics like *Dance Magazine*'s Bill Como and Norma McLain Stoop, we strolled past racks of highly polished copper pots, Cuisinarts, pasta-making machines, and tortilla presses, toward the festivities. Guests sat at long tables laden with platters of vegetables and cold meats, champagne and liquor, and pastries. No detail had been neglected. The string beans had been braided into thick plaits; white radishes had been sliced into razor-thin shards that curled up at the end; mounds of tiny cream puffs, coated with sticky caramel, had been piled high to form a pyramid.

The dancers, too concerned with their diet to indulge, studiously avoided the food, and many seemed uninterested in the dance band. Like Houston prima ballerina Andrea Vodenhal, dancers are able to perform onstage before thousands of people but shrink at the notion of dancing "in public." "I get embarrassed getting out on a dance floor and dancing," Vodenhal tells me, laughing at the contradiction. "When I dance onstage, it's like I'm someone else. But when I'm just me, it's different."

Parties like these, where the entire company is invited, are not to be confused with the exclusive and glamorous celebrity parties that feed ballet lore. Ballet is quite simply a two-class system. There are the very rich—the superstars—and the modestly impoverished—the corps members and soloists. After galas or special performances like *La Bayadère*, they comingle. But as Michelle Benash says, "Flowers are strewn at the feet of the principals, and you're constantly reminded that you're nothing. Very often, people invite touring company members to parties. But they invite soloists and principals, never corps dancers. It's almost as if we're not part of the company. If there's a gala or opening-night party, we're sometimes invited."

The same is true in regional companies. According to a young corps dancer at Houston Ballet, "When they have parties, lots of times they invite just the principals. It makes you feel really shitty when they do that. It's like they feel we're not worth a damn. But the corps de ballet is in a lot of ballets. We're proud of being in the corps. We get great reviews. Then there's a party, and only principals and sometimes soloists are invited. I mean, we know we're the lowest paid and all, but they don't have to rub it in."

Commercialization has affected more than the dancer's social life and media image. It has forced companies to mount prodigious numbers of ballets to accommodate the demands of larger and larger audiences who attend more and more frequently. American companies have now begun to carry enormous repertoires. Ballet Theater performs between thirty and forty ballets a year, which means that dancers must master dozens of new roles each season. The huge repertoire guarantees a company's ability to sell season subscription series, a current staple of ballet marketing strategy. Each subscription comprises a series of evenings, scattered throughout the season, during which the subscriber will see a different ballet or series of ballets. On one Tuesday he might watch *Swan Lake*; on another, a new version of an old classic like *La Bayadère*; on another, a selection of standard one-act ballets; and, on yet a fourth, a program that includes newly choreographed productions. The mix is concocted to avoid repetition and ensure variety so the program will attract both devoted ballet goers, always eager to see new works, and newcomers, who want a smorgasbord of offerings. These subscribers are a guaranteed, pre-sold audience upon whom companies depend for their financial well-being.

While companies adamantly support the subscription series, dancers are less than enthusiastic about this sales technique. Such varied programming forces dancers to rehearse dozens of ballets at once. Some companies, like New York City Ballet, set aside adequate rehearsal time, while others—most notably ABT—tend not to. "There are so many ballets in the repertoire, both at ABT and at City Ballet, that dancers are not carefully coached," says ABT superstar Cynthia Gregory. "People are just thrown into things. Dancers aren't given enough time to learn the ballets, and this means that attention to detail is lost."

"We always carry far too big a rep," says Michael Owen, a tall, solidly built, curly-headed ABT soloist who is an outspoken critic of his company's policies. "It's an injustice to the public, who is paying a small fortune to watch a performance. We're just not prepared. For instance, you'll dance a ballet, not touch it for almost a year, then dance it for a week, then not touch it for another year. That becomes very frustrating, because as much as you try to remember it, you can't work on it to correct and perfect it. When that happens, you lose certain feelings for the ballet and for your craft."

Owen also adds his voice to a chorus of complaints from male dancers who feel that commercialization and attention to the superstars have encouraged critics and popularizers to focus on the athletic-ism of male dancing. Choreographers have begun to make concessions to popular taste, pushing *danseurs* to ever greater pyrotechnical feats. Like gymnasts, *danseurs* regularly bound across the stage, leaping and turning like high jumpers; like weight lifters supporting heavy weights at an international match, *danseurs* parade around the stage, support-ing ballerinas on their shoulders.

If a company lacks sufficiently talented male principals who are also strong partners, those dancers whose muscles can presumably bear the strain must also bear the burden of additional roles. During one performance I watched in Houston, one male principal danced in three consecutive ballets filled with intricate leaps and acrobatics. In the last of the three ballets, he crisscrossed the stage with a ballerina held high above his shoulders, his face a mask of smiling forebearance. Ultimately, however, I and other members of the audience could not help observing that his body seemed to groan rather than soar onstage.

By emphasizing ballet's athletic, masculine challenges rather than its graceful, feminine aspects, popularizers have tried to circumvent America's ingrained antipathy toward anything that even hints at the homosexual. Comparisons between Nureyev and sports superstars like Joe Namath are not uncommon. Wayne Gretzky, the famous hockey superstar, was recently dubbed "the Nureyev of sports, the superstar's superstar." Anna Kisselgoff pointed out in a *New York Times* article that this kind of comparison proves that ballet has become part of American culture. Obviously, it serves no purpose to compare Gretzky to Nureyev unless people know who Nureyev is.

As Kisselgoff and other ballets critics have warned, ballet's special qualities—its dramatic intent, its subtleties of mood and gesture—may be lost in the new emphasis on athleticism. "When the dance world tries to sell dancers as athletes," Kisselgoff writes, "the result may be self-defeating. Unlike sports, whose athletes are capable of communicating imagery of beauty and grace on occasion, dance is concerned with a release of artistic expression. Its creativity resides in the idea that art is not limited by known parameters—such as goal scoring."

It is not difficult to understand why many male dancers, like Michael Owen, compare ballet pyrotechnics to sex and violence on television. "The emphasis on athletics makes our position more prominent," says Owen. "But our bodies just can't take it."

These excessive work loads shorten an already truncated career. Dance has always been the province of youth; and, in this sense, dancers are more like athletes than artists. Because they depend so heavily on bodies that will eventually wear down, they know that their careers are a race they will eventually lose. "Your body begins to give out," says thirty-three-year-old Robert Maiorano. "Just when your mind is at its best and you should be dancing your best, your body can't do it. It's a tragic career in a way," he adds, "because there's always this terrible frustration that as you grow older, it will be too late to apply what you've learned to your art. That's the tragedy of a career dependent on youth."

Dancers used to expect that they would inevitably retire in their mid-thirties. Today, however, they can no longer count even on that. For both men and women, choreography that relies heavily on athletics and schedules that involve learning large numbers of ballets rapidly wear down a dancer's body. A frame that might have lasted twenty years will not last fifteen; if it sustains too many injuries, it might last even fewer years. In addition, older, more experienced dancers—of the twenty-five- to twenty-eight-year-old variety—are out of fashion in many companies.

The new ballet vogue is youth. When Baryshnikov took over ABT, he began weeding out older dancers and replacing them with the youngest dancers he could find. Approximately twelve were not re-hired, and about twenty of those hired were in their mid- to late teens or early twenties. He has also passed over experienced soloists to give plum parts to inexperienced teenagers. Across the city at City Ballet, Darci Kistler was taken into the company at age fifteen, and a number of choice roles have gone to equally young dancers. These kids are thrilled with their luck, but ballet observers and older dancers caution that their meteoric rise may have adverse physical results. "Sure she may be dancing like crazy now," says Vane Vest. "But when such young dancers are pushed ahead, they have a hard time when they get older." During performances last year, Darci worked "full out" on a bad hip injury, covering the pain for hours at a stretch.

When a choreographer promotes young dancers and pushes them, perhaps further than their bodies can safely go, he is not only taking advantage of the dancers' talent and ambition; he is, in subtle ways, exploiting the dancers' fears. All dancers live with an almost permanent sense of insecurity. When Kri Soleri and her companions surrender their private lives to their art, they are not fueled just by ambition; they are also motivated by the knowledge that they can be replaced by any one of a dozen eager dancers. Age, an injury, a choreographer's whim: Anything can end their careers. Any year could be their last, not just to make it but to do what they love—to dance. And so they work, constantly and obsessively, to please the one person who determines their professional fate.

Ballet companies are dictatorships—sometimes malevolent ones, sometimes benevolent ones. New York City Ballet's George Balanchine is the prime example of the ballet dictator. One of the world's most famous choreographers, he is said to take extraordinary care of his dancers. The New York State Theatre, which is NYCB's permanent home, is America's finest ballet theater. Built to Mr. B.'s specifications, its studios and stage have specially constructed sprung-wood floors. At City Ballet, dancers have the pleasure of working with the greatest costume and set designers in the business, as well as with one of the greatest living choreographers. At City Ballet, dancers also have the opportunity to work with Jerome Robbins, Balanchine's co-choreographer. His moody, dramatic ballets are a welcome counter-point to Balanchine's abstract, technical works, giving dancers a chance to develop a more dramatic emotional range.

Like most companies, City Ballet carries an enormous repertoire, but dancers are well rehearsed and well coached. No expense is spared in the productions. No matter how impractical it may be to create costumes out of silk, silk it must be for the gowns in *Vienna Waltzes*, for how can ballerinas feel beautiful, dance a fantasy, if the accoutre-ments do not lend themselves to the magic? Balanchine has also ar-ranged a summer session at Saratoga, so City Ballet dancers do not have to suffer through long summer layoffs. If they are faithful, many of them can also expect some security in their old age: Balanchine generously provides work for aging dancers as ballet masters or mis-tresses, teachers or character dancers.

With the exception of their salaries—better than most companies but still relatively low—working at City Ballet would seem a dancer's dream, and it does to most dancers outside the company and to many within. Dancers, however, pay for the privilege. To enjoy the benefits Balanchine metes out, they must not only obey, admire, and respect Balanchine; they must worship him.

Appropriately, their training in loyalty begins when they are children, students at the School of American Ballet. There, dancers are schooled in the legend of Balanchine. To them, he is the greatest genius alive; to dance is to dance in City Ballet; not to dance in City Ballet is tantamount to not being alive. Women who started in the school when they were young children are especially susceptible to his phantom presence. "For years, you get all this stuff about Balan-chine," a former NYCB dancer explains. "It's like he's a god and you're supposed to worship him." Or as Rachel Isadora Maiorano, herself a former SAB student, says, "The women are raised in the school from a very young age. Balanchine is the most powerful male figure in their lives. He becomes either a father figure or a sexual figure. All the girls are in love with him; if they aren't, they don't stay. You're brought up, in the school, to think Balanchine is the pinnacle of the whole world you're involved in.

"Then, when you're a teenage girl," Rachel adds, "and you begin to get your period and breasts and hips, a very strange thing happens. You don't want them. It's very ironic. Ballet is the most feminine world, or so it appears. But it's really a very hard world. To have softness, breasts and hips, is not wanted in ballet. So you can't become a woman in the ballet world. You have to remain a child. And there's Balanchine, at the center of it all, this very powerful male figure. He reinforces the idea that you should remain a little girl, that you shouldn't go out, that you shouldn't be with men. Balanchine is supposed to be the only man in your life."

Balanchine's male dancers are not quite so closely watched. "In my ballets," Balanchine has often said as he did in a recent interview in *The New York Times*, "woman is first. She is queen. Men are consorts. Ballet is, for me, a feminine form: it is matriarchal. Women are not equal to men, they are better. God made men to be poets, and sing the praises of women. Women do not write poems to sing the praises of men. That is a big difference." Perhaps Balanchine realizes that men cannot be controlled quite as easily as women. They enter ballet at a later age, so their connection to the master is not as firmly developed. "It's not like with the women," Robert Maiorano says. "All the men know that Balanchine focuses on the women, that he's more interested in the women. As a man, you know that, but you can't do anything about it. You just dance as best you can and have him make use of you. He doesn't have as much hold on male dancers. But still, he's the god of his own little world. You're a man living in that world, and he's the ultimate power figure." Men may thus be dependent on Balanchine for advancement, but he is not the all-powerful figure holding the key to their identities.

"One of the principal dancers in the company once told me that she is totally dedicated to Balanchine," says Rachel Maiorano. "I had suggested that someone in the corps might not be getting parts and might want to go elsewhere, and this dancer said, 'No, you can't think like that. You must give yourself to Balanchine. You must have the belief that he's a god.' "

That is precisely how many City Ballet dancers view Balanchine. Toni Bentley, a corps dancer in the company, deifies Balanchine in her recent book, *Winter Season.*† She came to SAB when she was a child. At eighteen, she became a corps member and has since made City Ballet her entire world. Her recounting of a season at the ballet is not a simple professional autobiography; it is a tale of romantic passion.

"Most women have two important men in their lives—their father and their lover," Bentley says.

We have three. Mr. Balanchine is our leader, our president, our mother, our father, our friend, our guide, our mentor, our destiny.

He knows all, sees all, and controls all—all of us—most often by saying very, very little. . . . He is our third parent, the parent of our adulthood, when so many people have no one at all. We are all his children, but his adult children, his working, dancing, performing children. His power over us is unique. . . . He loves us all. He adores our beauty and extends it out of all conceivable proportion in his ballets. What more could a girl ask of a man than such an appreciation?

He is, Bentley says, the repository of their souls, a man whom one cannot cheat. Onstage, in front of Balanchine, a dancer is "bare, naked, exposed. . . . And how we love it, that exposure." For Balanchine, women do not just dance; they live.

Twenty-nine-year-old Erica Davis* is another of City Ballet's true believers. A slim, blond girl whose hair is pulled back into a

---

† Toni Bentley, *Winter Season: A Dancer's Journal* (New York: Random House, 1982), p. 59.

severe ballet bun, she has a pert, elfin-like appearance. Her ears form small hearts at the side of her head. Her clear blue eyes are like opaque crystals that seem to match the neat little pearls that pierce her ears. Were it not for a slight, brittle edge, she would have the supple, sprightly delicacy of a wood nymph.

We meet one spring afternoon in her dressing room at City Ballet. Reserved for corps dancers, it is a dingy cinder-block room, strewn with a dancer's usual paraphernalia. In it she has spent most of her adult life. She lives with her parents, as she has since she was a child. She has no current boyfriends, has never been married, and has never lived with a man for any extended period of time. "City Ballet," Davis alerts me almost immediately, as if introducing me to invisible relatives, "is my family. Most of us have grown up together, not only in SAB but in Professional Children's School. When you work with people every day, they become your family. If you have a boyfriend problem or a family problem, you can always talk to someone right here. You don't have to go outside the theater. It all emanates from Mr. B., who cares a great deal about his dancers and wants to know their problems."

Mr. B. is the source of all bounty, and tales of his generosity abound at City Ballet. To many dancers, he is a saint who miraculously appears in times of need. One dancer relates the story of "Mr. Balanchine and the Boots." In the dead of a dreary winter, she was walking near the theater on a snowy afternoon clad in a pair of flimsy, sodden shoes. Suddenly Mr. B. appeared. Looking down at her feet, he asked solicitously why she was not wearing warm boots. She explained that she could not afford to buy boots on her pitiable salary. Balanchine reached into his pocket, produced seventy dollars, and told her to immediately buy herself a pair of boots.

For Erica Davis and other dancers who have spent most of their lives sequestered in studios, Balanchine is more than a source of material well-being; he is a text in which they read the world. "Maybe

I'm a Balanchine groupie. But I'm very proud of it," Davis says. "Balanchine taught me more than any other person in the world, aside from my parents. Not only about dance, but about life in general. In class he goes off on tangents about his life. He tells us about cooking, about wines, about living. He tells us what Monte Carlo was like in the thirties. He shares his experiences with us. He's just fantastic."

He is also, Erica says, the mirror that reflects the dancer back to herself. "He's so willing to nurture us along, always pushing us beyond what we're able to do, always pulling things out of us. At times when I just want to cry in frustration and say I can't do that, he knows that I can."

What Davis says is something I hear from many other NYCB dancers. "He allows you to be yourself," Heléne Alexopoulos comments. "It's uncanny. He has a sixth sense, and he knows what you can do even when you don't."

The price for this super-intuitional attention, however, is high. Enchanted by Balanchine's ESP, his dancers are prisoners of his institution. Davis denies this, insisting that Balanchine gives his dancers freedom. But as we talk, this "freedom" seems ephemeral at best. When we first met, Erica Davis was extremely nervous. "We've just found out that the company doesn't like books, doesn't like us talking to people writing books," she informs me. She is so anxious about a possible breach of the rules that she insists I use a pseudonym; and even though I agree, she is still worried.

Later in the afternoon, she admits that for some dancers, City Ballet is not the happy family she originally depicted. "Newcomers are not always well received. It's very difficult for them with all this competition and no one to talk to. Some of them become psychologically disturbed. When I say they have nervous breakdowns, I mean the real thing, like they have to go into institutions. It's been pretty frightening. Suddenly one little thing goes wrong and they go crazy."

And though she does not quite see it herself, Erica is just as trapped as Solange MacArthur and Michelle Benash in the unending childhood they describe. Preferring her parents' comfortable apartment to the cramped quarters her meager salary could buy in today's market, she says, "I do give them [her parents] some money toward the rent out of self-respect. And I do all my own laundry and all that stuff," she adds proudly.

She also economizes on freedom, thinking twice about entering a relationship. "The decision is there: Do I move out? How serious is it? But that's good. I have to stop and think. I don't rush into things."

Dependent on Balanchine's emotional and material largesse, dancers like Erica Davis and Toni Bentley never have the security of adult self-sufficiency. Dancers who are subject to their "father's" whim for a pair of boots, a raise, or a sense of their own talent never find their own strength. Each apparent gain is, in reality, a kind of loss. Advancement is proof not of mastery but of the power of the mentor, and each step forward is a link in the chain that binds them to him.

Unfortunately, he who giveth can always taketh away. And Balanchine does. There is a darker side to Balanchine's benevolence. "When I was dancing in City Ballet," a former NYCB dancer recalls, "I was dancing out of fear. I was always afraid that if I did something wrong or if I didn't please Balanchine, I'd be out. I remember one day we were rehearsing, and no one could do anything right. Mr. B. was furious and he said, 'When I die, I'll be up there watching you; and when you're like this, I'll just—' he gestured like he was going to make us disappear. And we all just cringed. But I think people actually believed he could make us disappear because dancing there, at City Ballet, you do disappear. You're invisible. You begin to lose yourself. Only when you're noticed do you exist."

Balanchine is ballet's most talented and respected choreographic sorcerer. His loyal supporters admit that he is a dictator but insist that he is a benevolent one. When arguing for dictatorship in ballet, they maintain that it is not a danger but rather a necessity, essential if the art and artist are to thrive. But whenever one person has total control over other people's lives, terrible abuses of that control are inevitable. And when someone comes along who wields his control malevolently, there is no protection for the weak and vulnerable dancers who are dependent on him.

Many dancers tell particularly grim stories about one prominent choreographer whose personal and sexual preferences interfere with his professional judgment. This choreographer—we shall call him Sam Rivers—is homosexual and has routinely become attracted to male dancers who are involved with his female dancers. Suzanne Wheeler, a dancer who worked with Rivers, bitterly exclaimed, "Talking about him is like opening a can of worms!" She was only nineteen when she was in his company, and she fell in love with a young boy who was a particular friend of Rivers's. At first, Rivers did not object, but when he learned they were romantically involved, he became incensed. "He said if I continued to see Roger he'd kick me out of the company. I was very young and my career meant a lot to me, but this boy meant a lot to me." She did not leave the company nor did she stop seeing her boyfriend.

At this point, Rivers announced that she had been fired. Although other influential company administrators insisted she be reinstated, Rivers was never disciplined, and so the harassment continued. "He started to tell other members of the company that if they talked to me, they'd be fired. He had me followed and used to make horrible phone calls to me in the middle of the night. Once, when Roger and I were walking through the park, he followed us and started shrieking at me, calling me a whore. Another time he got into Roger's room and shredded his clothes with a pair of scissors."

The affair ended when her boyfriend left the company. Shattered by the experience, however, she also left and joined a Swedish company. "It was the most terrible experience I've ever had. I still dream about it."

This story is unique only in degree, not in kind. Although some choreographers—Frederick Ashton, John Butler, Benjamin Harkarvy —are known for their courteous demeanor, others do not hesitate to impose the full burden of their professional power on dancers, who are expected to submit to their every personal and artistic whim. Although Michael Smuin is a family man and so supports his female dancers in their decision to have children, he apparently does not approve of homosexuals, and gay dancers complain that he is particularly hard on them. When Nureyev steps out onstage to set a ballet for a new company, he does more than choreograph a series of elaborate steps and gestures. He goes on famous artistic rampages, yelling, screaming, and barking commands like a drill sergeant, demanding that dancers forfeit breaks and rehearse well into the night. And when Baryshnikov grows tired or irritated, he often takes it out on his dancers.

Ballet lore is filled with tales of choreographers or directors who treat dancers to a regimen of unbridled anger and callousness. When Margot Fonteyn writes of her life at The Royal Ballet and of the ballet's founder, Ninette de Valois, she describes her in tyrannical terms: "I had never encountered anyone so volatile. Miss Fleet [a former teacher] headmistress of my school in Shanghai, who struck terror in pupils, parents, teachers and governors alike, was a remote dragon lurking in her lair, whereas de Valois might at any time breathe fire and smoke upon one in the canteen, or the corridor, or the dressing room."†

Fonteyn attributes de Valois's conduct to Old School severity. Others tend to condone such behavior because it is the artist's prerogative to succumb to fits of "artistic temperament." Like gods, choreographers behave capriciously and unexpectedly; like gods, they expect their every desire to be satisfied, their every command to be obeyed. They are expected to be neurotic and eccentric, and to challenge them

† Margot Fonteyn, *Autobiography* (New York: Alfred A. Knopf, 1976), pp. 42–43.

is to risk blocking the very wellsprings of their creativity. However, such conduct seems to have less to do with artistic creativity and more to do with the inevitable abuses bred by the institutionalization of absolute power. Because such conduct is so integral a part of the ballet world, it is difficult to fight it. When a dancer complains about a choreographer's or director's attacks, the response of the choreographer or director is almost always the same: "This is the way things are. If you don't like it, you can leave." The needs of the dancers are rarely considered or met.

THE BATTERED BALLERINA:

6

INJURIES AND ANOREXIA

"You've got twenty seconds. That's right, come on now, phrase it, phrase it. No, no, it's got little squares, that's why you have trouble getting into the thing. Play with it, play games. Try it once again."

Choreographer Daniel Levans, who played temperamental artist to Anne Bancroft's prima ballerina in *The Turning Point*, is not acting today. It's real life here at the Met. He is rehearsing his ballet *Concert Waltzes* with Janet Shibata and her two male partners for ABT's 1980 summer season.

Moving rhythmically, through steps and leaps and lifts, they obey a constant barrage of orders from Levans. Shibata, a frail young Japanese woman whose face is a wide plane with high cheekbones and a strong chin, jumps over and over again. Abruptly, the grace is shattered. Coming down she lands and then crimps over in pain. Grasping her knee, she hobbles over to the side of the room. For a moment no one pays any attention, and she goes back to her place and continues to dance.

"Stop it," Levans calls out to her.

But she goes on, grimacing, obviously in pain.

"Stop it, Jan! Jan, stop it!" he barks. "Now what is it? Is it all right?" he asks.

"Something popped in my knee," the dancer answers.

"That sounds familiar," he replies casually, as she massages her kneecap. "Well, Janet, what's up?" he asks impatiently.

"It's been hurting for a long time, but it's never popped like that," she says softly. As her partners rehearse the boys variation, she walks over to the side of the studio, sits down, and continues rubbing her knee. Then she stands up and gingerly tests it. Five minutes later she is back on the floor, leaping, flowing, moving—in spite of pain—to the music.

Ballet dancers call this ritual scene dancing through an injury. Daily pain is as much a part of a dancer's life as daily class. The dancers' bodies may look as if they have defied the normal limits of the human frame, but the cost of that defiance is high. Not only do dancers frequently injure themselves while dancing; they almost invariably continue to dance while injured. After I leave Studio Three on my way to watch a stage rehearsal, I begin to chat with Lisa Houlton, a twenty-five-year-old soloist who is getting more and more roles this year. She appears stiffer than usual and informs me, in a nonchalant voice, that she tore the ligaments in her rib cage while rehearsing Glen Tetley's ballet *Voluntaries*. Injured or not, she will still dance the ballet two nights hence, despite the fact that *Voluntaries* is one of the most demanding partnering ballets in the ABT repertoire. Women are constantly lifted and pulled and swooped through the air, and it is hard to imagine how she will be able to ignore the pressure of her partner's hands as they rub and press against the tender area. "I'll just bandage it while I'm rehearsing," she said, as if trying to reassure both herself and me.

Bandages and Band-Aids, a day off here and there. By the end of the 1980 season, Makarova is out because of bursitis of the knee. Fernando Bujones is dancing with tendonitis; Patrick Bissell was out for several months with a back injury but is now back; Kevin McKenzie was out with a sprained back; and John Meehan has been out with a leg injury. Of the ten women soloists, Janet Shibata is out; Lisa de Ribere has been dancing with a pinched nerve in her foot; Cynthia

Harvey is out with a torn ligament in her ankle; Rebecca Wright has a back injury; and Jolinda Menendez has been dancing with injuries in the bones of her feet. Five out of the ten male soloists are out; five of seventeen male corps dancers are no longer dancing; and six of the thirty-seven women are out with assorted injuries to the spine, leg, knee, and back. "What is worse," Frank Smith says, "is that virtually everyone who is still dancing has something wrong. We're at the point where if one or two more people are out, they'll have to change ballets and rearrange programs. They come up to us and beg us, 'Please don't fall apart,' even though we're already falling apart."

Even after a long layoff, injuries reappear. During the following fall season, Lisa de Ribere will have an operation on her foot and will take a month off; in 1981 and 1982, Makarova and Baryshnikov had knee operations. Other companies have the same problems. While Janet Shibata was having her knee problem, Robert Weiss, a City Ballet dancer, hobbled around on crutches and watched SAB Workshop rehearsals: He had had surgery on a ruptured tendon. In San Francisco, Vane Vest limped in and out of class, onstage and off, after a similar operation. "All the dancers who are older have chronic problems," Vest says. "It's funny. We always kid around and say, 'Hire the handicapped' because people here are walking around lame, limping, or they're unable to use an arm, or have strained their backs."

Dance and injury go hand in hand. Why? There are several reasons. The simplest is that dance is hell on the body. We see dancers sitting in positions that make them look like they are made of rubber; those dancers can only "relax" in such positions because they have pulled and twisted and distorted the natural patterns of their bodies for years. Says Dr. Liebler, "They must actually distort their bodies to achieve the number one requirement of ballet: turnout."

Once the student's body begins to undergo the process of molding to suit the dance, he or she begins to accumulate injuries. Both Liebler's study of one thousand consecutive injuries in ballet dancers and another study by a young New York podiatrist, Dr. Thomas Novella, catalogue an impressive series of injuries common to dancers: sprains; stress fractures; fractures of bones, which happen when a man drops his partner, when a dancer falls or when he or she trips over something onstage; tendonitis of the knee, or Achilles tendonitis; inflammation of the sesamoid bones, small bones in the foot; as well as problems particular to women's feet, the result of wearing toe shoes. Tortured for years in pointe shoes, women may develop early forms of rheumatoid arthritis in their feet, as well as corns and swollen and painful bunions.

In large companies like ABT, injuries are due, in part, to what dancers claim to be an unwieldy repertoire. "Dancers get injured," says Frank Smith, "because they're tired and under great strain. Well, if you're worried about what you're supposed to be doing next, obviously you'll run a greater risk of being injured."

Dancing on the hard, concrete floors of many of the nation's opera houses and theaters can also lead to injury. To safely jump and pirouette onstage, dancers must perform on specially constructed stages made of a latticework of wood that will give when the dancer lands with great force. Most stages are made of poured concrete, which is far less costly than wood and can also support heavy operatic sets. "If we blackballed every theater we shouldn't dance in [because of hazardous floors or other equipment], we wouldn't dance at all," Michael Owen says, after suffering through a stint at Washington's Kennedy Center. This past year, City Ballet refused to perform at the Kennedy Center because of its hard stage. No other major ballet company has followed suit, and regional companies cannot afford to boycott theaters in which they count on making dozens of appearances.

In smaller companies, injuries are due not only to inadequate rehearsal time and dancing on hard floors but to a company's inability or unwillingness to hire enough dancers. Although dancers in the Pennsylvania Ballet say their company tends to be far more solicitous of their welfare than are New York companies, Jeff Gribler admits that dancers often dance when they are injured in order to help out one another. "There are only thirty of us," the young *danseur* explains. "If you lose two people, you're down to twenty-eight. If someone is badly injured and you're not so badly injured, you feel you ought to cover for him to help out."

Too much dancing and too little rehearsal time contribute to injury. But the main factor that impels dancers to dance when injured is the terrible competition of a field in which only a tiny number of jobs are available for more and more, and better- and better-trained dancers.

"You can always be let go," Elizabeth Tienken points out. "Some bigger stars might be able to go in and say, 'Well, I won't dance on Friday night.' Here you just have to do what you're told. If you don't dance, someone else will have to dance your part or your partner will be let down. It just goes on down the line. If you're a strong dancer, a choreographer will take advantage of your strength and abuse it."

It is common knowledge that dancers love to dance and refuse to take time off, even if doctors order them to do so. So fanatical is their dedication that they appear to have no aptitude for health. But this fanaticism is as much a product of fear as of devotion. They learn, as students, that dancers are penalized when their all-too-human bodies cannot tolerate the strain. Instead of growing into their bodies and respecting their limitations, dancers work against themselves. When they are scheduled to work every day and perform almost every night, they leap to the task because they want to fill their short careers to the brim. And they are encouraged in this by the companies, which increase performance time without increasing the number of dancers and push their members to dance when injured.

"It's a pressure they put on you," a young Houston dancer says. "They make you feel that you're awful for being injured. When you come back from taking time off, they don't pay any attention to you."

The worst thing that can happen to a dancer is to get a bad reputation —a reputation for being "injury-prone." Dancers who gripe about their aches and pains and refuse to dance through them get labeled. "It's a head trip they do on you," she continues. "You just feel that you can't say, 'Hey, I have this inflamed Achilles tendon, and if I keep dancing on it it will rip, and then what will happen to me? I won't ever be able to dance again.' "

Since most dancers seem to be somewhat injured most of the time, the injury-prone dancer is probably just a dancer who is prone to talking about injury. As a consequence, most dancers put more energy into concealing injuries than treating them. Lauren Rouse, a dancer at Pittsburgh Ballet Theatre, for example, was perfectly willing to discuss the difficulties of her career but suddenly became circumspect when we began to discuss her injuries. From talking in the first person, she quickly began to speak abstractly, using the third person to distance herself from the problem. The injury was no longer hers. Why such sudden reluctance? Because she feared she would lose her company's respect if she had too many physical problems.

Like soldiers volunteering over and over again for dangerous missions, dancers dance no matter how much pain they are forced to endure. And the pain can often be excruciating. Victor Barbee's experiences are typical. In his second year with ABT, he began to have problems with his shins. He did not know the exact nature of the problem, nor did he want to know. For a year he danced in ignorance, until the pressure of an elastic sock against his leg was so agonizing that he finally sought medical advice. The verdict? One leg had three stress fractures and one had five. "If I jumped and pushed off the ground, I could feel the bone opening a bit in front," he now acknowledges.

He procrastinated so long before getting medical advice because, he says, "I just didn't want to lose time. People were saying if you want to cancel a performance, fine. But then you know that nobody cares if you're around or not. I thought I had to keep going. I was just starting to get good parts," he continues in his slow, quiet, North Carolina drawl. "I thought it was bad timing to stop being around. The doctor told me to stay off my legs for six months. I took three weeks off and then came back."

In this case (and in most other companies where injuries occur), ABT knew Barbee was injured and did not intervene to protect the dancer. For ballet companies, a dancer's almost self-destructive zeal is an advantage. After all, companies stay, while dancers just come and go. A dancer, however, does not get a new body when the old one wears out. "From the company's point of view," says Barbee, "it's been months since you did anything. From your point of view, it's been two weeks and for those two weeks you've hardly been able to walk. I regret now that I didn't just take six months off. It's been three years since the problem started, and it still gives me pain."

Chronic problems like Barbee's do not necessarily stabilize so that a dancer can learn to live with a fairly constant level of pain. The injuries get worse and worse. Vane Vest was finally forced to have surgery. "I've danced with torn muscles, torn ligaments in my shoulder, severe tendonitis, and pulled hamstrings," Vest tells me almost boastfully. He says he always thought he could beat his injuries by the force of his will. One day, his injury, chronic tendonitis, beat him.

"I should have stopped way before it happened," he admits, now that it is too late. "I had a partial tear in my Achilles tendon five days before it happened. But I was stupid, I just went on dancing. Then the whole thing ruptured in class. My calf rolled up like a window shade behind the knee, and I had to have surgery."

The experience did not, however, teach Vest to listen to his body's warning signals. To someone accustomed to working day in and day out, Vest found being inactive as unendurable as physical pain, so he started taking class and performing long before his doctors recommended. "I had surgery in March and started performing full out in August. I shouldn't have begun to perform for a year, since I know I'm running the risk that it will snap again."

Dancers run that risk, Vest says, because they are stupid, young, ambitious—and perhaps because they are undervalued by the companies they serve. "If you can't choose to stay off your feet, someone should choose for you," says Gelsey Kirkland. "But this is not the case now. There are some injuries you can dance through and some you cannot. Someone should say, 'It's not wise for you to dance, and we'll reschedule you so you won't be penalized.' If companies would do this, it would help immensely. Dancers would feel valued, and they wouldn't constantly have to prove themselves."

Doctors can repair the damage once, perhaps twice. But if dancers do not cooperate with a doctor's treatment, chronic injuries can have lasting, even crippling, effects. If Vane Vest's tendon rips one more time, that's it. "Next time it will be the end," he says. "It will snap. They'll be able to sew it back together again, but they'll have to snip out a piece, and I'll never dance again." Yet Vest continues to dance.

Dancers drive doctors to distraction. Dr. Liebler is horrified and frustrated by their response to treatment. "Treating them is very hard because they get so worked up about taking time off or even taking medicine. If you want to give a girl with an inflammation an anti-inflammatory drug, she doesn't want to take it because it will make her retain water. Or you tell a kid to take a pill three times a day with meals, and the kid says she doesn't eat three meals a day. She doesn't eat breakfast; she doesn't eat. Period. These dancers won't take the food that is needed to offset the side effects of the medication. You're up against a stone wall treating them. They are pushing their bodies beyond what is normal, and they won't let the body heal when it breaks down."

So they develop long-lasting, degenerative bone and muscle and joint diseases. According to Dr. Liebler, ballet dancers have various forms of arthritis in their later years. Jacques d'Amboise has advanced degenerative osteoarthritis; Baryshnikov and Makarova both have serious knee problems; Nureyev's body looks positively tortured; and Edward Villella danced so much when he was young that he is now crippled. "It's so sad," Michelle Benash muses. "He was such a beautiful dancer, and now he walks with a limp and he's not even that old."

Michelle could be talking about herself. At thirty, she too is partially crippled. She walks with a limp and sometimes finds it painful to walk at all. After years of working on a knee injury, dancing with a brace under her tights, she finally quit ABT. She had planned to teach ballet to make a living and to take acting classes on the side. But staying off her knee did not improve it. When it got worse, doctors recommended surgery. They found that half her kneecap had disintegrated, and the surgery was of little help. She will never be able to dance again. Indeed, she will always have trouble walking. "I have to wear a brace every time I teach a class, and I can't do any jumps at all. I'm only thirty, and I'll never be able to play tennis or ride my bike. Some days I just can't deal with it."

"When I was young I ruined my body," Michelle Benash says quite simply. "It wasn't just the dancing that did it; it was the dieting. You were supposed to be thin, super thin, so I starved myself. I lived on three hundred calories a day. On weekends, I'd just eat ice cream instead of anything good for me. Sometimes I'd be so hungry that I'd go home and cry because I was in such pain. My muscles ached from not eating. And I'd just collapse in bed at night."

At that time, Michelle was dancing with a small New York company. The company encouraged strict dieting. A company doctor prescribed a variety of diet pills and injections, and a five-hundred-calorie-a-day diet. "They used to give some girls shots of serum from pregnant monkeys," Michelle recalls. "The idea behind this had to do with a pregnant woman's ability to live off her fat reserves. They thought that with the injections, girls would burn up an extra thousand calories a day. I never took the shots. They gave me diet pills instead. I have no idea what they were. All I know is that one day, after taking them, I fainted on Lexington Avenue.

"Of course, I can't prove it medically," she adds, "but I know my knee problem is related to all that. I was a growing child, and I was depriving myself of food, taking weird medicine, and now I'm paying for it."

What Michelle Benash describes, self-induced starvation, resembles the symptoms of anorexia nervosa. This psychosomatic disease—and its more violent counterpart, bulimia (eating and then vomiting)—is ballet's dirty little secret. To conform to an idealization of womanhood that denies the very qualities that make them womanly, dancers have to starve themselves.

Anorexia nervosa†, the most prevalent form of neurotic behavior in the dance world, is one of the most serious psychosomatic disorders. Generally, it afflicts adolescent and pre-adolescent girls (in rare cases, boys get anorexia), and it is on the increase in the United States.

Psychiatrists, like Dr. Hilda Bruch, who specialize in the treatment of anorectics write of young girls who starve themselves, sometimes to death (the mortality rate among anorectics is 15 to 17 percent). Bruch calls anorexia "the relentless pursuit of excessive thinness." The disorder is not due to loss of interest in food; quite the contrary. Anorectics are obsessed by food. "But," writes Bruch in her

---

† There is some psychiatric debate about who qualifies as a genuine anorectic. Some doctors believe only women who are so thin they must be hospitalized are anorectic. Others feel that there is a wider range of anorectic behavior. A real anorectic hovers on the borderline of starvation or may simply be someone who must eventually be force-fed in order to survive. In this chapter, I will use the word "anorectic" to describe dancers who actually starve themselves and those who manifest anorectic-like behavior—not eating, going on crazy diets, vomiting, abusing laxatives, imagining that they are fat when, in fact, they are very thin or almost skeletal.

study *The Golden Cage*, "they consider self-denial and discipline the highest virtue and condemn satisfying their needs as shameful self-indulgence."†

Anorectics characteristically believe they are fat when, in fact, they are emaciated. They do not respond appropriately to hunger (by eating, that is), and have "a paralyzing sense of ineffectiveness, the conviction of being helpless to change anything about their lives." In true anorexia nervosa, the disturbance borders on the psychotic. As if she were hallucinating, an anorectic looking in the mirror sees a fat girl. Bruch and other experts in the field also stress that anorectics are often hyperactive. (It is not uncommon to find sixty-pound anorectics jogging in place by their hospital beds because they fear gaining weight.) And they are frequently overachievers.

Anorectics' sense of powerlessness, says Dr. Jane Oldden, a psychiatrist who has treated anorectics both inside and outside ballet, forces them to adopt primitive mechanisms of self-control, like refusing to eat or eating and then inducing vomiting. "This kind of behavior is a result of what we call a symbiotic relationship between the parent or parent surrogate and the patient. In ballet, it seems like the ballet school or company has been a kind of anorexogenic family. The individual has been or is essentially controlled in her goals and self-image by another person. In revolt against this entanglement, of which she is part, she regresses to an emotional level of about two years old. That is, she will do anything Mommy wants her to do but eat. This is her only way to develop a sense of separateness and autonomy."

The other eating disorder prevalent in the ballet world, bulimia, can exist as an entity unto itself or as part of the anorectic syndrome. Psychiatrist Arnold E. Andersen, who specializes in both eating disorders, writes that "bulimia patients find themselves, after a certain point in weight reduction, unable to continue to restrict their appetite.

† Hilda Bruch, *The Golden Cage: The Enigma of Anorexia Nervosa* (New York: Random House, 1979), p. x.

They experience intense hunger, which leads to episodes of overeating. These food binges are usually followed by self-induced vomiting, or laxative or diuretic abuse, in order to avoid the feared response of weight gain from the food eaten."

Like most ballet goers, I never imagined that anorexia was one of ballet's major occupational health and safety hazards, until I was researching my *Geo* article and stumbled across the disease. I had come to interview SAB's Lesley Clifford; and as we sat talking in her studio apartment, her friend Valerie Marshall came in, muttered a shy hello, and sat down to nibble, unenthusiastically, on tuna salad.

My grandmother would have called Valerie "a long drink of water," a tall, thin, rail of a girl. She is blond, nineteen years old, and would be the envy of any woman who knows that Gloria Vanderbilt jeans will not do for her what they do for TV models. I asked Lesley if Valerie was also a student at SAB. Lesley whispered that she had been, but had quit last year. Well, I was there to find out all about ballet, so I invited Valerie to join us and tell me why she had decided to stop dancing.

A sweet, timid girl, almost painfully unsure of herself, she was nonetheless eager to talk about her experiences. She told me she had been a scholarship student at SAB. She had come to New York from a small town in upstate New York when she was fifteen. During her first year at SAB, she lived with a family and went to high school. In her second and third years, she shared an apartment with fellow students. Before she entered SAB, she said she had never worried about her weight. Tall and very thin, hailing from a tall, thin family, why should she have worried? She did not know then that an obsession with dieting and weight was as much a part of the school's curriculum as partnering and pointe classes.

"The first year I came, I thought I could eat as much as I wanted," she recalled. "Then every single day I'd go to class and I'd hear girls say, 'Oh, I ate a yogurt and an apple, I feel so full.' All they talk about is food till finally I began to think that if they think they're fat, maybe I'm fat, too."

By the time Valerie entered her last year at SAB, dance dominated her life. She did nothing but take classes. Just as she was obsessed with dance, so was she obsessed with food. "That's all we talked about—food. If you gain weight, the teachers announce it in class. So finally you start worrying about every single thing you put into your mouth," she goes on, becoming more and more impassioned as she speaks. "Either you don't eat at all, and I mean that literally, or you decide that this is the one day you can splurge. Then you eat an ice cream and feel disgusted and guilty and you think 'Oh, I feel so fat today.' After hearing all this talk about food every single day, you become so scared of gaining weight that if you eat your heart starts beating a mile a minute. And after looking at yourself in mirrors day in and day out, you just can't see yourself anymore. I thought I looked just perfect, and I had lost fifteen pounds. I weighed ninety-five pounds. It's like a sickness," she concludes. "It really is." In the end, she left SAB because she had starved herself, not only of the strength to dance but of the desire to persevere.

What Valerie Marshall recounted sounded so startlingly like the behavior manifested by anorectics that I began to question more deeply. When I asked if other girls had similar problems, Valerie and Lesley nodded and began to list innumerable students who had been forced to leave school because they had lost twenty or thirty pounds and were unable to dance; girls who were on crazy diets and who discovered that if they vomit after they eat, or use up to seventy or eighty laxatives a week, they can remain thin.

Later, when I interviewed other students at the school, they described their own "little bouts" with anorexia. Even when I was not expecting it, the stories came pouring forth. During an interview with Carol Goza, one of SAB's ballet mothers, anorexia was the last thing on my mind—and one of the first on hers. She told me she had just asked a little fourteen-year-old to whom she rented a room to leave. Why? I asked. Because the child was a problem, she replied. What kind of problem? "Well, she was an anorectic," said Mrs. Goza. "She would eat and throw up, eat and throw up. I did everything. I would turn off the commode. I'd tell my daughter, Tracy [who herself is painfully thin], to run in and take a bath, and then I'd run in and take a bath, you know, to give the food time to digest. But she'd throw up in the garbage can or out the window. It was awful. I used to find her in tears because, she said, she was so fat. And, of course, she wasn't; she was like a skeleton." Finally, Mrs. Goza asked the parents to take the child away, and they did. She is still at SAB, living with another family, burdened with the same fears and the same means of allaying them.

This problem exists in ballet schools all over the country. "Texas has its share of anorectics," says the school's director, Clare Duncan. Several students have had to leave the school because they were too thin; and one young girl nearly died of the disease. At the San Francisco Ballet School, Richard Cammack told me they have three or four cases a year; Pennsylvania Ballet, where the standards are far less stringent than in New York, has its occasional case; and the Boston School of Ballet is famous for its excessively thin students.

Recent medical studies confirm that anorexia is a growing problem in the ballet world. Dr. Eugene Lowenkopf, a New York psychiatrist, and Dr. Lawrence M. Vincent, a physician who was once a dancer, have studied anorexia in student ballerinas in New York and contend that this sort of conduct is epidemic in the ballet world. Their data indicate that as many as 15 percent of student ballerinas in the country's most prestigious schools may suffer from a true anorexia nervosa syndrome, and many more are borderline cases.

Janice Greenburg,* a former ballet dancer who, as a psychology student at the University of Chicago, studied anorexia in ballet dancers, says that when she was a ballet student and weighed 120 pounds (at 5 feet 8 inches), she was told to lose ten pounds before she would be accepted in the Cincinnati Ballet. "I thought, to be safe, I'd lose twenty," Janice says. She lost the weight, but when she got into the company, she did not stop dieting. "I thought I still needed to lose more weight. So I kept on dieting, and working six or seven hours a day, and spending my free day swimming. I finally got down to 103, and I kept thinking, 'I have to lose three more pounds.' I didn't trust my ability as a dancer because I was just starting out. But I did trust my ability to be thinner and thinner. I worked as hard at that as I did at my dancing."

At one point a teacher told her she was getting too thin, but she disregarded her advice. When fellow company members suggested she might gain a few pounds, she also dismissed their concerns. "I was sure they were jealous," Janice recalls. Finally, like Valerie Marshall, she became so thin that she no longer had the energy to keep dancing, and after two and a half years she left the company. During the entire time only one teacher exhibited any concern about her condition. "The director never came up to me and told me, 'Okay, you can stop now, you're fine.' "

"Not eating becomes the way a dancer has of achieving some power," says Elisabetta Kintzoglou, a former anorectic dancer with Pittsburgh Ballet Theatre. Because hard work and talent are not necessarily the keys to success, dancers lose touch with reality. "Their teachers propagandize this thin-is-beautiful thing," she adds. Kintzoglou, a rail-thin dancer, speaks with the passion borne of experience. For years she has been battling the emotional and physical consequences of her training. She knows that thinness brings the dancer not beauty but fatigue, depression, illness, and self-hatred.

We do not ordinarily associate disease with ballet. First of all, the average American ballet goer is a product of a culture that believes that thin is beautiful, so the thinner you are, the more beautiful you must be. Secondly, those of us who are not privileged to go backstage or to attend ballet school never glimpse the physical reality. Lights and costumes and photographs add weight to the body and make a terribly thin dancer seem simply slender. But doctors like William Liebler know that dancers are not just thin; they are often malnourished. And that is malnourished as in Biafra, not fashionably trim as in Bloomingdale's catalogue. Even Makarova, one of the most exquisite ballerinas, seems a mere stick figure when she is viewed offstage. The arms, which appear so graceful and fluid when she dances, are so thin that they resemble the human figure as it appears on an anatomist's chart. Makarova's arms look as though they have been flayed of their skin, so that one can follow the pattern of vein, muscle, tendon, and bone underneath.

In many instances, women who fail to conform to this ideal are penalized. Michelle Benash says she suffered in her last years at ABT because she refused to punish her body. "I did enough of that when I was a young dancer," she says ruefully. Now, she maintains a weight of 105 (at 5 feet 3 inches) and is delighted that she looks like a woman. Her company did not share her pleasure. "They wouldn't use me in better roles," she said. "They said I was too fat. They like this totally asexual look. One choreographer actually had the nerve to tell me that I should put Ace bandages around my chest to flatten my breasts," she remembers with outrage.

Michelle Benash is a rebel. Most women acquiesce to these demands. Some get so thin that they risk hospitalization or even death (a dancer from a major ballet company is currently dying of anorexia in a New York hospital, and anywhere from 15 to 20 percent of all anorectics die from the disease). During the 1980 ABT season, a young soloist was beginning to worry her diet-conscious colleagues. Whispering about her in the dressing room, they nervously assessed her condition. "But there's nothing you can do with these anorectic dancers," one concluded. "If you tell them they're getting too thin, they think you're trying to fatten them up so you can steal their roles."

In this case, the soloist in question became so alarmingly frail that she was unable to dance with the company the following fall. Unable to resist what would ordinarily have been a minor illness, she was out recuperating for five months. This year, another young girl is growing alarmingly thin; and the company, after instilling her with the fear of "fat," is now busily trying to get her to gain weight.

Excessive thinness was a problem under Lucia Chase's tenure as artistic director of ABT, and it has worsened since Baryshnikov's arrival. Dancers report that both France and Baryshnikov have had "chats" with many female dancers to urge them to lose weight. "I was standing in the hall the other day," a super-thin soloist told me recently, "and Misha came up to me and started looking over my thighs. He said that he could tell I was beginning to put weight on there," she said, looking down at her thighs, which have no extra flesh on them at all. "I got very concerned. I suggested that maybe it's the new birth control pills I'm taking. He nodded, and then, as he rushed off, he shouted back, 'Why don't you try taking cold showers instead?' He wasn't kidding."

Baryshnikov seems to have no tolerance for dancers who do not fit the mold. Thus, one evening, he fired ABT corps dancer Pamela Nearhoof simply because she was too "fat." In a fit of pique, he ordered that the dancer be rejected from the company—without any notice whatsoever—because "he couldn't stand to see her onstage any-more." (The case was later taken to arbitration, and Nearhoof was reinstated.)

The fact that a dancer can be fired because she does not meet current ballet standards ought not to surprise us. Image is, understand-ably, a central concern to any performer who appears in public. But ballet's aesthetic does not value mere thinness; it values excessive thin-ness. "It's necessary to be thin if you're a dancer," says ABT principal Martine van Hamel, who is often cited as an example of an overweight dancer. "I've always had sort of a weight problem. It has definitely handicapped me at certain times, though not so much anymore. But the thin thing is being carried too far. There's thin where you can see your line and dance properly, and then there is too thin. But a lot of dancers get into it because when you tend to be fat, you think it's great to be so skinny. So much emphasis is put on being thin that it's neurotic. It gets to be a sickness, and it's crazy."

The reason for this emphasis on thinness may seem obvious. Dancers must be super thin so that they do not unduly burden their partners. But there is a difference between trimness and starvation. When we examine the rationale for the anorectic look, it does not seem to be a product of the demands of partnering. Ballerinas outside New York and ballerinas in Europe almost invariably weigh more than their New York or American counterparts, and men manage, nonetheless, to lift them off the floor.† Some of America's greatest ballerinas, like Cynthia Gregory and Martine van Hamel, are slender but not skeletal. In fact, male dancers say that it is as difficult to partner a terribly thin dancer as it is to partner a dancer who is overweight. These women are so fragile and have so little cushioning between flesh and bone that male dancers get nervous when they consider touching their brittle bodies. "It gets carried too far, it really does," says Patrick Bissell. "It's not easy to partner very thin dancers like Natasha. You partner a super-thin dancer, and they scream out all of a sudden because you pick them up. I feel like I'm hardly doing anything, and they're screaming in pain. It makes you very tentative about how you touch them."

Jeff Gribler shares this sentiment. "It's easy to bruise a woman when you partner anyway, and if she seems too frail, you don't want to

---

† While attending a gala performance given in honor of ABT's fortieth anniversary, I sat next to a New York ballet critic. During one segment of the program, Zhandra Rodriguez, a former ABT principal who dances with Ballet de Caracas, came on. A stunning woman, she had visible breasts. I commented on that to my seat mate, and she instantly replied, "She can't be an American."

grip too hard. It can be really painful for her to be partnered." Vane Vest goes even further: He finds partnering anorectic dancers positively distasteful. "I'm good at partnering," Vest says quite candidly. "That's my forte. I can make any woman look good. But these anorectic ballerinas"—he shudders—"I can't bear to touch them. I mean, you partner a woman and lift her at the waist and you want to touch something. These skinny ballerinas, it's awful. There's nothing there. How can you do a pas de deux with one of those girls? Their bones become brittle.

"Let me put it another way," Vest elaborates. "One of the most exciting experiences I've ever had is dancing with Cynthia Gregory. Cynthia is built like a woman. She's not heavy, but there is a body there. She looks like a woman, but, goddamn it, she looks like a ballerina, too. These other girls, they're hideous. And it's hideous that management condones this stuff and does nothing to stop it, because what they're saying is that thin is good and that looking normal is bad."

That is, in fact, what companies all over the country are saying. They are not pushing "the look," (as dancers refer to the emphasis on excessive thinness) as a concession to the male dancer's aching back but, as most critics and dancers agree, as a concession to one man's taste. That man is George Balanchine, America's chief arbiter of ballet taste, style, and aesthetics. It is Balanchine who has both encouraged and promoted the thin look. Describing Balanchine's third wife, the young Maria Tallchief, in *Balanchine*, his official biographer wrote that when Balanchine first knew her, Tallchief still had a little "plump flesh" on and was not "pared down to the bone yet, the way Balanchine likes his dancers."† Balanchine has often stated that he likes his dancers super thin because "he can see more that way," and the Balanchine "pinhead" has become famous in the ballet world.

† Bernard Taper, *Balanchine: A Biography* (New York: Macmillan, 1960), p. 230.

While almost everyone with whom I spoke credits Balanchine with the anorectic look, no one man can dictate taste if his taste does not coincide with that of the culture in which he lives and works. Balanchine's predilection would not have been accepted if he lived in a culture that values feminine definition. But Balanchine lives in America, where society is obsessed with thinness.

Women who idealize thinness and who, themselves, have trouble attaining their ideal tend to view the world through a prism of envy. Hollow cheekbones look like classic distinction; absence of breasts and hips becomes the hallmark of a stunning figure; gauntness becomes beautiful. We lose the ability to understand that there is such a thing as being too thin—until we are confronted with a young woman who slips over the border between dieting and death.

Despite its distortions, the Balanchinian aesthetic has become the norm in ballet; it is not an anomaly in a culture in which men define standards of female beauty. The men who regulate women's images would argue, as does Balanchine, that they are merely servants of the female ideal. In fact, throughout history, women have distorted their bodies to conform to particular ideals of feminine beauty. In China, where women's feet were supposed to be small and dainty, women were literally crippled in an attempt to defy nature. In nineteenth-century Europe and America, where waists were supposed to be small, women were trussed and corseted. If a woman's breasts were supposed to be flat, she was bound and bandaged despite the fact that this created an epidemic of breast cancer.

Some observers would argue that in ballet, as in the world of fashion, the predominance of male homosexuals is the cause of the disparagement of a female aesthetic. Says Robin Schimel, a former dancer, "Homosexuality is very strong in the ballet world, and as a female dancer you get a lot of hostility from men. It's subtle and peculiar. The hostility isn't necessarily directly expressed. It's indirect. They don't like you. You get the message that they don't like you because they don't like the features that make you a woman. You aren't faced with directly hostile comments, but when a director forces you to look so thin that you lose all female definition, when in his eyes you become more beautiful the less you look like a woman, that tells you something."

It is an uncontested fact that most choreographers and company directors are men, and that the bulk of them are gay. Even if they claim to "love women," homosexuals often have very ambivalent feelings about them. And a dislike of the normal female form might easily lead to the desire to distort it, ostensibly in pursuit of aesthetic goals.

This explanation, which may not sit well in the gay community, is open to debate, but it certainly cannot be easily dismissed. What seems to be incontrovertible is the fact that the Balanchinian aesthetic, whether it be adopted by homosexuals or heterosexuals, men or women, is punitive and destructive. It is, finally, a misogynist aesthetic. You cannot protest that you love women, that they are your muse, your ideal, your very soul, when once they are under your control you maim and sometimes destroy their bodies.

Apologists for the super-thin aesthetic insist that by encouraging its adoption, choreographers like Balanchine have simply improved on nature. In *The New Republic*, critic Richard Poirier lauds Balanchine because he is "the most heterosexually vibrant of choreographers," and is "astonishingly intuitive about the resources locked into the bodies of particular dancers, especially the American woman whose [long-limbed] shape pleased him from the beginning."†

Unfortunately, the narrow-hipped, long-limbed City Ballet dancer is an artificial creation. "If you take a girl at twelve years of age and keep her below about 17 percent body fat," Dr. Vincent explains, "she won't menstruate. Puberty is arrested, her hypothalamic function is suppressed, and she has low estrogen levels. Estrogen, of course, affects breast and hip development. These girls go into a

† Richard Poirier, "The American Genius of George Balanchine," *The New Republic*, October 11, 1980, p. 28.

puberty holding-pattern. The claims of ballet mistresses that they can pick out a future ballet body are false; they're simply selecting late developers and, with the help of poor nutrition, keeping them that way. It's almost as if ballet had created a new species of woman: low estrogen and androgynous."

The quest for the look takes its toll on the body—and on the mind—in countless ways. Self-imposed starvation, like real starvation, leads to abnormalities in thyroid function and to hormonal imbalance; hypothermia, or loss in body temperature, which makes one extremely sensitive to cold; and hypotension, or low blood pressure. Anorectics become amenorrheic, which means that they do not get their periods. Many girls do eventually menstruate once they begin to eat normally, but many will be permanently sterile. Anorectics are also more susceptible to leukopenia, or a drop in the number of white blood cells, which lowers the body's resistance to infection. A decrease in the number of red blood cells produced in the bone, which also lowers resistance to infection and simultaneously retards the healing process, is also associated with anorexia. Edema, swelling due to fluids pooling in the body, and bradycardia, a reduction in the heart beat, also occur. Moreover, in a growing child, inadequate nutrition can affect myelination of nerve fibers, the process that allows impulses to speed through the nervous system. When myelination is inhibited, the complexity and efficiency of the normal nervous system is significantly reduced.

Because a body deprived of food begins to eat itself—first consuming fat reserves and then going on to eat its own muscles—one of anorexia's lesser-known side effects is a condition of drying, cracking, and bleeding of the palms of the hands and soles of the feet. On both hands and feet, fat glands excrete oil. When the starving body begins to feed upon itself, these fatty reserves are permanently depleted.

Lack of awareness of the medical consequences of anorexia often leads dancers to romanticize some very unromantic symptoms. The great Russian ballerina Anna Pavlova was known for her legendary dedication to the ballet. Accounts regale us with tales of a dancer who was so committed to her art that she continued to dance despite her bleeding feet. She was also said to have been sparrow thin—a waif, ethereal as a cloud. Because so few in the dance world, both then and now, fully understand the hazards of anorexia, they do not stop to consider that Pavlova's bleeding feet may have had more to do with excessive thinness than extraordinary dedication.

Weight control by vomiting or laxative and diuretic abuse often induces another series of physical complaints. The stomach acid churned up by repeated vomiting eats away at the tooth enamel and can cause serious dental problems, as well as a chronic sore throat and esophagitis. Pressure on the esophagus can lead to a tear or rupture, and vomiters may also have chronically infected salivary glands. Vomiting and abuse of laxatives and diuretics also change the body's balance of essential minerals. Anorectics or bulimics may be hypo-kalemic, which means that they have drained their body's reserves of potassium, a mineral that is essential to muscle and heart functions. The high mortality rate among anorectics is often a result of com-promised coronary functioning due to potassium depletion.

Needless to say, women who suffer from any or all of these prob-lems are not in optimum physical shape, yet they are trying to sustain the stress of dance. They are thus far more injury-prone than are well-nourished dancers. "The whole basis of the physical fitness of a dancer is good nutrition," Dr. Liebler states emphatically. "If a person doesn't eat the correct number of properly balanced meals, he or she will not have the ability to cope with this tremendous demand on the body. Ballet puts great catabolic stress on the body. In other words, it's constantly tearing the body down; and if you don't build the body up at the same time, you are wide open to injury."

It is hard to accurately gauge the extent of the anorectic dancer's physical problems. Few medical studies correlate the malnutritive aspects of the disease with the bone, joint, or muscle problems so common among dancers. Studies that focus on anorexia tend to emphasize the psychological dimensions of the problem and the hormonal consequences. These studies do not correlate profession—like dancing or modeling—with the frequency of the disease. Nor do orthopedic studies of dancers, like the one by Dr. Liebler, correlate anorexia, or severe weight loss, with frequency of injury. No study seems to address dancers' overriding problem: healing. Yet it is crucial to the dancers' welfare to document how, like any form of malnutrition, anorexia retards the healing of the many injuries that dancers sustain in the course of their careers.

Reading such a vast list of medical symptoms, one wonders how dancers manage to function. Deprived of necessary nutrients, doctors explain, dancers feed on sheer will and off their own fat and muscle tissue. "It's because these women are such superb athletes that they can do what they do," says Dr. Vincent. "They manage to keep working in spite of what they do to themselves, not because of it. And they can continue working because the human body is such an extraordinary machine: It makes the necessary adaptations to starvation. Instead of eating working muscles, the body will take energy stores from muscles that aren't working. So if someone who is protein-deficient is dancing, the body won't eat muscle on the legs but on the arms and clavicles. When you see these dancers with very muscular legs, arms like toothpicks, pronounced clavicles, and ribs showing through, this is actually the body's adaptation to starvation."

Just as anorexia stunts and cripples the body, so it affects the mind. Women who try to starve themselves to conform to an idealized body image have complex emotional problems that are very hard to treat. Fearful that someone will uncover their dirty secret, they isolate themselves and become increasingly lonely and withdrawn. Many of them have trouble forming relationships, particularly romantic ones. Their disease is, in effect, a denial of sexuality. Says Dr. Lowenkopf,

"They don't learn, as they grow up, to accept their sexuality and integrate sexual feelings into normal functioning. They don't grow up; they want to remain children."

The Balanchinian aesthetic has not only altered dancers' visions of themselves, it has clouded the vision of the average ballet goer. Audiences who have been trained, by their culture and by the ballet world, to think that thin is beautiful begin to scorn any dancer who is not a pinhead. Just as they expect to applaud increasing feats of technical virtuosity that may compromise the male dancer's health, so they begin to demand feats of dietetic virtuosity that jeopardize women's psyches and bodies.

And most telling, perhaps, the pinhead ideal has been endorsed by the dancers' mothers. One day, as I am observing a class at Robert Denvers's studio, I meet Carol Goza waiting for her daughter, Tracy, to finish class. We pass the time comparing notes about a performance of *Swan Lake* we both attended the previous night. I thought the ABT production, with Cynthia Gregory dancing a stunning Odette/Odile, extraordinary. Mrs. Goza liked the production well enough and thought Gregory's technique an exercise in perfection. Nonetheless, she found the ballerina's performance flawed. Why? I wonder. "She's too heavy," Mrs. Goza replies without hesitation. "She's too matronly. She just doesn't look like a ballerina."

Anorexia is clearly one of the most serious problems the ballet world faces, yet it is one very few companies or schools openly acknowledge or cope with effectively. When I was working on my *Geo* article, a conversation with the photographer assigned to the piece brought home just how closed the ballet world can be. A man who had worked with Balanchine many times, he was very familiar with all of ballet's problems. When I suggested that he might want to take some pictures of "skinny" dancers, he replied instantly, "Oh, you mean the anorectics." Yes, I answered and mentioned the names of several distressingly thin dancers. "Listen," he said after a few moments. "I don't want to offend Balanchine or Baryshnikov. You'll do this story and split, but I have to live in this world."

His attitude mirrors that of many people in the ballet world. But not all.

Clare Duncan is far more concerned than most ballet administrators about anorectic dancers. "I'm not a trained psychiatrist," Duncan says adamantly. "But I won't let them in class. Absolutely not. I speak to their parents. I put them on the weighing machine and say, 'If you don't put on a pound by next week, you can't come to class.' This is the only way I found that I can handle it. That," Duncan adds, "and helping kids get therapeutic advice."

Richard Cammack readily admits that anorexia is on the increase in his school. Cammack, who says he tries to create a healthy environment for his dancers, is, in fact, more humane than many New York teachers. But not quite humane enough. The school and company, he says, are both "very body-oriented and weight-oriented. But," he adds, "we've loosened up somewhat because we found our percentage of anorectics growing in the top classes." To him, "loosening up" means weighing kids six times a year rather than nine times a year. It also means telling super-thin kids to gain weight, but waiting as long as a year to see if they do.

Unfortunately, you cannot cure anorexia by waiting and watching; you cannot even begin to prevent an incipient epidemic of anorexia unless you significantly decrease the emphasis on weight. The worst offenders—New York companies and schools—seem to resist any attempt to deal aggressively with the problem. At the School of American Ballet, administrators often identify the problem when it is too late; they intervene (often by sending the dancer home) only when a dancer becomes almost skeletal.

Female ballet dancers, states Dr. Lowenkopf, are an "at-risk population." They are women who need help. Physicians speculate that their conduct is, like any form of extreme behavior, an attempt to call attention, indirectly, to a problem they cannot define or face. Schools and companies, however, have refused to heed this cry for help.

When Dr. Vincent approached Lincoln Kirstein with his physical and psychological findings, Kirstein dismissed him. "So they don't get their periods," Kirstein said. "So what?" "When we tried to discuss these problems with girls in New York companies," Lowenkopf said, "we were rebuffed. The School of American Ballet has gotten a lot of press about being America's finest, most elite school," Lowenkopf continues. "But if you really look at it, you're impressed by their irresponsibility. There are no child labor laws that regulate what they do with dancers when they're in a company. They have no health forms that follow their physical development. If you play YMCA ball or intramural ball, they have health forms. But at SAB there's nothing. And they justify it all in the name of art."

"I think the schools and companies recognize that dancers have serious emotional problems," says Dr. Vivian Diller, "and they're afraid because those problems seem so overwhelming. That's why I felt having a psychologist to consult would help."

Dr. Diller's idea of having a psychologist on call is by no means revolutionary. It is the norm in most schools, universities, and corporations. The idea, however, was too controversial for SAB or NYCB to handle. "Betty Cage, General Manager of City Ballet, told me that they recognized that my findings were accurate. Nonetheless, they felt that I had exaggerated the gravity of the situation," Dr. Diller says. "They said the company and the school were one big happy family. The dancers are happy, and if they aren't, they come to the administration with their problems. They seemed to feel that if the dancers were dancing, they were okay; and if they weren't okay, they shouldn't be dancing."

Dr. Diller was not surprised at this response. "Schools and companies traditionally view dancers as uncomplicated beings," she explains. "They're artists, not people; they are tools for Mr. Balanchine. Like an anorectic's family, the school tends to want to hide the problem, to make believe it's not there." And again like an anorectic's family, they refuse to confront the facts until the child is in desperate straits. "The difference between an anorectic's family and the ballet world," Dr. Diller points out, "is that in a real family, you can't just get rid of the problem child; in the ballet world, you can always ship the child back home, or fire the dancer and then replace her with another."

In the modern world, dancers must adapt to heavy performance loads, to choreography that depends on athletic pyrotechnics, and to a new vogue for youth and excessive thinness. Their bodies are no longer treated like precious instruments, repositories where ballet's great treasures are stored. Instead, they become mere machines— machines their companies do not properly service and which they regard with an odd mixture of anxiety and disrespect.

By refusing to care for their bodies, dancers aggravate their injuries. A strain or sprain or rupture is the inevitable consequence of such general mistreatment. To make matters worse, dancers do not let their injuries heal; and when they dance on injuries, these injuries persist even longer. A strain or sprain that might have taken two weeks to heal takes twice as long to mend if it is not properly treated. And the longer the healing process takes, the more anxious the dancer becomes. So he pushes himself to return to work sooner than he should have. After a month or two, the injury flares up again; this time it is even more serious, requiring even more healing time. The dancer, now out for six weeks instead of two, grows even more panicked. Once again he begins performing, until finally the injury becomes so painful that it requires surgical intervention. Now, instead of taking a month off, the dancer is told he will have to take it easy for a year. To the ambitious young man or woman, this seems an eternity. Once again the dancer starts performing full out sooner than is safe. And then the damage is complete. The tendon snaps one time too many, the knee disintegrates, the joints become swollen, crippled, and stiff with arthritis. The pain can no longer be ignored. The career the dancer danced to protect has now ended because he failed to protect the body upon which that career had depended.

It is opening night here in Houston, and the curtain has just come down on the last of four one-act ballets. A janitor begins to cross the back of the stage, pushing a huge broom over the resin-covered floor. Stagehands clear the props, and company dancers return to their dressing rooms to prepare for an after-opening-night party. Andrea Vodenhal is in no hurry to leave the theater. Dressed in a white spandex leotard and tights decorated with intertwined coils of multicolored leaves, she stands listening intently to British choreographer Ronald Hynd. Tonight was the premiere of his new ballet, *The Four Seasons*, to Vivaldi's score. The dancer and choreographer immediately set about dissecting the evening's performance. Hynd details refinements, while Vodenhal, almost diffident in her attentiveness, nods eagerly.

Hynd's ballet was not the only one she danced in this evening. In the second of the four ballets presented, she played the mother in modern choreographer Richard Kuch's *The Brood*, based on Brecht's *Mother Courage*. In this stark, wrenching ballet, Vodenhal was covered in rags, hardly recognizable as she danced to the cacophonous music that accompanied the drama of death and destruction, war and loss. The piece required a far greater emotional range than is called for in most classical ballets, which is perhaps why the forty-two-year-old ballerina was one of the few Houston dancers who was both capable of immersing herself in a new technique and who would accept this assignment. (Many ballet dancers are unwilling to venture into modern techniques and themes.) This past year, Vodenhal has become all too familiar with death and loss.

In just two short years, Andrea Vodenhal has lost two of the people who provided her with the moorings of her life. After a sixteen-month illness, her mother recently died of cancer. The woman who had brought her to ballet was more than a mother; she was also coach, masseuse, adviser, supporter, and companion. As if that were not enough to cope with, Vodenhal and her dancer-husband have just divorced. Reflecting on her inability to end an unhappy marriage earlier, she places part of the blame for her inaction on her ability to form only a very few intense relationships and to depend on others rather than herself. Her husband was one of those people she feared she could not do without.

After more than twenty years as a dancer, Vodenhal has climbed ballet's ladder of success to the top. She is one of Houston's best-known and most respected ballerinas, and she has danced principal roles in almost all the major ballets. One would think that a woman who has achieved so much would have more confidence in her ability to stand on her own. But ballet, as we have seen, is not a career that encourages independence. Marrying a dancer—her partner—made things worse, says Vodenhal. Rather than moving out into the world with someone who had different interests, she incorporated her marriage into ballet.

Nothing in her emotional and professional training has taught her about the outside world, yet now all the problems that come with a ballet career are about to catch up with her. Unable to sustain the strains of the profession much longer, she will soon have to retire. All dancers, of course, fear this moment. But Andrea Vodenhal has actually experienced it: She knows what she will be losing and how little she will have to gain.

When she was thirty-two, she left the world of dance. After ten years with Ballet Russe and National Ballet of Washington, she simply became disgusted with seeing friends hurt because they did not have the talent for ballet politics, with the personal disappointment of being passed over for roles, with the fatigue and the pressure. For nine months, she and her dancer-husband taught ballet in Puerto Rico, where they staged ballets and danced with the Ballet de San Juan. Then her husband was offered a job teaching in Vodenhal's hometown, and the two returned to Houston.

Once home, Vodenhal discovered that a dancer's talents are useful only onstage. When she moved off, she found that she needed marketable skills to earn a living. Vodenhal had none. Fortunately, her brothers owned a machine and welding company; and her mother, then in her early seventies, ran its office. Vodenhal learned basic bookkeeping skills with her mother's help, and then was able to relieve her mother three days a week.

She punched in at nine, quit at five, and moved about in a predictable world of accounts payable and receivable, where morning coffee breaks, lunch, and quitting time were the only things to look forward to. "It was *horrendous*," the thin, tomboyish ballerina says emphatically, as if underlining the word with her whole being. "All I did was sit. I just couldn't take it. I ended up more exhausted at the end of the day than if I'd been rehearsing for ten hours. I just didn't like being in a rut, which is where I was."

Compared to this, ballet seemed a career filled with challenge and endless promise, the company a community of people whose camaraderie she began to miss. "Even when everyone is tired and uptight," she comments, "it is still like being part of a big family. You can go off with different groups, do all kinds of things, play poker, go to the movies. We get very close."

Like many dancers who leave when they are still young, Vodenhal was becoming bitter and frustrated. Five years after she had been away from dance, Houston Ballet offered her a job, and she began to dance again.

When I talked with her in the fall of 1980, she was forty-two, and she knew her dancing career would soon be over for good. "I want to stop before it gets uncomfortable for people to watch me," she says. "There are some ballerinas who are terrible to watch. Their backs are gone; they can't jump. There are a few roles they can do, but not many. I hope someone will have the good sense to tell me when that time comes."

Although she worries about not embarrassing herself onstage, Vodenhal, like so many dancers, has not prepared for what she will do when she must live offstage, outside the theater. Despite the fact that she has already tasted the boredom and loneliness of the outside world, she has done nothing to secure a more exciting and fulfilling professional future. Instead, she has pushed thoughts of retirement out of her mind, dancing through them as she would dance through an injury. Considering the future, she lists a series of potential professions but rejects each in turn. Teaching or coaching is out, she says. Having done a bit of both, she does not feel temperamentally suited to either. "I love coaching roles that I've danced, but I find teaching very frustrating," says Vodenhal. "Perhaps it's because I've never taught a group of students long enough to see their progress. But it just seems such a slow process. You're giving and giving and giving, and you don't see any change for a long time. And then, you can also get into a rut going over the same thing in class after class. I just don't think it's for me."

Most people assume that retirement should not pose problems for dancers, since they can always turn to teaching. But teaching requires very particular skills and a very particular sensibility. When a dancer performs, she is immediately rewarded with the audience's appreciative applause for her virtuoso display. Teachers, on the other hand, stand on the sidelines, where their reward is the pleasure they take in their students' accomplishments. A dancer like Vodenhal must find another profession. And that will not be easy.

"I don't have any college at all," she says ruefully. "I keep thinking that every summer I'll do some college, at least on correspondence, but I never get round to it." Her face clouds with confusion, and she stops for a moment to consider the image she presents. "Isn't it horrible?" she asks suddenly. "Here I am at forty-two, and I haven't the foggiest idea what I want to do."

Andrea Vodenhal is a principal dancer. She has reached, in a regional troop, the pinnacle of professional success. Yet her response to retirement is typical of the majority of dancers I talked with. The way most dancers cope with their anxiety about retirement is to do what Vodenhal has done: not deal with it at all.

To anyone who has spent a lifetime working at something he loves, forced retirement is a dreaded event. Far from being a new beginning, it merely ushers in a series of losses: loss of income, of workplace community, and, most importantly, loss of identity. But even the most dedicated workaholic in another field probably has an easier time facing retirement than does a ballet dancer.

The average professional simply does not lead such a uni-dimensional life. She may eat and drink and breathe her profession, but she nevertheless has other relationships—family, lovers—and contact with the world. And from a successful career she can garner a sense of her own autonomy and self-esteem.

Most men and women who retire at sixty-five live, for example, in a complex matrix of professional, community, and familial relationships. With their spouses they have constructed a social life that steers them out of the narrow berth of their profession into the community. Even if they are not active in church, community, or politics, their work is proof of adulthood; it confers professional and social status, and it usually affords some financial cushion in the form of a retirement or pension plan, which they can rely on in their later years.

Compare this to what dancers experience when they quit. When most people are coming into their own, in their early thirties or forties, dancers lose their work and with it their sense of self. Few have families of their own; some have even postponed any romantic attachments whatsoever; and most have had limited time to form friendships outside of dance. When they lose their dancing community —which they inevitably do if they do not remain within the dance world as teachers or coaches—they lose their only social network. If they want to move from ballet into another professional career, they must complete four years of college before they can apply to graduate schools. This means that dancers who want to become nurses, doctors, lawyers, or architects will not have completed the initial training until they are in their late thirties or mid-forties. If they choose careers in a related art, like acting, they will still have to make up for their lack of training; and they will have to start at the bottom in a profession that is as overcrowded and as ruthlessly competitive as dance.

And how will dancers finance such a career change? Ballet is the football of the arts. Yet football players, who must also retire when they are young, earn twice or three times as much as dancers. Although the average player will play for only 4.2 years, he will make $83,000 a year. During the five months he has between seasons, he may set up a part-time business to which he will return when he stops playing. And, of course, most players have had a college education.

Few dancers, except the most highly paid principals, amass any savings. They have spent thousands of dollars learning their craft; yet when they retire, they find that their skills are nontransferable. Coming from upper-middle-class families who ordinarily would have sent them to college and perhaps even graduate school, they also have very high career expectations. But once their ballet careers are over, they can look forward to the kind of job Andrea Vodenhal took when she retired. After a life in the public eye, where people idolized and respected their talents, dancers find it difficult to adjust to the prospect of becoming a clerk, secretary, or salesperson.

No one knows for certain when the majority of dancers actually do retire, since no one has compiled official statistics about ballet dancers. Dr. Liebler observes dryly that ballet dancers are "like bag ladies: Suddenly they appear out of nowhere, and then, just as suddenly, they disappear, and no one knows where they've gone to." Some dancers, like Nureyev or Fonteyn, may be able to dance until they are quite old: Audiences attracted by their fame will forgive their declining technique, and choreographers will tailor roles to suit their dwindling abilities.

Most dancers are not so indulged. The majority are forced to quit far earlier. Their bodies simply give out, and either they suffer a serious injury or they lose the stamina they once had. "I think if I quit," says twenty-six-year-old Lisa de Ribere, "it will be because of injuries. Someday I just won't be able to take it anymore. It will be too painful, and it won't be worth it." Others realize that they will never be the stars they had dreamed of being when they were younger. Discouraged and washed up by age twenty-five or twenty-eight, they have run out of patience.

No written code or mandatory retirement age—only a choreographer's caprice—determines when a dancer must retire. Today, dancers are forced out of their companies at an even earlier age to make room for younger dancers, who are now in vogue. A dancer who thought she would be able to dance with her company until she was in her late thirties is abruptly informed that she is "too old." Like a castoff lover, she is replaced with a blushing ingénue, who is, conveniently, far more grateful for the opportunity to dance and thus far more tractable. At ABT, Amy Blaisdell and Hilda Morales, two company veterans, were recently fired because they had had the misfortune to grow older. Blaisdell is thirty-seven; Morales is thirty-five.

A corps dancer who had been with the company for seventeen years, Amy Blaisdell told me several years ago that she was certain ABT would repay her unstinting loyalty. Not one of the company's stellar lights, she nonetheless had been content to stay in the corps because she knew she did not have the ambition to move ahead. Though she had never been a star, or even a soloist, Blaisdell still had a great deal to offer ABT. Because over the years she had become a walking archive of the ABT repertoire, the company was getting two for the price of one: a dancer and a supplementary coach who could help younger dancers learn their roles.

Blaisdell knew she would have to retire eventually, but she trusted ABT to ease her out gently. Her trust was misplaced. When Baryshnikov decided to change the ABT image, Blaisdell was given notice. After sixteen years of service, she was denied severance pay and was not allowed to stay on as a temporary ballet mistress until she could find other work. Referred to in jest by ABT executive director Herman Krawitz as "our dear departed," she became a kind of bad administrative joke.

Hilda Morales is another dancer who feels she was cheated of several more good dancing years with ABT because of Baryshnikov's youth fetish. In the winter of 1981, Charles France, like a doctor hinting that a patient might have a terminal disease, informed her that, at thirty-four, she was too old to dance some of her "cute" roles, and suggested that they discuss "more meaty" ones.

Throughout the winter and spring seasons, however, no such discussions took place. When Morales returned to work the following fall, the silence continued, but it had taken on an ominous cast. On the ABT's fall tour, Morales learned that she had been divested of her traditional roles, and she spent her days sitting in hotel rooms doing nothing. Instead of explaining their plans for her and allowing her to make plans of her own, the company decided, it seemed, on a campaign of slights and innuendo. Finally, when ABT returned to New

York, Morales asked to have her promised talk with Baryshnikov. Armed with suggestions about suitable parts she might dance, Morales came to the interview. But Baryshnikov was not interested in discussing her dancing. Her urged her to consider accepting work as a ballet mistress with the company. "You will be doing less and less," he told her, adding that she could help him train the young fifteen- and sixteen-year-old dancers he had hired to replace older dancers. She insisted she was not ready to retire but agreed to ease herself into a ballet mistress position. "I said okay," Morales recalls, "because I needed a job. I wanted to stay with the company, so I thought I'd just see what happened."

What happened was hardly what she expected. Rather than help her make a smooth transition to ballet mistress work, the company thrust unfamiliar ballets upon her. "It was incredible!" Morales says. "And what's more, Misha had fifteen-year-olds who were supposed to be the ones who would carry the company, but the strain was too much for them and they were always out. So they'd ask me to dance. I was supposed to be too old to dance, but when they were in trouble they didn't hesitate to call me."

By January 1982, the hints had turned to hostility. "I was in Miami, and Misha began to ignore me. The man just wouldn't look me in the eyes. It was then that I understood what was going on. Finally, on Friday, February 19, at three-thirty in the afternoon—how could I forget that day?—Misha called me into his dressing room and bluntly said, 'There's a time in every dancer's career when she must quit dancing. I don't think you belong in my theater anymore.' I was listening to all this, and I just said, 'Misha, why don't you just come out and say you're firing me?' "

And that was that. There was no more talk about meaty parts or position as ballet mistress. After nine years with the company (just one year before she would have qualified for a pension), Morales was dismissed because she was thirty-five years old. She feels ABT's conduct was both callous and inexcusable, and she has filed a suit against the company alleging age discrimination.

Morales believes that directors who are pushing youth—extreme youth, that is—do so because they cannot deal with the fact that they themselves are getting older. "Misha feels old," she says. "I think he's petrified of what he's going to do when he gets older. And he imposes how he feels on everyone else. Of course there comes a time when every dancer must quit. But it's getting ridiculous today. He's setting a trend for dance in America that's very unhealthy."

After months of anxiety, Morales has bounced back. She is now planning a program of dance lectures to alert young dancers to the hazards of their profession, and she has been offered guest slots in companies all over the world. Other dancers, however, may not be so fortunate. Indeed, the way many companies choose to deal with retiring dancers exacerbates an already difficult situation. In most professions, and in dance in many European countries, a mandatory retirement age is set, and the worker or dancer knows when he or she will have to leave. In America, no rules govern retirement in the ballet profession, so dancers can never fully prepare for it. One dancer may discover that she is too old at twenty-eight, while another dancer may not be considered too old even though she is nearing forty. Given such inconsistencies, retirement always comes as a shock. Even in ending their careers, dancers are once again reduced to the status of children who wait and hope, dependent on the good will of their parents, unable to act as adults to direct the course of their lives.

The major problem the ex-dancer faces with retirement is how to make a living. The most successful resolution of this dilemma is usually a career that connects the dancer to the ballet world. Superstars often become choreographers or artistic directors, or they form their own companies. Although men have considerable difficulty adjusting to retirement, the ballet world seems to afford them greater opportunities to successfully cope with retirement than it does women. Because there are fewer men in ballet, there is less competition among them for the available jobs. They are also in a better position to get work as choreographers and artistic directors. Ballet boards simply favor men when they choose a new artistic director for an established company or when they form a new company. There are a few notable exceptions, among them Maria Tallchief at Chicago City Ballet and Violette Verdy at Boston Ballet.

Almost all the major ballet choreographers are men, at least in part because company directors do not tend to encourage women to develop choreographic skills. At New York City Ballet, Balanchine distinctly frowns upon women choreographers. "If you want to choreograph," says a former City Ballet dancer, "you won't get any help from him. He believes that women should provide the inspiration that triggers men's creativity. But he does not believe that women should develop their own creative choreographic talents, and he's quite explicit about his feelings on the subject." Women who have displayed such talent have been forced to go elsewhere to cultivate it. Linda Rodriguez, former administrative assistant to City Ballet, left the company when Balanchine, who had allowed her to choreograph a ballet for SAB students, suddenly withdrew them from rehearsals.

Some former soloists and corps dancers remain in their old companies as ballet masters or mistresses, coaches, *régisseurs*, or dance notators. But there are, in any given company, far more candidates for those positions than there are openings.

Dancers like Amy Blaisdell or Hilda Morales, who cannot secure positions with their old companies, often open their own school. But starting a school is like starting any business enterprise. Capital is required to buy, rent, or refurbish studio space, as well as to cover expenses. At the same time, great amounts of energy are needed to attract and build up a clientele.

Another alternative is teaching in smaller ballet schools or professional academies. Teaching, however, like dancing itself, is a highly competitive field, and there are not enough schools to accommodate all the dancers who retire each year. Even if a dancer finds a teaching position—say, at an existing studio—her income is by no means guaranteed. At large New York studios, for example, teachers are assigned classes if they are popular with students. Until their names are known and they are in demand, they may teach only one or two classes a week. So the novice may make as little as $5000 a year. For many dancers, teaching is not an option, because they have sustained too many injuries; for Michelle Benash teaching is extremely stressful.

What happens to those dancers who do not remain in the world of ballet? While some women marry, have children, and stay at home, most are too accustomed to being active not to pursue a vocation of some kind. Among both men and women, those who fare best are the ones who, having confronted the inevitability of retirement, have prepared for a second career.

Robert Maiorano is one of the few dancers who has planned for his future. He began dancing at SAB when he was eight, and he is now a City Ballet soloist. He probably has two or three more years of dancing left. But Maiorano, whose dark good looks remind me of Al Pacino, will not be one of those dancers who, fearful of the end, waits to be dragged offstage. He has recently embarked upon another career, that of writer. He has successfully published a ballet book for children, *Worlds Apart: The Autobiography of a Dancer from Brooklyn.* He is now at work on both a novel and a book of nonfiction, *A View of Balanchine.*

Robert, Rachel, and I meet in a Broadway café one night to talk after a rehearsal. He says he has had no regrets about his career. Since his mother first took him to ballet classes, over twenty years ago, he has loved dance. "It's a great life, very exciting," he asserts. He began to dance, and suddenly a career in dance became his only goal.

In his mid-twenties Maiorano reached what he considers the dancer's "danger point." "When you're fifteen, your whole life is built around dance. Later you start questioning yourself." For him, this began when he was twenty-five. He had gone to Russia with City Ballet, and one night at a party, he injured himself doing Russian folk dances. Depressed and withdrawn, he discovered how dispensable dancers really are. "For about two years I was pretty much out of the picture, and other people got their turn," he remembers. "It's not that you're completely forgotten; it's just that you're not needed."

During this enforced respite, he began to think about his life. "They were not nice thoughts," he says bluntly. "I came to the conclusion that I wasn't going to be as good as I thought I would be. I began to wonder what was wrong with me, why was I doing this. And when you start questioning your performance, you can't perform. So you begin to wonder if you're here because you love it or because you're just afraid to go into the outside world and face the abyss."

Once he realized he was going to have to live in that world after his dancing was over, Maiorano began to explore life outside the theater. While recovering from his injury, he began to write. First he jotted down his thoughts, and then he began to compose stories. When he went back to the company, he kept on writing. He also kept on injuring himself. But as he worked harder at his new vocation, he gained a sense of himself and of his own potential. "Writing is something I started on my own." Writing taught Maiorano that there was a world outside ballet, a world in which he could function quite successfully.

Maiorano is still dancing, but unlike most of the people with whom he performs, he is also prepared to glide quite gracefully into another profession when he does have to retire from ballet. He says that he has lost the childlike devotion he used to have; he no longer refuses to question either the system or the self. He may have lost his "100 percent dedication" to the art, but he is proof that one can be a dancer and cultivate other interests, other loves; he is proof that life after dance does not have to be a series of losses, that it can be a series of unexpected gains.

Maiorano came to writing through what appears now to have been a fortuitous accident: an injury that literally forced him to take stock of himself and his options. David Coll, a thirty-five-year-old former ABT soloist, planned his retirement more deliberately. Short, dapper, and blond, he meets me in the fall of 1981 dressed in a neat, tailored business suit to usher me around his jewelry store in a pleasant, hilly section of Oakland, California. Since his retirement, Coll and his wife, another former dancer, have purchased the Coll family business. To go from dancing to selling watches and diamonds may seem an unusual transition, but Coll knew for many years that this is what he would do when his dancing career ended.

He tells me that what he wanted was to leave ballet while he was ahead. "I wanted to have a full career. I wanted to do the parts I had always wanted to do so I wouldn't have second thoughts. When I felt that I had gotten what I wanted out of my career, I left." To ensure easy passage from one stage in his life to another, he read up on gemology, and spent whatever spare time he had with his wife and young son. Having a family helped smooth out the rough edges of his imminent retirement. Indeed, by the time he was ready to leave, he had already begun to weary of both life in New York and a touring schedule that prevented him from spending as much time with his family as he wanted. Because he paid attention to timing offstage, as well as on, Coll says, he did not regret leaving ballet: His retirement marked a real closure.

Retirement from the "family of ballet" does not often enable dancers to go on and lead independent lives. Instead, they are forced to turn to their real families, to finance a college education, buy a business, or pay rent on studio space.

Solange MacArthur received a great deal of financial and emotional support from her parents when she finally left ABT. Like Maiorano and Coll, MacArthur had been considering leaving ballet for some time; in fact, she says, she had never accepted ballet's military-like discipline and wished to leave ever since she began dancing.

The summer before the 1979 ABT lockout, she took a philosophy course at The New School in New York. Not only did she enjoy the class, but she was stunned to learn that a professor wanted her to assist him in preparations for a book he was writing. "I thought, 'Who, me? I'm just a dumb dancer.' But I jumped at the chance." She read books he did not have time to read and alerted him to subjects of importance. His response encouraged her to continue studying during the ABT lockout the following fall. In between stints on the picket line, she took a chemistry course and got an A. "That really opened my eyes," she says, "because until then I'd thought I could never do well in school."

After the lockout, when the company returned to work, MacArthur asked for a leave. "I thought I'd better strike while the iron was hot, before I got all excited about being onstage again and got sucked back in." Even though she was primed for escape, the prospect of retiring was unsettling. All through her last days at work, she cried and spent hours questioning the wisdom of her decision. The sobering vision of her future as a thirty-five-year-old ex-corps dancer fortified her resolve.

What concerned her, as she contemplated going out into the non-ballet world, was the loss of her "celebrity status." "I was worried my family wouldn't like me anymore. My brothers loved to tell their friends that their sister was a dancer. My mother loved to tell her friends that I danced with ABT. My family loved to come and watch me perform when I was in Chicago. Strangers who know nothing about ballet don't know how boring and monotonous it is. They think it's exotic being a dancer. So you're afraid that if you quit, you'll be nothing."

Quitting, MacArthur feared, would mean going backward, not forward. Back to nothingness, to the kid she remembered being in high school when she was neither a swan nor a sylph but a mousey girl with no self-confidence. Without the glamour of ballet, what would she have to offer? "I thought I would disappoint any boyfriend who knew me as a ballet dancer. If I quit, I felt they wouldn't be interested in me, because the thing that made me appealing would no longer be there." MacArthur had seen friends disappointed by men who were dazzled by the dancer, not the person. "One woman in the company was married to a man who was totally enamoured of her as a ballet dancer. He came to all the performances, and bravoed and supported her. But when she decided to quit, he was totally unsupportive. He just loved having this dancer-wife."

With her family's emotional and financial support, MacArthur overcame many of her reservations and enrolled at Hunter College full-time. When I first met her she was a freshman, and she planned to study veterinary medicine. She has since decided to become a doctor and is applying to medical schools. "I realized that I chose to become a vet because I didn't have enough self-confidence to go right for medicine. How could a 'dumb dancer' become a doctor? But as I got more confidence, I decided that I really didn't want to treat animals, I wanted to treat humans. I guess it's just that when I left ballet I was where I should have been when I was seventeen—just graduated from high school and with the whole world opening up before me. But I'm not seventeen. I'm almost thirty, and that's been hard to deal with—being so young when chronologically I am so much older."

Corps dancers and principal dancers alike share an overwhelming anxiety about what will happen to them when they quit dancing. Whether they teach or choreograph, they fear they will lose their identities; they will no longer have the special quality that has made the world love them. Without ballet, who will they be? What will they do? Will they be loved, respected, admired? Nothing they accomplish after dance, they fear, will compensate them for the world they have lost.

Sue Knapp, a former soloist with ABT, now works in the presentations department of the Metropolitan Opera, booking summer festivals and dance companies. Although she has managed to stay in close touch with the ballet world, she still yearns for those luminous moments she dreamed of as a child and lived through, on occasion, as an adult. "There were experiences I had as a dancer that were so glamorous. When we were touring Europe, Carla Fracci's husband put together a party for her in Verona, her hometown. She hadn't danced there since she left as a corps dancer, and now she was returning as a prima ballerina. The party was at an open-air restaurant atop a beautiful hill overlooking the town. The company sat at one long table, covered with white linen, flowers, and candles.

"It was a beautiful summer evening," she continues, alight with the memory. "There was a full moon. Carla's husband stood up and told us how privileged he felt to be sharing this moment with us, to return Carla to her home. The whole city just rose up in pure joy and appreciation, and her husband gave fresh flowers to every woman in the company. I carry that memory with me; it is still very, very vivid."

It is also a memory she doubts she will ever relive. Such a glamorous fête may be a rare occurrence for soloists and corps dancers, but for the average administrator, salesperson, or secretary, it will be forever out of reach. Living on the fringes of the ballet world, Susan Knapp has become an ordinary person. Her life is spent shuttling back and forth between her home, seventy miles outside New York, and her job at the Met. To get even this job, she says, she has had to "really put my nose to the grindstone." She started from scratch, volunteering to work in the administrative offices of a ballet company so she could develop administrative skills, then working as a company manager for next to nothing, and finally landing a job at Lincoln Center. She is married to a musician, who is also struggling to establish himself, and she seems weary, at thirty-three, of a kind of Sisyphean pursuit of advancement.

Like so many other dancers whose sense of specialness is intimately connected to their mastery of their bodies—that recalcitrant instrument dancers both love and hate—Knapp has also had to adjust to living with a body that has lost its aura of immortality. "A lot of dancers are very maladjusted when they leave dance," she remarks. "They're so concerned with their bodies that they can't bear to put on a pound. They keep yanking their hair back and wearing this very stagey makeup. I try not to be like that. I run most days, but I don't go to class like some former dancers do. I don't want to do a double pirouette when I remember what it feels like to do six. It's over, and I won't dabble in it. It would be too painful."

"As a dancer you're always in tune," says Clare Duncan, one of those fortunate dancers who, though retired, has stayed at the center of the dance world. "Then suddenly you have to learn that that tuned-up feeling is not the only thing in your life. You have to come to terms with your body. So you're going to put on a bit of weight; you've got to learn that it doesn't matter."

Most fans imagine that life cannot be too difficult for a retired ballerina because she will have her choice of a mate. But talking to dancers destroys that myth. "You don't meet that many people as a dancer," a beautiful, lithe, olive-skinned Heléne Alexopoulous says. "It's like living in a glorified convent. You don't come across a lot of heterosexual men, and it's hard to meet people outside. There are probably lots of interesting men in the audience who would like to meet me, but I'm helpless to do anything about it. How do you know if someone wants to meet you? So it can often be very lonely."

When women like Heléne retire, they feel as inexperienced as a girl going through puberty. "Many women I know who are former dancers," says Susan Knapp, "don't know how to interact with men. They end up having a hard time forming long-term relationships."

One of the side effects of the asexuality of the ballet world is female dancers' lack of confidence in their femininity. "Why would anyone find me attractive?" asks one super-thin former ABT dancer. "I mean, our bodies may be fine for dancing, but they're not really women's bodies." She looks down shyly at her nonexistent bosom. "Why would anyone want me rather than someone more voluptuous?"

Young dancers have been told that if they leave romance till they finish their careers, they will easily make up for all they have missed. But psychological and sexual development are gradual processes. To integrate sex, love, and work into one's life requires trial and error. Adolescent encounters and dating have developmental significance. Adults who have been deprived of such crucial growth experiences do not just catch up as soon as they leave the stage.

With retirement, the analogy between ballet and family truly breaks down. Families do not rudely eject their members when they are no longer useful. Nor is it to a family's advantage to produce people who lack the means to stand on their own. Families are supposed to liberate their offspring, slowly and gently, so they can trade the dependence and obedience of childhood for the autonomy of adulthood.

Ballet's children have no such training. After years of being told what to do, how to think, where to be, they do not know how to go about choreographing their own lives. The real void they must fill is the vacuum of indecisiveness and passivity.

This is why so many dancers dread retirement, Gelsey Kirkland explains. Huddled on the floor of an office at Fifth Avenue and Forty-second Street just after the ABT lockout, Kirkland hugs her knees to her chest. She is dressed in a baggy shirt that hangs down over her jeans, and her hair is covered by a bright bandana. Her agent, Barna Ostertag, a gray-haired woman dressed in black, sits close-by.† Ostertag, who turned eighty today, is more than the ballerina's agent. She plays the roles of grandmother, mother, protector, therapist, and friend to a dancer whose only family has been ballet ever since she began studying at Balanchine's school as a young child. At fifteen, Kirkland was promoted into the company, and she forged rapidly ahead. She had no childhood or adolescence, just one performance after another. Her career has been interrupted by emotional problems and problems with drugs. Many dancers see Kirkland as an extreme example of what happens when a dancer is cloistered in a world of make-believe, where there are, unfortunately, few princes to come to her rescue.

As I watch Kirkland, I think about those beautiful, delicate figurines under a globe of glass, the kind children shake to watch the snowflakes flutter gently around the frozen figure. For years Kirkland, too, seems to have been frozen. Success has not meant that she has control over her life. Rather, it has meant that she has learned to acquiesce to others.

"People in ballet skip development," she tells me. "They are not encouraged to be temperamental ["which is the word they use to brand you if you try to think for yourself," she explains later]. They're encouraged to be part of the whole, to be thought of as a dancer. At least that's how I grew up with Balanchine. You learn things like balance with your legs and feet and arms, but your brain is an unexercised muscle. It's taken me a long time to realize that what brought me to where I am is my ability to use my mind and to concentrate; to see that if I brought that to other areas in my life, it would be no different. But when you spend your life only dancing, you feel that there are too many steps to take to get to where you want to be, and so you question taking that first step at all."

Barna Ostertag nods as Kirkland articulates her feelings. It is her

† Since this meeting Gelsey Kirkland has gotten a new agent.

job, she has told me, to help Gelsey find her self-esteem, because living onstage, being a star to millions of fans, does not mean that a dancer has any appreciation of herself as a person behind the gestures and the roles. A dancer becomes dedicated to one facet of her identity, she and Kirkland both tell me. When a dancer wants something else, she discovers how afraid she is that the one facet is all there is of her. "It's so hard to stop," says Kirkland. "I've thought about it a lot. As hard as it is to go on, it would be even harder to quit. It would mean starting again, from the very beginning." She pauses, and then adds, "I have a very close friend who described her retirement. She said she no longer knew what to call herself. I am no longer a dancer, so who am I? People tend to see this as a glamorous occupation, and rewarding. But the reality of it does not become rewarding to many dancers. It's just difficult to explain that to an outsider."

That is not what the dancer sees in herself, Kirkland goes on to say. Dancers are not light-hearted souls who bask in the limelight. Quite the contrary. "They are often miserably unhappy people. How can you possibly deny yourself all those things you deny yourself in order to dance, and put your body through all that you do, and still be happy?" she asks.

"The ballet world doesn't help you make real-life decisions, not because it is glamorous but because it is such hard work. You put those decisions off; you think only about the next class, the next year. You think, 'I have to learn to jump this year; I have to learn to move fast this year.' But now," she concludes regretfully, "I have done it all. It is over. But the difference is, now I don't know where I'm going, and I used to know exactly where I was going."

"I remember my first professional performance. I was fifteen, and I shared a dressing room with two older professional dancers from New York," recounts Edward Myers of Pennsylvania Ballet. "They were carrying on and on about their low salaries, and all I could think was, 'How can you worry about your salary when you're actually being paid to dance and be with dancers?'

"Throughout the first couple of years with a professional company, that's the way I felt. It just seemed so strange to be paid to do something I loved. My views on this subject have changed considerably over the years."

"When I was young," agrees Hilda Morales, "I never saw the reality of ballet. Now I put the realities in front of me, and the tutus and pointe shoes and makeup come afterward. Ballet is hard work."

Edward Myers and Hilda Morales are both in their mid-thirties. Each has danced professionally for over fifteen years, and for them ballet is no longer a spiritual experience: It is exhausting, demanding work. Now that they are company veterans, they no longer feel that they must sacrifice themselves to their art; rather, they want to be well paid and respected, and they want a voice in determining the conditions of their work.

Dancers, like symphony musicians, actors, and screenwriters, have a vehicle through which they can make their demands known and bargain for improvements: their union. Formed in 1936, the 4700 member American Guild of Musical Artists (AGMA) represents dancers, opera singers, opera stage directors, choreographers, and stage assistants. Most major regional companies—Pennsylvania, Houston, Boston, Ballet West, San Francisco—and large New York companies—NYCB, ABT, the Joffrey Ballet—belong to AGMA. Regional companies are covered by one master agreement, negotiated for all companies outside New York; the New York companies bargain individually.

Although most dancers say they feel fortunate to have union protection, many complain that, unlike the musicians union, the International Alliance of Theatrical Stage Employees and Moving Picture Machine Operators (IATSE), and the Dramatists Guild, AGMA is not a strong or aggressive bargaining agent. Among its members and in other unions in the arts and entertainment fields, AGMA has the reputation of being a "let's not make waves" organization, which is not much better than a "company union." Befitting this reputation, AGMA has only recently been involved in its first major struggle against management of a ballet company. And in this instance, the union did not lead the dancers: The dancers led their union, kicking and screaming all the way, according to many dancers.

In the fall of 1979, dancers at the American Ballet Theatre decided to reject the small salary and benefit increase offered them by ABT management during protracted contract negotiations. In response, the company locked the dancers out of their studios and canceled its winter season. Dancers and management haggled for ten weeks, during which time the dancers took their case to the public. Nightly television news shows ran clips of dancers, dressed in tutus and tights, carrying picket signs emblazoned with union slogans. Speaking out in television and newspaper interviews, at cocktail parties and fund raisers, the dancers gave ballet fans a look at the real world of ballet: the long hours, low pay, paltry benefits, and occupational hazards. After years of silence, dancers had found their voices.

ABT's dancer's did not break their silence for arbitrary or capricious reasons. The conditions of their lives were described by the group spokesman, soloist Frank Smith, as "nothing short of slavery." By 1979, they had had enough. Older dancers like Smith and other members of the dancers' negotiating team began to realize that ballet is not only art; it is work. They began to see that if they wanted conditions to change, they would have to act to change them. And they began to understand that if there ever was a time to institute change, that time had come.

By 1979, ballet companies could no longer plead poverty. Ballet had definitely come of age. It was big business, drawing huge crowds, selling itself to television and the movies, receiving larger and larger grants from governmental agencies and large corporations. To dancers, one proof of ballet's coming of age was right there, on ABT's board of directors, which is headed by Donald Kendall, chairman and chief executive officer of Pepsico.

Dancers had only to look around them to see how much money ABT was earning and spending: to purchase lavish costumes and sets; to hire superstars; and to pay musicians and stagehands. Without dancers there would be no ballet, yet they received the smallest slice of an ever-expanding pie. "They've taken the money out of the dancers' pockets to pay for the labor of other union workers and designers and superstars," Frank Smith says, summing up the dancers' complaints. "It's hard to take when you know a corps dancer is dancing in a costume that cost twice as much as she might have made in a week."

Dancers also found—much to their surprise—that management's approach to bargaining had also changed with the times. Having grown up with ABT, many members of the company were accustomed to Lucia Chase's "family style" of negotiating. Every three years, when the AGMA contract with ABT was about to expire, Chase would assemble a "family council." She would listen to "the kids," commiserate with them, and then lay down the law. The kids would accept a slightly larger weekly allowance and a few other small improvements in the agreement, feeling that their meekness at least purchased maternal protection.

After Kendall became head of the ABT board, there were to be no more "family councils" held at contract time. During the 1976 negotiations, ABT hired Alan Jaffe, a lawyer with Proskauer Rose Goetz and Mendelsohn, one of the largest management law firms in the country. AGMA's sleepy staff negotiators and relatively passive members were no match for this high-powered negotiator. Presented with their new contract, dancers felt that they had been done in—by their company and their union.

In 1979, dancers were determined not to be "screwed again." Kri Soleri's husband, Joel Timm, suggested that the dancers follow the lead of symphony musicians, who had hired a militant labor lawyer, Leonard Liebowitz, a partner of the labor law firm of Sipser Weinstock Harper Dorn and Liebowitz, to bargain for them during contract negotiations. ABT dancers acted on the suggestion and met with Liebowitz. AGMA consented to pay a quarter of the lawyer's fee, dancers raised the rest, and in the spring of 1979 the members of ABT hired him.

Liebowitz and his new clients quickly got down to work, discussing the dancers' problems and possible bargaining strategies. He recognized immediately that he had to tackle an image problem. "I remember going to a meeting of the whole company," the attorney recalls, "and the first thing I said was, 'Before anything else, can we all just stop calling each other "boys" and "girls"?' It wasn't only that management referred to them as 'boys' and 'girls,'" Liebowitz tells me with a certain alarm. "It was that they referred to each other that way."

Liebowitz also informed the dancers that although he would advise them and negotiate for them, he would not become "their militant." They would have to fight their own battles, form a negotiating committee, research the economics of the business, formulate contract demands, and—most importantly—provide the kind of internal leadership that could hold a group of seventy-seven ambitious individualists together.

The dancers surprised everyone. They took on this new task of forming a cohesive union group with the same rigor, discipline, and single-mindedness they had always applied to their careers.

Setting aside part of their weekly earnings, the ABT dancers began to contribute to a strike fund, something for which their union had never made any provision. Their negotiating committee met for months and developed detailed bargaining proposals. The dancers wanted significant pay raises, increases in per diem allowances, and realistic pension benefits. They also wanted a job tenure agreement similar to that negotiated by the musicians union. Under this agreement, a conductor can fire a musician for artistic reasons only if a jury of the musician's peers agrees with the conductor's assessment. Finally, dancers wanted to be referred to as "ladies" and "gentlemen."

Initially, ABT management rejected these proposals. The company offered to raise the dancers' salaries by a mere 5 percent, an increase that would have cost ABT only $150,000 during the three-year life of the contract. That was all it could afford, insisted ABT. Shortly thereafter, the company offered Russian defector Alexander Godunov a yearly salary of $150,000—equal to the total sum ABT was prepared to spend on raises for seventy-seven dancers over three years. The dancers refused to accept this final indignity, so the company closed its doors and locked them out.

This did not curtail the dancers' efforts, and once the ABT superstars understood that the corps dancers and soloists were not attacking their status but merely seeking to reduce the pay gap between the top and bottom of the scale, they joined in. Dancers like Kirkland, van Hamel, and Bujones were vocal in their support. Kirkland was especially helpful, devoting hours to speaking out publicly against management's position. Colleagues from other companies also championed the cause of the ABT dancers. And ballet fans from across the nation sent thousands of dollars to the dancers' strike fund, along with letters urging ABT to settle in the dancers' favor.

The company management resisted. "Management did things during the strike that we couldn't believe," Kri Soleri recalls. "They sent long letters to each dancer signed by the chairman of the board questioning what the negotiating committee was telling them. The committee got quite nervous, but the dancers held together. Management's letters just got people more angry."

After a ten-week lockout, the dancers won significant improvements in wages and working conditions at ABT. The starting salary for a corps dancer went from $235 a week to $405 a week by the end of the three-year contract; a fourth-year corps dancer, who earned $285, now makes $420; and a tenth-year soloist, who used to earn $422, now earns $610. During tours, the company agreed to pay for dancers' hotel rooms and to provide a $24 per diem food allowance. The company also increased from thirty-six to forty the number of weeks dancers are guaranteed employment, and agreed to pay $25 per week supplemental unemployment coverage during the twelve off weeks. The terms of the 1979 contract call for rehearsal and performance schedules to be posted a week in advance, and dancers must now be referred to as "ladies" and "gentlemen." The dancers also won a provision that prohibits management from firing them without a "just cause," such as absences from rehearsals and performances. They were unable to win job tenure clauses; and although an artistic director can still use his authority to dismiss a dancer for "artistic reasons," he must now go through a fairly elaborate procedure to do so.

During negotiations, the union also initiated discussion with management concerning dancers' touring problems. Because hard concrete floors contribute to injuries, ABT dancers want the company to construct a portable wood floor that could be laid over the concrete stage of many of the theaters where they perform. At this writing, management is still balking at the added expense of constructing and transporting a portable floor.

Pensions also remain an unresolved problem. One reason retiring dancers have nothing to fall back on is that even when they do have a pension plan, it does not go into effect until the dancer is sixty-five. Since most dancers must retire before they are forty, the pension plan is not very useful. Furthermore, many dancers do not stay with one company long enough to be eligible for pension benefits. A more realistic pension plan would be designed to take these facts of dance life into account. One solution to the problems unique to dance would be a group tax-sheltered annuity plan. Under this plan, employers would deposit their contribution of the dancer's pension into individual accounts established for the bargaining unit, and the dancer could withdraw the sum upon leaving the company. So far, management has not objected to this approach, but AGMA has not supported it, preferring to maintain its own pension plan.

In spite of their contract's shortcomings, the ABT dancers' spirited struggle in 1979 provided inspiration for dancers everywhere. "We were fighting for all dancers all over the country," Hilda Morales says exuberantly. "We were fighting for their futures as well as our own. Dancers can't just daydream about *tendus* anymore. We have to pay the rent and earn respect."

That fact has become apparent to many dancers around the country. Shortly after the ABT lockout, dancers at the Pittsburgh Ballet Theatre voted—over management's strong objections—to join AGMA. "We work just as hard as steelworkers," says corps dancer Jackie O'Dell, "and yet we earn next to nothing. We can't afford to buy a house or save money. It can't go on like this."

The most impressive result of the lockout has been its effect on dancers' self-esteem. "ABT set the example," another young corps dancer says, "and we're following it." After years of being treated like children, ABT dancers learned they could act to help themselves and each other. "It was such an idyllic situation during the lockout," Solange MacArthur observes. "I thought I'd never see the day that dancers would take a job action, threaten to go on strike, refuse a contract, and band together. I was so proud of the company, so proud of us."

Or, as Gelsey Kirkland says of her experience: "I came very late to the lockout. This was the first time I really sat down and listened to a group of dancers. It was a real education. I learned that I was certainly paid out of proportion to them. I was one of the people sopping up the money that was unevenly distributed. I couldn't do anything about that. But I could certainly support them."

Even though the dancers did not win all their demands, their victory emboldened them to continue asserting their needs in this next series of contract negotiations. "This contract is like a good pool shot," Frank Smith explains. "It's a setup for the next shot."

It is clear that dancers can improve their wages and working conditions by effective collective bargaining. Unfortunately, however, AGMA has been relatively uninterested in aggressively pursuing their interests. The union is staffed by three paid labor professionals in New York, who do the bulk of the bargaining and whatever organizing the union conducts. Many AGMA locals are run by lawyers rather than active union members. The union conducts very little educational activity: Occasionally dancers are given a cursory hour-long lecture explaining the value of a union.

AGMA's top officials are Joan Greenspan, associate executive secretary, a woman who replies with testy impatience to members who call up inquiring about their union's action, or inaction; Alan Olsen, another associate executive secretary, is a cautious gentleman who expresses as much sympathy for management as for dancers; and DeLloyd Tibbs, the secretary-treasurer. None of these officials seems particularly interested in expanding the union's membership or power. When Jodie Pattee was an AGMA rep with the Chicago Ballet, she complained to Joan Greenspan that the company threatened not to renew her contract because of her union activities. Greenspan told her that she ought to quit if she found management pressure too much to bear.

Responses like this help explain why the union is so weak. Most union reps feel they should not rock the boat. At the San Francisco Ballet, AGMA rep Vane Vest admits that he is now working in a semi-management position—a conflict of interest the union has not protested —and that he is not even pro-union. "I don't necessarily believe in the union," Vest tells me. "It's a necessary evil and must be dealt with as such. This means that you bend the rules when you need to. You talk privately with the director and say, 'Hey, we've got a problem here.' Above all, you don't call a company meeting and allow the dancers a voice in solving the problem because you don't want to 'get the dancers upset.'"

One of the most disturbing indications of AGMA's lack of local and national leadership manifested itself during recent negotiations involving dancers at New York City Ballet. In the fall of 1980, City Ballet dancers began to worry more explicitly about their financial and professional futures. The previous spring, they had submitted a list of demands to management; management promptly lost the list. When their contract expired that August, the dancers continued working without a contract. A week before the season was scheduled to begin, they realized that they were about to lose their only leverage: the threat of a strike before the season began.

AGMA was neither negotiating on behalf of the dancers nor preparing them for the possibility of a strike. More and more worried,

City Ballet dancers met and decided that, like the ABT dancers, they might benefit from outside help. They had an initial consultation with Leonard Liebnowitz, but when they asked AGMA to pay part of his fee, the union refused. According to AGMA leaders, the union could not afford to pay an outside lawyer because City Ballet dancers' dues had been in arrears for over two years. Although the City Ballet contract contained an automatic dues checkoff clause, management had simply stopped deducting members' dues from their paychecks, and AGMA had never protested this violation of the contract.

City Ballet management reacted strongly against the idea of dancers hiring an outside negotiator. Accustomed to the passive bargaining position of the dancers and their union, management was not looking forward to dealing with Liebowitz. Before it was discovered that the dancers could not afford to hire the attorney, City Ballet's top-level management threatened to dismiss dancers who had been trying to hire Liebowitz. "We were told that in the mood Balanchine is in these days, he just might fire everyone," one young dancer tells me. Management announced that it would refuse to deal with Liebowitz, and that any attempt to hire the lawyer would constitute grounds for legal action against both the dancers and their union. "They said that because we'd already submitted a small list of demands in the spring, we'd technically begun negotiations, so we could be sued for harassment if we hired Liebowitz."

City Ballet dancers were intimidated by the company's response. It had not been easy for them to consider bucking Balanchine, and they felt they had to justify their actions—to their company and to themselves. They formed a committee to collect details about the high cost of living in New York in order to convince management they needed a raise. They submitted bargaining proposals about touring conditions and hotel accommodations, and requested new guidelines for the discharge of employees. (They wanted six months' notice for any firing.) "The company's gotten so huge and impersonal," a dancer active in the negotiating committee explains, "That we don't feel protected anymore. Balanchine's not around. He doesn't know who everyone is; he doesn't have the energy to take care of us. Besides, he's going to die, and we're worried about what is going to happen to us."

In violation of the National Labor Relations Act, management tried to interfere with the dancers' right to select their own bargaining representative. Dancers who went to Liebowitz for counsel were threatened with dismissal. AGMA leaders did not protest. When dancers spoke with union representative Alan Olsen, he encouraged them to have more sympathy for management's point of view because, as one dancer reports, "He said he felt management had been so nice to dancers in the past."

When I interviewed Olsen in the spring of 1980, he acknowledged that management occasionally takes advantage of dancers' trust and loyalty at the bargaining table, but that, for the most part, "the relationship between management and the dancers has been very good, very caring."

When I asked Olsen about the ABT settlement, he did not seem as pleased as I had expected. Still concerned about the old status of ballet as an unpopular art, he worried that the dancers' demands would place undue strain on the company. That's why AGMA has been so cautious in the past, he explained. That is why "we want to get our members 100 percent of the possible, which may not be 100 percent of what's necessary."

Every union worries that unreasonable demands will reduce employment, but AGMA's position is unusually meek. On financial issues, Olsen seemed equally resigned to management's position. Dancers do complain about an unwieldy repertoire, he agreed, but it is management's prerogative to worry about the box office; and without a wide variety of programs, subscription attendance would decrease. Olsen also expressed concern about the additional costs to management of building and transporting portable floors to alleviate the stress of concrete stages, though he conceded that the union and management should consider the dancers' request.

AGMA, Olsen believes, has not been able to do much to curb dancers' injuries. "It's very frustrating," he said. "It seems to be an inherent part of the job—like football. Attempts to minimize the injury rate have been, at best, marginally effective. Years ago we had an engineering survey done and made recommendations on construction of floors, which are a standard part of our contract and have had a noticeable effect. But the problem is still there. Today it's even worse. Years ago, when a dancer had a minor injury, he would stay home and recover. Now there are therapies available that mask the symptoms. This means dancers go on dancing and only exacerbate the injury.

"I don't see a readily available answer," Olsen concluded. "And the problem is confounded by the fact that dancers are so enthusiastic about dancing that they often dance with broken bones, and that's not what you should do with broken bones."

Olsen was unable to explain why AGMA had failed to collect dues at City Ballet. This is perhaps the most incomprehensible of all AGMA's responses to contract violations and harassment. As one labor lawyer and organizer pointed out, "It's hard to understand why a union wouldn't insist on enforcement of an automatic dues deduction clause in its contract. Even the most docile and the most corrupt unions get very militant where dues are concerned because dues money pays the salaries of the union officials. If a union doesn't collect dues money and fails to negotiate a contract after it expires, then it's hardly a union at all. What can it do?"

Leonard Chassman, executive director for the Writers Guild of America West, the union that represents screenwriters, was appalled by the interaction between AGMA and NYCB. Under such circumstances, he said, the Writers Guild would not hesitate to file unfair labor practices charges on all counts. "When you are talking about that level of harassment—threatening members for union activity and trying to interfere with the union's right to select its representatives—it's unbelievable. That's a clear violation of the law, and if you filed charges with the National Labor Relations Board, you'd undoubtedly win."

If dancers are to survive the increasing commercialization of ballet, they will have to become more aggressive in their conduct with respect to management. The ballet boom has brought more than a new influx of fans to the art; it has changed the methods of ballet's management as well. Today, as members of the old guard of ballet die out, they are replaced not by seasoned patrons of the art, but by corporate board chairpersons whose solution to budgetary problems is to imitate the increasingly tough bargaining position adopted by most American corporations. The ABT lockout illustrated what these new management methods mean for dancers in established companies who seek to improve their wages and working conditions.

At the Houston Ballet, in the heart of the Sun Belt, the new corporate approach is even more explicit. Fifteen years ago, Houston Ballet was an undistinguished, struggling provincial company. It was formed after World War II, by a group of Houston oil and mercantile millionaires whose vision of ballet was shaped by companies like the Ballet Russe de Monte Carlo, which toured America's hinterlands.

For years Houston Ballet limped along with neither the creative nor the financial abilities of a first-rate company. Then in the sixties large corporations from the Northeast began to relocate in Texas; and in order to convince executives and their wives to leave New York City, Chicago, or Boston for Houston, these corporations had to offer more than low income taxes and an unregulated business environment. "From the chamber of commerce point of view, arts had to be a major attraction of the city," explains Eugene Loveland, president of the board of Houston Ballet, a former vice-president of Shell Oil, and president of his own oil company. "When Shell moved down here from New York, one of the questions our people asked was, 'Do we have to go to New York to see ballet or opera?' The need for culture is becoming more obvious in the corporate world."

A seventh-rate ballet company would no longer do: Houston decided it wanted to be number one. To achieve that goal, Houston Ballet recruited Loveland to its board. A trim sixty-year-old with neatly clipped gun-metal gray hair, Loveland is a latecomer to ballet. "I guess I'm like every American boy who says he's never been to a ballet. I had the usual male chauvinist hang-ups," says Loveland. When he came to Houston, a patron invited him to a ballet per- formance. He could not refuse. "I'm nuts about athletics, and when I watched the ballet, I was so impressed to see the athletics and music combined that I just got hooked." Loveland was asked to serve on the Houston Ballet board and shortly thereafter to become its president.

"I wanted to know what we were selling. If what we wanted was to be the strongest regional company, I knew that we had to stay in the black. Because you can't succeed without money. I looked at this as I would look at any new business," Loveland says. "What we needed was to develop a product; that's what sells. Then we had to finance that product; that's the development part. So I saw it as a company—a manufacturing organization, a sales organization, and a finance organ- ization. First, of course, we needed to have a good school to develop a style." After a thorough real-estate search, the company purchased an old candle factory and constructed studios there for the company and the school. "Then, to develop our product we needed a manu- facturing unit with a head of manufacturing being an artistic director." Corporate Houston contributed the requisite funding, and the com- pany hired choreographer Ben Stevenson as artistic director. "And to finance our product," Loveland continues, "we needed a marketing unit with a head of marketing being a developmental director." To market the product and raise developmental funds, Houston Ballet appointed Irl Mowery as developmental director. Mowery appeals to corporate self-interest, pointing out the public-relations value of donations. "Oftentimes corporations give because we offer them the opportunity to look good, which they need nowadays. Oil companies can look like they're doing something other than raking off profits on oil," Mowery says quite frankly. "They're not just taking away from the community; they're giving to the community."

The company also offers the services of its dancers when corporate Houston needs help. When I was in Houston, Gulf Oil Company staged an afternoon spectacular to announce its contribution of $500,000 to the city's new ballet and opera theater fund drive. As workers in Gulf Plaza streamed from their offices at lunchtime, ballet students, musicians, and opera singers distributed handbills trumpeting Gulf's magnanimity. The announcement of the company's donation was printed on the back of a glossy, four-color ad that appeared in a saturation campaign of the nation's cultural magazines. The ad pictured a performer's dressing table with an array of cultural props: a gleaming French horn, an opera helmet with spiked horns, a pair of pale satin ballet slippers, and one long-stemmed red rose. The ad copy was discretion itself. Next to the Gulf emblem was one line: "Gulf Oil Corporation is pleased to help keep the lively arts lively."

With such a sales pitch, corporate Houston has created a company of thirty-eight dancers, which operates on a budget of nearly $3 million. But despite the fact that the Houston company is one of the richest in America, its dancers reap few of the rewards. Their salaries are as low as those of most other regional companies, their benefits as minimal, and their pension plan practically nonexistent. Loveland cheerfully counts the passivity of the dancers' union as one of his blessings. "The dancers' union is not a strong union," he says. "It's made up of people who want to dance and who are dedicated to getting out there. They're a lot less well paid than symphony musicians or opera singers. So far"—he knocks the rim of the wooden coffeetable in front of him—"it has not been a militant group."

Tied to their companies in a quasi-parental relationship, most dancers are afraid to take aggressive action, and the union to which they belong has never performed a leadership role. Yet in European countries, where there are strong dancers and strong leadership, the working lives of dancers have been dramatically improved.

In England, dancers belong to British Actors Equity. Though it is hardly the strongest of the unions representing European dancers, it has fought for and won improvements in working conditions. Dancers at both The Royal Ballet and London Festival Ballet elect committees to oversee safety conditions in theaters in which they dance. Women are given paid maternity leave, which enables them to raise families and continue pursuing their career. Shorter performance schedules extend the British dancer's career; and when dancers do retire, financial aid and retraining are provided to prepare them for a new one. Though British dancers do not receive pensions until they are sixty-five, these pensions are more generous than the pittance American dancers obtain, and the union is fighting to lower the age of eligibility to fifty-five.

Elaborate provisions also protect British dancers from arbitrary firings. At The Royal Ballet, dancers must be given a year's notice before they are dismissed. During the interim year, the company must help them improve their dancing by providing coaching and additional time off. If a dancer has not improved after six months, the company must give him or her paid time off to audition for another company.

Dancers in such Scandinavian companies as the world-famous Royal Danish Ballet or the Royal Swedish Ballet enjoy even greater union protection, impressive job security, and occupational safety and health programs that enhance dancers' careers.

At first glance, the Royal Swedish Ballet seems no different from any other ballet company in the world. Morning class, held in a studio under the eaves of the Royal Swedish Opera House, is a familiar scene: dancers engaging in a daily battle with their bodies, their exhaustion, and their hopes. But there is something different here. I notice a far greater percentage of older dancers—and fewer very young ones—than I am accustomed to seeing in the States: At least ten or twelve dancers seem to be in their late thirties or early forties. The female dancers, nowhere as thin as their American counterparts, actually look like women: They have breasts, hips, and soft curves. Three women in the company even seem a bit overweight. I find out that they are pregnant, and that most of the older women in the company are married and have families. During the course of the working day, children come in and go out of the studio, planting themselves on a mother's lap while she makes up prior to performance or waiting in the wings as she is dancing.

Comparing these dancers to American dancers, I notice differences not only in the dancers' bodies, but in the attitudes and aura they project. Is it that they have more confidence in their abilities? Is it that they are more mature? No, there is something else. What all the Swedish dancers I meet and talk with have in common is a powerful sense of their own dignity—not just as artists, but as people and workers. We are to be valued, they explain over and over again. We have certain rights, and we will exercise them.

An extensive system of collective bargaining and "work environment" legislation in Sweden gives all workers in the country the opportunity to participate in workplace decisions that affect their lives. In addition to generous pensions and health plans, educational benefits and paid time off, Swedish dancers have a form of permanent job security, not unlike tenure in a university. According to their union contract, Swedish dancers who have been with the company for three years are either hired permanently or dismissed. Once dancers are hired permanently, they are not easily fired. This kind of job security protects dancers against a choreographer's caprice: No new company director can dismiss dancers with years of seniority. It also alleviates the pressure on dancers to perform when injured, to diet to death, or to deprive themselves of a moderately fulfilling social and family life.

Though ballet companies in Scandinavia still tend to be dominated by one man or woman at the top, dancers are given some voice in company operations. At the Royal Swedish Ballet, dancers cannot be denied roles without receiving some explanation, and they must be consulted about the selection and the methods of a company director. When I meet with several dancers in the Royal Swedish Opera House canteen, they explain their philosophy. "We feel secure enough to say no to someone," says principal dancer and union rep Kerstin Lidstrom. "We are quite flexible. If a director or choreographer treats us well, we cooperate fully. But if someone is rude and engages in unsuitable conduct, we don't feel we have to take it."

Several years ago, when Nureyev came to work with the Royal Swedish Ballet, dancers exercised their rights. Accustomed to playing the prima donna, Nureyev yelled at the company, and often asked dancers to work through breaks and late into the night. Unused to such treatment, the dancers refused to work with him. Nureyev reformed, and the company returned to work.

Dancers at the Royal Swedish Ballet have an active safety committee that meets regularly with management to discuss health needs; they are also able to choose their own company director. With the help and support of Company Director Gunilla Roempke, who herself was a soloist with the company and their trainer Dan Rudholm, the Royal Swedish Ballet has begun to institute programs that protect the dancers not only from management pressure but also from themselves.

Rudholm has a small studio in the basement of the Royal Swedish Opera House and will soon be moving to refurbished quarters, equipped with the best exercise and rehabilitation equipment available. A former hockey player, he feels that dancers merit the kind of care and attention given to valuable athletes. Rudholm has inaugurated programs that prevent dancers from returning to work too quickly after sustaining an injury, and he has started a special training class to heal a dancer's morale as well as body. "What I want to do is work the rest of the body and allow the injury to heal," Rudholm explains. "This means that injured dancers don't just stay at home, where they become more and more depressed. They come to a special session where we exercise everything but the injured part. Then when the dancer's injury is healed, we have a special class that brings her back to work slowly." Aware that dancers often try to minimize bad injuries, Rudholm insists that they be checked by a doctor before they return to work; he does not hesitate to stop an injured dancer from performing.

Like all Swedish workers, dancers have a five-week paid vacation during the summer. Retirement is made easier for them because of annual pension benefits equal to their average salary during the fifteen highest paid years of their working lives. If dancers desire to move into another field, they can apply for retraining funds from the government.

Security is the key to well-being for European dancers, yet it elicits negative reactions from most of the leaders of the American ballet world. When ABT dancers tried to insert job tenure clauses into their contract, ABT management adamantly refused to countenance such provisions. Baryshnikov argued that he needed total artistic control over his company—in other words, the ability to hire and fire at will. When I ask critic Norma McLain Stoop what she thinks of job security, she responds without hesitation: "One thing that happens when a dancer gets a little bit of security is that a little bit of ambition is chipped away. You're so comfortable that you lose the feeling that you have to go to class and rehearsal. When I went to rehearsal at the Paris Opéra Ballet, I was quite shocked by the lack of enthusiasm about rehearsing. If a dancer wasn't on a specific segment, instead of watching, she went to get a cup of coffee or read a book [something I've seen American dancers do many times, although Stoop apparently has not]. In Europe, they're so terribly secure that they have less enthusiasm. I feel the competition and insecurity in America fuels a wonderful desire on the part of the dancer to keep on getting better and better."

The argument that security breeds laziness in the individual dancer fails to take into account the hierarchical system that under-values the contributions and achievements of all but the star dancer. Ballet training tends to steep students in fantasy and steer them away from reality. It directs them toward the apex of ballet's pyramid of success. But because there is so little room at the top, most dancers end up at the bottom. There, they languish. There is no sense that an experienced corps dancer is a valuable asset to a company. In America, corps dancers tend to be replaced by younger recruits fed on the same dreams of glory.

One could easily imagine a different system: one that encourages dancers to excel and improve even within the less glamorous universe of the corps dancer and soloist. But most teachers and directors are still compelled by the old image of the pyramid; and in trying to extend their students' horizons to stardom, they ironically limit their futures. Taught to seek stardom at all costs rather than to seek fulfill-ment within the limits of their own talents, some dancers lose their ambition along with their fantasies.

Both American dancers and their union could benefit from the experiences of European dancers. If a union is only as militant as its members, it is the union's task to educate its members. In most unions, members either come from union families or learn about their union on the job. Dancers rarely know anything about trade unions. They come from affluent homes where neither parent was a union member. The ballet schools they attend teach them to ignore their financial, emotional, and physical needs. When they get into companies, they are so delighted by their good fortune that they do not worry about their rights as workers. The union is an afterthought, a technicality of joining the company.

Dancers tend to remain passive because there is no one to teach or encourage them to fight for themselves. But the ABT lockout demonstrated that they can and do benefit from strong leadership. Over and over again, young men and women involved in the lockout explained the importance of the role played by Leonard Liebowitz. "He showed us how to take the first step," Gelsey Kirkland says. "He made us feel that what we were doing wasn't wrong," Hilda Morales echoes. That dancers need such help is a testament to their training in diffidence; that they respond so positively is a testament to their potential strength.

FINDING BALANCE:

9

A NEW VISION OF BALLET

I t is a luminous spring afternoon. Sunlight streams through the high windows of the School of American Ballet and falls in dappled patterns, on the highly polished oak floor. Incandescent figures, dressed in pale pink, fluid as finely spun gossamer, glide across the floor. Still regal and supple after decades of dancing, Alexandra Danilova commands the center of the classroom, her transparent nylon skirt shimmering with each movement as she coaches her students for the upcoming SAB Workshop. Four hopeful ballerinas—the smallest swans in the second act of *Swan Lake*—cross arms and, grasping each other's hands, spring across the floor to the staccato rhythm of Tchaikovsky. Younger students gather in the doorway to watch this enactment of their future. Two ballet mothers judiciously survey their daughters' accomplishments. An out-of-town critic takes notes. Charlie, SAB's resident balletomane, a wiry bald man with spectacles, occasionally utters a long sigh of admiration. Transfixed, the audience pays homage to the dancers.

Beholding these girls, says Charlie, is "like watching music dance. As if a Beethoven symphony suddenly takes form, each note, each cadence, flickers before your very eyes." To be a balletomane or a critic is a constant challenge, for one must discern, in performance after performance, the subtle changes, the intricate magic of the dancers' bodies in which the mysteries of delicacy and grace are forever distilled. With their bodies dancers—these children of our imagination—paint a perfect picture. But when you remove the veil of art and look at them closely, the four girls leaping like kittens across the center of the floor reveal a not-so-perfect reality. They are among the most painfully frail dancers SAB has to offer this year. Their leotards pucker across their flat chests and gather in folds along their incredibly thin arms. Danilova herself seems a fragile relic. There is something brittle in her tenacity, something almost too fierce in her loyalty.

The audience sees none of this. As the thick glass doors of SAB close behind them, they enter an enchanted realm. For dancers young and old, this vision can be a kind of trap—a trap set by companies, schools, and often unwittingly by balletomanes who see only the art, not the dancers who make the art possible. They approach ballet as they would a painting or a text, dissecting its aesthetic imperfections and accomplishments, ignoring the fact that dancers are human beings with real bodies, real needs, and all-too-real problems. In fact, critics often glorify the worst conditions of the ballet world by preserving the romantic myths that celebrate not just what is difficult and exacting in a dancer's career, but what is destructive and brutal.

With a few notable exceptions, like the criticism of *New York Times* dance critic Anna Kisselgoff, who actually compliments dancers who are healthy and well fed, countless books, articles, and films tell audiences and dancers alike that ballet can thrive only if dancers are totally submissive to teachers, choreographers, and artistic directors. They say dancers must be so devoted that they will tolerate injuries and will dance despite their pain. Female dancers must sacrifice their health to the ballet look. And all dancers must accept low salaries and poor working conditions without complaint. There is no need for change in the ballet world, they argue, because ballet is just one big happy family.

In critic Franklin Stevens's book, *Dance as Life*, readers are told that dancers are not ordinary professionals in ordinary professional relationships. To be a dancer is to join a family. "Everyone in ballet," Stevens writes, "is connected, a relation close or distant, but ever-present, members of a family who may not be merely sitting close-by at a party, but one day—perhaps the next—may become partners or dance beside you, or be the choreographer who directs you, or the *régisseur* who rehearses you, or the company director who hires or rejects you, or the older dancer who shows you, finally, why you are having trouble with a particular turn or series of beats."

It is a family—a family that is so special, moreover, that its wards can easily do without kindness and nurturing. "The teacher," Stevens says, "is like the parent. . . . As parent, he is totally biased, totally prejudiced, and plays favorites with quiet intensity from the very beginning. . . . This one is fat and it doesn't look like the kind of baby fat that comes off. Forget her. After two years, that one still moves as if she were on stilts. Forget her. Forget the . . . one who could have been possible a few years ago, but not now. Gone forever now. A pity. Forget her."†

Ballet's children live in a world outside time, a world in which they can never accede to power. Speaking of the ballerina in his great ode to ballet *Balletomania Then and Now*, Arnold Haskell beatifies her eternal childhood: "She has never finished learning. At the height of her triumph, she must submit herself to the discipline, and often to the abuse, of her ballet-master. To him she is never 'madame' but always the small girl whose arabesque lacks perfection or whose elevation is weak."‡

In book after book, article after article, the passivity and powerlessness of the dancer are sanctified. "That is what makes dancers such a delight!" says critic and balletomane Norma McLain Stoop. One fall afternoon, the seventy-year-old writer invited me to tea in her spacious apartment near Lincoln Center and told me how lucky she feels to have entered this golden world. "I just love the ballet world," she says. "Dancers are the most hard-working people I've ever known. I love

† Franklin Stevens, *Dance as Life: A Season with American Ballet Theatre* (New York: Avon Books, 1976), p. 61.
‡ Arnold Haskell, *Balletomania Then and Now* (New York: Alfred A. Knopf, 1977), p. 4.

the fact that they go on eating peanut butter sandwiches because they love to dance."

Peanut butter sandwiches? I query, thinking yogurt was a more likely diet. "Yes," she answers easily. "They really do not get paid. For people as good as the corps de ballet dancer is at his or her job, I really think that dancers practically live on peanut butter sandwiches or the equivalent. And I love the fact that there's no kicking about that."

The dancers' absolute dedication and willingness to be disciplined enchants Stoop. "Besides sweat, I think their discipline is the thing I love. The very top dancers are told, sometimes not too nicely, that they're doing something wrong. I've heard company members being screamed at and told they're absolutely terrible, and except for the very little kids, there are no tears. There's never any argument. There's a smile exchanged. I love that smile that dancers have when they're told they're doing something wrong."

In the theater, where Stoop spends much of her time observing actors talk back to directors, there is far less submission to authority. In ballet, someone yells at the dancers, and they nod meekly and do as they are told; someone insults them, and they smile sweetly. "This is an ideal setup for a productive world," Stoop says. "You don't get talking back in the dance world. People acknowledge the right of the person who knows more to tell them what to do."

It is in the criticism of Arlene Croce, *The New Yorker*'s dance critic and grande dame of balletomanes, that the rigid standards for physical conformity and submissiveness in ballet are applauded with the greatest enthusiasm. In "Balanchine's Girls," an essay in *Afterimages*, Croce praises Balanchine because he has taken the American woman, whose athleticism, independence, and intelligence are a challenge to the female role in ballet, and tamed her. Balanchine has managed, Croce says, "to get American girls to stop thinking and start *dancing*."†

---

† This and all subsequent quotes on pages 208–210 are from Arlene Croce, *Afterimages* (New York: Alfred A. Knopf, 1969), pp. 422, 423, 426, 427, 425, 40, 28, respectively.

Having convinced them to dispense with thinking and divorce their bodies from their minds, Balanchine's next logical step was to get them to relinquish their bodies altogether. The dancers who win Croce's greatest praise are no more than flashes of light, deft strokes, insubstantial as air. Take Patricia McBride as Croce sees her. She has "the body of a pubescent girl, the bones of a sparrow, the stamina of a horse. Having dispensed with all angles in her body, she appears to be dispensing with her body as well, with recalcitrant flesh. In 'In the Night,' she jumps curled into Moncion's arms, and so lightly that he seems to have received nothing but spirit.

"How does a dancer get to be so transparent?" Croce asks. How indeed? Croce tells us, but obliquely, withholding the real mystery: sheer starvation. "In one sense," she writes, "New York City ballerinas *are* like nuns: they're a sisterhood. They survive in an atmosphere of an aesthetic style that happens to exist nowhere else in the world, that absorbs modern tensions and transcends them; and they put up with untold miseries because they know it's the only way to look the way they want to look—ravishing, like mortal goddesses, yet reachable."

Croce is also a great defender of the ballet mother and her role in achieving the desired image. "After Balanchine and his organization," she says, "the credit for this goes to one group of people. Not to the dancers, who are generally too young to know what they're getting into at the age when they have to get into it, and certainly not to the critics; but to the dancers' mothers. This maligned tribe, and may it increase, has over the years chosen to give its most talented daughters to Balanchine. Ballet mamas are the great realists of the business. And when their weary charges come home full of aches and pains they'd say it, night after night: Darling, all I want is that you should be a pinhead."

Pinheads, sylphs, sparrows: these are Croce's models of perfection. Dancers who look healthy are scorned. "Karin von Aroldingen," Croce writes, "projects something else: blazing, powerful good health *and a kind of plodding animal vigor*" (my italics). Or, in another passage, von Aroldingen is described as "tall and blocklike, with big muscles and the face of a Nordic movie goddess (the outdoor type)." Croce criticizes dancers who are not spritely, ineffable, and diaphanous. "Because of some extra poundage gained since last spring, Judith Jameson did not dance effectively this season."† So too Gelsey Kirkland, who should be applauded and cheered for gaining so much as a pound, is instead exhorted to thinness. Croce describes her performance with Patrick Bissell: "They danced the *Don Quixote* pas de deux, and my misgivings about their physical condition—they'd both gained weight and Kirkland is now decidedly plump all over—were heightened by their performance. Though Kirkland has gained strength along with her weight, she was using it to slam out the sort of crude bravura spins and balances one might expect of a Bolshoi second-rater."

"Dance is the art of sacrifice and deprivation, not fulfillment and gratification." That is what dancers hear—from critics, teachers, choreographers, artistic directors, and even from fellow dancers. In her book *Winter Season*, New York City Ballet corps dancer Toni Bentley says she was aghast at City Ballet's most recent union negotiations. How could dancers consider contradicting Balanchine? How could they debase themselves by focusing on financial demands? "The issue to me is a moral one," she writes.

Those who refuse to see it in such a light but say it is purely political or economic are protecting their moral guilt for such an action. But we are not fighting against an organization but against one man—an artist.

And so the choice is to stand up for ourselves, our security, our financial security, or to give second place to such values and act on respect, devotion, love and deep belief in one man. I opt for the second without hesitation. Balanchine is more important and valuable than we are individually. If

---

† This and the following quote are from Arlene Croce, *Going to the Dance* (New York: Alfred A. Knopf, 1982), pp. 340, 344.

personal security is our primary aim, dancing is not the career for us. It flourishes and feeds off all the qualities created by a lack of security.

"Like children, his children," she concludes, "we feel sure and safe in trusting him."†

Bentley confesses that she often suffers from the isolation of her career, its lack of financial reward, its physical demands, and its competitive, hierarchical structure. Yet she adamantly rejects any hope of change. So, too, the ballet world is hopelessly enmeshed in the myths established when ballet first arrived on American soil. At that time, there was some justification for these myths. Untutored in the subtleties of the art, American audiences had to be enticed and cajoled to ballet performances. While audiences were scarce, impoverished companies had to convince dancers to dance even though they had little money to pay them. Romantic myths about the dedicated artist who sacrifices all to his art proved useful. By promising an experience that combined glamour with spiritual transcendence, ballet companies convinced audiences of the value of the art and ensured the dedication of the dancers they depended on.

Today, the myth machine continues to produce its romantic rhapsodies. But in the contemporary dance environment, these fairy tales are not only increasingly destructive; they are also increasingly anachronistic. Conditions in the ballet world have drastically changed. First of all, the art itself has undergone an enormous aesthetic transformation. Ballet no longer draws solely on the classical tradition. Over the past decades, most classical companies have broadened their aesthetic horizons and have incorporated into their repertoires ballets with a definitely modern cast. This new infusion of modern content and style affects the dancers as well as the dance. Classical fairy tales and nostalgic romances about the virtues of pain and loss create an

---

† Toni Bentley, *Winter Season: A Dancer's Journal* (New York: Random House, 1982), pp. 87, 88.

atmosphere that extols self-sacrifice and denial. Modern dance is far grittier, far more realistic. Instead of removing the dancers from the real world, it brings them into that world, and can help them better understand the nature of their own personal and professional problems.

Modern choreography also places far less emphasis on homogenization. Classical ballets depend on corps works—on regimented rows of female dancers, all of whom look, dance, and act alike. Modern technique does the opposite: It releases the individual from the mass. In great part, modern dance is a conscious feminist revolt against ballet. When women like Isadora Duncan danced uncorseted, they were rebelling, as Roger Copeland writes, against the constraints, "both physical and psychological—imposed on women by Victorian culture."† Modern dance lifts those restraints. "We don't try to look like angels or sylphs," says modern choreographer and Julliard teacher Ruby Shang. "We're generally more chunky, more female than ballet dancers." Women directors and choreographers have also played a central role in shaping the modern tradition. Modern dance companies, unlike ballet companies, are not dominated by male choreographers. By drawing on the legacy of the modern tradition, younger ballet dancers may seek a greater creative role in the arts. As more women become choreographers and company directors in the ballet world, they can act to change the heritage of ballet's vision of women.

Slowly but surely, ballet companies are beginning to change. And some of the schools and teachers that serve them now recognize that that change must begin soon. A new generation of teachers is beginning to heed the advice of psychiatrists and psychologists like Dr. Eugene Lowenkopf and Dr. Vivian Diller, who argue that dancers need affection and support as well as technical instruction. In Britain,

---

† Roger Copeland, "Why Women Dominate Modern Dance," *The New York Times*, Arts and Leisure, April 18, 1982.

the Royal Ballet's Upper School has recruited a number of counselors whose express mandate is to deal with students' emotional and physical problems. Caroline Kennedy, a counselor who worked with students at the Royal Ballet School for three years, described the evolution of a very positive approach to students' worries and concerns. "Ballet students need help building bridges to the real world," she says. "The training is very negative, so students focus on failure. What we have to try to do is help them see their strengths. Psychologists need to help them deal with their emotions as well as their physical problems. They have to make themselves available to students so they aren't afraid to come and confess feelings they consider signs of weakness. They need to have more discussions with teachers and administrators. All of this is essential if we're to change the emphasis of the training."

In New York, Eliot Feld's New Ballet School is an impressive American experiment in new styles of dance education. The staff recruits its students from the New York public schools. Classes are filled with black, Hispanic, Chicano, and Oriental children. The Feld look is in direct contrast to the homogenized look of most ballet schools, and so is the Feld attitude. In the classroom, teachers practice a positive, supportive approach. They do not tell the students only what they are doing wrong; they praise what is right. Outside class, teachers encourage students to develop intellectually, socially, and emotionally.

Such changes in ballet style and teaching have been accompanied by financial changes that will make it far easier to improve dancers' lot. While many ballet companies must still scramble for financial support, they have succeeded in attracting private, corporate, and public sponsorship, and many professional companies are thriving. New York City Ballet's theater is packed night after night. It is the richest ballet company in America. ABT is on sound financial footing. Regional companies are proving themselves to be economically viable. Yet ballet boards and directors have not used the progress they have made to pay dancers more equitably or to alleviate some of the hazards of their career.

Nor do ballet companies take advantage of the dramatic changes in ballet audiences. Audiences are told exactly what they were told thirty years ago about the necessity for self-sacrifice, conformity, and submissiveness. They are not trusted to weather any change in the ballet world. Audiences, like dancers, no longer need the myths, which sustained the art in its early years. Americans are now devoted ballet goers. They have grown in number and have acquired more sophisticated tastes, welcoming companies and choreographers who bring to ballet new themes and styles. During the ABT lockout when audiences heard the voices of dancers themselves for the first time—voices asking for the most basic necessities and improvements—they responded with support and understanding.

Hundreds of letters poured in ABT's offices. "Dear Mr. Kendall and Ms. Chase," wrote Ginger Perkowsky. "Please resume negotiations with the dancers of ABT. They deserve more money for their dedication as artists. Dancers work harder than anyone else in the performing arts and are paid less than the musicians who play for them. The performing life of a dancer is very short, as you know. Please consider their plight." This letter was accompanied by a two-page addenda that read, "We the staff, friends, and members of The Hope of Israel Senior Citizens Center endorse Ginger's letter and add our names to this appeal."

The increased assertiveness of American ballet dancers, the responsiveness of American audiences, the innovations in ballet content and style, as well as new attitudes toward ballet training, all could alter fundamentally the world of dance. These developments demonstrate that there is no shortage of remedies to the problems dancers face, nor is there a dearth of sympathetic supporters who are willing to help dancers challenge traditional training, education, and company practices. But until dancers and audiences come together to share a new image of the dancer, new programs and ideas will produce only minimal changes in the ballet world.

As long as we continue to regard dancers as special beings, a breed apart, we condemn them to the status quo—to their eternal childhood. If we insist on their childlike charm and innocence at the expense of an adult relationship to the world of work, love, family, and friendship, it is they who will pay for our pleasure. And as long as dancers accept this self-image, forfeiting the rights most professionals fight for and enjoy—the right to respect, to financial remuneration, and to have at least some outside fulfillment—the price they pay will be inordinately high.

In Europe, dancers fare better because ballet is forced to play by society's rules. Ballet may create a magical world on stage, but dancers know that there is nothing magical about low pay and poor working conditions, sacrifice and injury. They've learned how to fight to protect themselves. There are some American dancers who have also learned that lesson. They are the superstars who insist upon high salaries, a measure of control over their working lives, a great deal of security, and even more respect. The difference between Europe and America is that across the Atlantic star dancers are not singled out: When dancers are truly protected, all are protected equally.

If American dancers follow the example of their European counterparts, they will not be jeopardizing the enchantment of the ballet performance but will be replacing a romantic world-view that focuses too much on self-sacrifice and too little on self-worth. They would teach their audiences, and most importantly each other, that as artists they are not different from the rest of us but rather express our longings, our fears, and our fantasies.

The practice of art, says Gustave Flaubert, the human desire to approximate heavenly perfection, is such a difficult, frustrating struggle because "the abundance of one's soul sometimes overflows with empty metaphors, since no one has been able to give the exact measure of his needs, his concepts or his sorrows. The human tongue is like a cracked cauldron on which we beat out tunes to set a bear dancing when we would make the stars weep with our melodies."†

Most of us will succeed only in setting bears to dance. But dancers, with their talent, their dedication, and their grace, do make the stars weep with their melodies. And for this, they deserve far, far more than what they receive.

---

† Gustave Flaubert, *Madame Bovary*, ed. and trans. Paul de Man· (New York: W.W. Norton, 1965), p. 138.

About the Author

Suzanne Gordon, author of *Lonely in America*, spent two years researching *Off Balance* and interviewing over a hundred students, dancers, ballet mothers, teachers, and choreographers in American and Europe. Associate editor of *Working Papers* and contributing editor of *Mother Jones*, she has written articles for the *New York Times Magazine*, *Ms.*, the *Village Voice*, *Psychology Today*, *Mademoiselle*, *Family Circle*, and *McCall's*, as well as a cover story on ballet for *GEO Magazine*.

About the Photographer

Earl Dotter, photographer for the American Labor Education Center in Washington, D.C., specializes in labor subjects. Some of the photographs in this book appeared in a solo exhibit, "American Labor," at Gallery 1199 in New York City.

Catalog

If you are interested in a list of fine Paperback
books, covering a wide range of subjects
and interests, send your name and address,
requesting your free catalog, to:

McGraw-Hill Paperbacks
1221 Avenue of Americas
New York, N.Y. 10020